P9-CDE-024

LIBERALS *on* LIBERALISM

LIBERALS
on
LIBERALISM

edited by Alfonso J. Damico

Rowman & Littlefield
Publishers

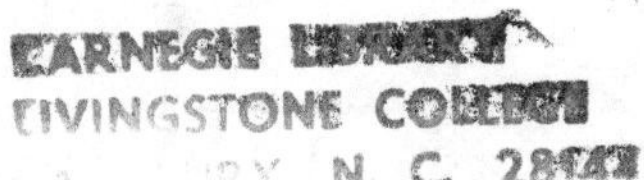

ROWMAN & LITTLEFIELD

Published in the United States of America in 1986
by Rowman & Littlefield, Publishers
(a division of Littlefield, Adams & Company)
81 Adams Drive, Totowa, New Jersey 07512

Library of Congress Cataloging-in-Publication Data

Liberals on liberalism.

Includes bibliographies and index.
1. Liberalism. I. Damico, Alfonso J., 1942–
JC585.L384 1986 320.5′1 86-13777
ISBN 0-8476-7484-3
ISBN 0-8476-7485-1 (pbk.)

88 87 86
10 9 8 7 6 5 4 3 2 1

Printed in the United States of America

Contents

LIBERALS *on* LIBERALISM

Introduction

I

Bringing together for the first time many political theorists who share a sober optimism about the intellectual and moral resources contained within liberalism, this book will disappoint partisans on both sides in the debates over liberalism. Critics of liberalism, anticipating a replay of old quarrels, will discover, instead, that many of their concerns can be usefully diagnosed and addressed within the terms of the liberal tradition—indeed, that they have often misunderstood liberalism. For those more sympathetic to liberalism, this book will disappoint any who imagine that some one formula (Locke's or Mill's, rights or utility) defines or exhausts the meaning of liberalism. These essays, all written especially for this volume, neither elaborate upon standard responses to liberalism's critics nor privilege some one version of liberalism's meaning. To be sure, the authors in this book often reply to liberalism's critics and frequently canvass the accomplishments and limitations of one or another formulation of liberalism. But the accent lies elsewhere.

Convinced that we have not yet fully exhausted liberalism's potential for generating a set of systematic principles for interpreting and guiding a politics that is at once both just and practical, these essays are more prospective than retrospective. The goal is to use *and* reconstruct liberalism, to tap neglected characteristics of the liberal tradition, to test its potential by critically probing its resources. Each reader will want to look more closely at the distinctive ways in which each of these essays refashions our thinking about liberalism. But, most generally, there is a shift away from the association of liberalism with what has come to be known as methodological (and political) individualism. Starting with (abstract) individuals and their self-defined or preexisting interests as its unit of analysis, liberalism has been subjected to three related criticisms: incompleteness, insufficiency, and incoherence. The accusation of incompleteness argues that liberalism neglects the social formation of individual interests and how these formative processes impact upon individuals' public and private lives. The theory is said to be insufficient because it cannot sustain the praise or importance that liberals often accord such things as the public interest and political participation. And, finally, critics have often said that the theory is incoherent in that it cannot account for such things as subjects' obligations without drawing upon concepts alien to the individualistic model.[1] In effect, the complaints imagine a liberalism too impoverished and constrained to engage some of the major issues of politics.

To what extent these criticisms, together, singularly, or in some combination, apply to one or another version of liberalism (they are most commonly targeted at contractarian and "neutrality" renditions of liberalism) is a topic of continuing controversy. Yet the criticisms have encouraged a useful redirection of philosophical and political energies. This book is a report on the new directions being taken by liberalism. Here are arguments about the philosophy and politics of liberalism, more carefully and critically considered, as a theory of the good as well as rights, of duty as well as obligation, about citizenship *and* individualism, about the separateness of persons *and* their interdependency. These, and others to be found in this book, are new liberal themes (at times, "recovered" within the liberal tradition). Their exposition is an initial step toward a liberalism more complete, sufficient, and coherent than what has been previously available.

II

As any reader of this volume knows, criticisms of liberalism and responses to such criticisms have been a staple of political theory activity for the past twenty years. Titles announcing *The Poverty of Liberalism,* or *The End of Liberalism* regularly alternate with those proclaiming *The New Liberalism* or *The Real World of Liberalism.*[2] Such confrontations between a reigning public philosophy and its critics may even be indispensable to political theory—at least, insofar as the characterization of theory as a sort of discourse or conversation is intended as something more than a curtsey toward the principle of tolerance. Real conversations are not very neat and tidy; there is a lot of movement back and forth. But formal political discourse aims to produce a more careful and systematic inquiry and outcome. One effect is that it often proceeds according to some elementary oppositions. So we have become accustomed to juxtapositions that use Rousseau to counter Locke, Marx to check Mill, needs to correct "wants," virtue to displace obligation, community to indict rights-based doctrines.

This book moves us beyond such familiar quarrels in that it attempts to avoid certain risks that attend such juxtapositions and dualisms. As currently structured, the debate over liberalism encourages the view that experience itself must consist of irreducible modes. Discouraged are attempts to explore the ways in which the arrangements signalled by our various concepts and categories are sometimes complementary, possibly necessary one to the other. More commonly, such "divisions" are seen as antonyms implying some necessary, invidious contrast between the two sides of the division, giving pride of place to one or the other. Critics of liberalism have been especially quick to press the advantage that such a pitfall poses for liberalism, accusing it of denigrating ideas and experiences equally necessary to a fully coherent theory of political life.

The critics, in turn, have often succumbed to a different temptation. They have sought to transcend the divisions of political life and some of its inevitable clash of ends by conflating and flattening out distinctions between public and private life, independence and community membership. This style of thought tends to posit some master concept or uniquely valuable experience that can transcend the plurality of ends and modes of experience. Rather than acknowledge a variety of values and a plurality of experiences which might, at times, be mutually supportive and, at others, in conflict, liberalism's critics have chosen to praise the harmony and suppress the conflicts. But liberalism warns against that sort of conflation of experiences and values that is false to their meaning and, subsequently, mocked by the socio-political context within which such experiences are undergone and such values realized.

There is, however, an alternative to characterizing the variety of values and multiple modes of experience as either irreconcilable or, if only we can discover the right translation mechanism, as neatly isomorphic. That alternative is to seek a fit among them without either dissolving their differences or simply engaging in crude trade-offs. Summarizing the major strategy of Benjamin Constant's liberalism, Stephen Holmes provides a precise statement of this alternative:

> Viewed as a whole, Constant's argument was this: civil liberty and political liberty are mutually interdependent. The abolition of one will eventuate in the abrogation of the other. Contrariwise, an increase in one form of freedom does not logically imply a decrease in the other. Indeed, each presupposes and vitalizes the other, and neither can survive in isolation. That is why Constant, in summarizing his position, urged his fellow citizens to integrate public action and private independence in a new pattern. Ancient and modern liberty should not be merely balanced but *combined*.[3]

Since public and private values vary and the conditions necessary to their operation are inhospitable to rigid determination, our combinations will always be marked by some looseness and indeterminancy, incapable of forecasting or controlling all future combinations. In light of that (weak) indeterminancy, we should be equally wary of theories whose concepts and categories are either rigidly dichotomous or perfectly continuous. So this strategy will not satisfy those who find intolerable the burden of living with a variety of goals that "are neither opposed to nor at one with each other" or who dislike theories that allow room for such tensions.[4] Yet the cumulative effect of the essays in this volume is to demonstrate the viability and attractiveness of this refashioned and more complex liberalism. This book argues that we are not confronted with a simple harsh choice between liberal individualism and some higher, more principled understanding of politics in order for citizens to have experiences that engage them in the practice of some good common to them all. Insofar as the quarrel between liberalism and its critics persists, it should now be seen for what it is: a judgment about how best to combine the practices and values signaled by various concepts and categories, not which set to choose.

This book does not claim to present a uniform version of liberalism. As is to be expected with any redirection of philosophical energies, even those travelling in the same direction are going to disagree about the best and safest route. So these authors are all willing to speak together, united, however, by a common project, *not* a common voice. This book is not a liberal manifesto, if that means that each author is an unambiguous partisan of liberalism. While some are self-identified liberals, others identify with liberalism not as it is but in terms of what it might yet become. There is, as Thomas Spragens points out, little likelihood of *a* reconstruction of liberalism. Instead, he advises that we are more likely to see reconstruction*s*. But he also offers reasons for welcoming that "family of reconstructed liberalisms." And he would, I think, agree that whether this signals some sort of liberal success is probably less important than the contribution the reconstructions of liberalism can make to that more decent politics that is the common project of all partisans.

III

The three essays in Part One provide the reader with both an assessment of liberalism's current standing and some more particular statements of how its reconstruction might usefully be undertaken. Ronald J. Terchek, in an overview of liberalism's successes and current dilemmas, starts by observing that the liberal language of rights has, indeed, produced an impressive series of political successes, including the extension of those rights to more and more members of society. But, he argues, that very expansion, along with the increasing number of desires that are pressed as rights-claims, has created a series of problems for liberalism. Those problems (Terchek canvasses six of them) revolve around the absence of any clear or common standard for arbitrating among rights-claims. Anticipating a theme that recurs in subsequent essays, Terchek notes that the individualism attending the vocabulary of rights can undercut a liberal political order by populating it with citizens whose actions are uncontrolled by anything more noble than self-gratification. Terchek reminds us that this concern, often associated with Rousseau and other critics of liberalism, was very much a part of the thought of liberals as diverse as Locke, Smith, and Mill. Each understood that "some of our desires can mislead us and retard our full moral agency." Warning against jettisoning important parts of the liberal tradition, Terchek points us toward a reconstructed liberalism in which the practice of virtue reassumes the leading place that it once occupied in the thought of earlier liberals.

Thomas Spragens had not read Terchek's essay before writing his own. Yet his reconstruction of liberalism begins just that contemporary account of the place of virtue (e.g., reason) in a liberal culture that is called for by Terchek's analysis. Organized around the issue of the public/private distinction within liberal thought, especially the relationship between the liberal state and a liberal society, Spragens contrasts the contractualist and neutralist models of this relationship with those of their (liberal) traditionalist and radical critics. He explains, first, why liberalism cannot be indifferent toward its own "enabling conditions" and, second, why it need not be. Liberals may have gone too far in their "political disenfranchisement" of reason, paradoxically jeopardizing the viability of the liberal state that such disenfranchisement was intended to serve. The very value liberals attach to a noninvasive state (i.e., regarding the formation of judgments about ways of life and moral beliefs) depends for its success on a liberal culture with norms governing the formation of such judgments and beliefs. A liberal theory of the state that is indifferent or neutral toward the society that constitutes the environment within which that state must operate is too vulnerable: "A citizenry without public spirit, without self-restraint, and without intelligence accords ill with the demands of effective self-government." What is called for is some more positive marshaling of forces on behalf of a liberal order. And Spragens concludes by explaining how "practical reason" can be such an ally. In an argument at once judicious and bold, he defends the idea of a society that is more liberal because it is more rational.

Although addressing a very different topic, alternative strategies for justifying liberalism's core values, James Fishkin's essay also positions the idea of a "self-reflective political culture" at the center of liberalism *and* its justification. Reviewing the various thought experiments that liberals have recently deployed to ensure impartiality in the choice of political principles (e.g., Ackerman's neutral dialogue, Rawls's veil of ignorance, and others), he believes that all suffer from "indoctrination" and "jurisdiction" problems, i.e., none is able to counteract bias or demarcate the range and types of claims properly admitted to the hypothetical choice situation. And, in any case, he notes that the real problem is not how to counteract bias in imaginary situations but in the actual environment where we and other citizens live. This self-conscious political judgment is important to his agenda for reconstructing liberalism. Contrasting his (fourth) strategy with those (three) that he finds deficient, what he proposes is that the central propositions of liberal theory not be seen as conclusions generated by some justificatory process, but as the "necessary conditions for *conducting* the evaluation." What matters about a self-reflective culture that instantiates important liberal values is that it encourages the continuous reevaluation of its own arrangements and practices. Importantly, Fishkin's philosophical essay reminds us that the process of justifying important liberal values is a political and practical activity.

Part Two moves us further into the specific characteristics of the philosophy of liberalism. Its four major topics are the liberal idea of freedom, the liberal sense of justice, a liberal theory of community and self-identification, and the possibility of a liberal public morality.

In "Liberalism and the Human Good of Freedom" Richard Flathman fills a surprising lacuna in liberal theories of freedom. Namely, such theories rarely respond with much detail or care to the question of why freedom itself is valuable. But that question, he notes, is implicated in any judgment about the comparative value of freedom and in every situation demanding some choice among conflicting freedoms. Understanding why freedom itself is a good is one way to better orient ourselves in such circumstances; it can also better reveal the range of possible agreements and accommodations available to rivals who, after all, are engaged in a family quarrel, i.e., their disputes occur within a particular type of society, one that accords considerable importance to free agency. That general valuation of freedom, Flathman argues, can best be explained and defended because freedom is instrumental to the "human good" of individuals who are end-seeking and purposive. Fully aware that others have attempted a "deeper" account of freedom, he faults such views for claiming too much for freedom (it is an intrinsic or self-evident good) and, consequently, actually saying too little about why it is a good. But even in a society that attaches a high value to freedom of action, there will be disagreements about the comparative value of freedom and the variety of freedoms. A "general presumption in favor of freedom" affects but cannot permanently forestall the question of how best to argue for it. Taking up that task, Flathman next unravels the complex of meanings and values summarized by the liberal notion that it is a prima facie good for human beings "to form, to act upon, and to satisfy interests and desires." What he has to say about this much abused liberal principle is both complex and commonsensical. In this connection, readers will note that he defends that principle from both critics of liberalism (e.g., perfectionists) and those liberals (e.g., Rawls) who would restrict freedom of agency in the name of some preferred system of ends or in order to preclude reconsideration of the structure of justice. In an important demurral from views expressed elsewhere in this book, Flathman defuses some of the more intense concerns about "desires" and "interests" that animate attempts to corral the liberal principle. He is closer to Fishkin in believing that a liberal culture must retain the freedom to evaluate and reconsider, to "settle and unsettle" the realm of freedom itself.

The two essays by Steve DeLue and Emily Gill converge, albeit in very different fashions, on how those processes of a self-reflective culture are implicated in the formation of a self capable of free agency and, yet, open to modes of discourse and experiences whereby one's membership in a liberal society becomes an important constituent of one's self-understanding. Both believe that the core liberal values of moral autonomy and free agency are consistent with, indeed facilitate, a way of life in which shared understandings, fellow-feeling, and intersubjective judging play a large role in each citizen's life. They start with the fact that liberalism is about individuals situated or living in a certain type of society (cf. Flathman). As such, the individuals who are the subject of liberal theory are necessarily enmeshed in a web of beliefs and institutional arrangements that importantly affect, first, what they expect of others and themselves, and, second, how they seek to satisfy those expectations. So, for example, DeLue's analysis, cast at the level of "ideal liberal theory," focuses upon the importance of a "sense of justice," i.e., the duty to make judgments about the moral worth of one's society, to the completion of ideal theory's account of a well-ordered society. (DeLue's reading of Rawls differs from Flathman's in that he argues that Rawls's just community requires that persons continue "to be agents of their own choice.") In DeLue's revised interpretation of Rawls's structure of justice there are strong demands upon individuals to satisfy themselves that the scheme is, in fact, "basically worthy of them." This sense of justice generates a moral culture whereby persons learn "how the activities of others in a just scheme contribute to our own agency and how we in turn contribute to the agency of others." This interdependency is worth underscoring, since it argues against the easy verdict that the disagreements and diverse interests characteristic of liberalism are necessarily fragmenting and divisive. They are, DeLue suggests, also the occasion for a political and moral education in which self-respect and respect for others are reenforced.

Emily Gill is also interested in the interconnections among individual purposiveness, virtue, and the identity of persons. In a provocative, yet powerfully persuasive, synthesis of the recent work by three distinctive thinkers—Michael Sandel, Alasdair MacIntyre, and Michael Walzer—she argues that the communitarian's concern with whether the individual's social environment elicits a self capable of meaningful choices makes the communitarian a natural ally of those who argue that all must participate in the formation and refashioning of their shared understandings. Gill's essay might be read as an account of the articles for reconciling communitarian and liberal ideals. And the first article of reconciliation is to understand that the alleged choice between "unencumbered" (liberal) and "situated" (communitarian) selves is no choice at all. Arguing that individuals always are situated within an ongoing community of shared understandings, her essay provides a novel statement of the importance of that "self-reflective culture" promoted by a liberal vision of political life.

William A. Galston's inquiry into "liberalism and public morality" marks the border between liberalism's philosophy and its more overt political practices. It makes for an easy transition between Parts Two and Three of this book. Galston sees a relationship between juridical liberalism and the recent political prominence of religious fundamentalism. The former is often understood to require that the state be mute on matters involving the morality of its citizens. That requirement led to the public dismantling of all sorts of practices (e.g., prayer in school) that, in turn, provoked the fundamentalist counterreaction. That counterreaction threatens the very foundations of a liberal order in that it demands the commingling of public and private spheres. If liberalism is to meet this threat, Galston argues, it must reconsider its own understanding of the relationship between the moral preconditions of a liberal order and the powerful juridical characteristics of that order, especially its alleged neutrality toward competing ways of life and its indifference on matters involving the choice of values.

Galston does not here reconcile the relationship between juridical liberalism and public morality. But he does something indispensable to such a project. First, he sorts out for us various versions of the neutrality postulate; indeed, he reminds us that there are important variations of this postulate. With that theoretical backdrop in place, he also denies that we are confronted with a simple either-or choice, in this instance between juridical liberalism and a concern for public morality. Rather, the issue is how best to hold on to certain features of juridical liberalism without abdicating any concern for civic virtue. The alternative, he argues, to a liberal theory of public morality is not state neutrality, but a state that becomes morally invasive in ways that undermine rather than support a liberal order.

Galston's essay, arriving at this point, should lead the reader to ponder again the importance and political implications of such topics as virtue, practical reason, and community covered in earlier parts of this book. Galston's analysis fills in that more philosophical landscape with political actors struggling over some very controversial issues. Politics itself is, of course, a mixture of competition and cooperation among citizens who finally have (or should have) the last word on many of these matters. Therefore, Part Three of this book more explicitly focuses upon political actors as we know them from everyday experience and the political institutions within which they pursue their ends and exercise their choices.

Part Three on the politics of liberalism covers the relationship between liberalism and democracy, offers a defense of such liberal institutions as representative government, and concludes by positioning liberalism closer to the activity of everyday political participants. But those three subjects are preceded by a pathfinding explanation of liberal political sensibilities and liberal reasoning. Deborah Baumgold's "Liberal Individualism Reconsidered," a careful exegesis of that theorist, Thomas Hobbes, who arguably stands at the liberal headwater, directly challenges those who use Hobbes's thought to tie liberalism down to an individualistic model of political reasoning. Struck by how few commentators have attended closely to Hobbes's political purposes, she argues that the "abstract individual" is not the subject of his *political* theory. On her reading, the problem of how, based on individualistic premises, to account for cooperation among the citizens of a liberal order is simply not the problem of Hobbism. Nor, she argues, need it define the agenda of liberal political theory. (This will surely confound a host of liberalism's critics.) Central to her revisionist model of liberal political reasoning are three key points. First, that Hobbes's political theory is about how best to constitute or organize the state so that important and necessary political functions get done. Second, that Hobbes's purposes commit him to a form of prudential, political reasoning that is clearly distinguishable from that more genetic logic that reasons from a hypothetical, psychological self-interested "everyman" to political theory. And, finally, that corresponding to Hobbes's structural-functional or constitutional picture of the state is a political analysis of roles and how this division of labor elicits the performance of civic duties. And, affirming the lessons of this more political Hobbes, she concludes:

> When political ties are impersonal, and government a distant organization, as Hobbes imagines these to be, political and structural solutions to collective goods problems are not only more practical than psychological, including moral, solutions; they are also more consonant with everyday political experience.

Yet the advantages of divorcing liberalism from an individualistic model of society are, she admits, contentious. The most immediate question is how a political division of labor fits with the liberal-democratic principle of equality, especially popular participation.

Elaine Spitz's study of "Citizenship and Liberal Institutions" and my own essay on the relationship between liberalism and democracy can be read, in part, as taking up the question posed toward the end of Baumgold's essay. Both of us argue that democracy is consistent with, indeed promoted by, characteristic liberal political arrangements and values. Spitz explains how liberal representational institutions provide citizens with "cohorts, intermediaries, inventors of bargains and agreements, leaders of coalitions": all of which enhance democratic equality. Similarly, I argue that democratic equality, i.e., public recognition of one's status as a citizen, is underwritten by the general valuation of free agency at the center of the liberal principle. There is also overlap in what Spitz and I have to say about the political style appropriate to that more impersonal State order discussed by Baumgold. Neither of us see liberal democracy as a poor relative hovering outside the mansion of direct democracy. Spitz is especially keen to tour what goes on inside direct democracy to dispel some of the more grandiose claims made on its behalf. And I have argued against the widespread view that liberal "strangers" make for poor democratic citizens by attempting to show that liberal-democratic arrangements encourage respect for "distant others." The effect, I suggest, is that popular rule and liberal individualism are mutually reenforcing. That suggestion echoes a reminder urged upon us by Spitz. In a voice more self-confident than liberalism's detractors, she tells us that

> modern liberalism does not flee "The babble of raucous interests and insistent rights," as one communitarian has disdainfully put it, but embarks instead upon the adventure of fashioning a world from agreements endless in their number and variety, and building institutions to process fairly those "raucous interests and insistent rights."

To renew liberalism we will also need to retain it.

More exactly, citizens themselves will have to keep it. Therefore, it is appropriate to end this book, in Charles Anderson's words, "closer to the everyday life" of citizens. In "Pragmatic Liberalism" Anderson recalls us to that ordinary world where we always "enter public life in mid-stream, never at the beginning." Liberalism, as this book has argued, is a compound of values, constitutive principles, and empirical calculations whose various parts admit of a more or less satisfactory assembly, a more or less satisfactory philosophical grounding. Liberalism is at risk, therefore, albeit not uniquely so, in three rather different ways.[5] It is epistemically at risk, potentially mistaken in how it conceives political relationships; ethically at risk, in that it might miscalculate the moral force of its proposals for a just regime; and practically at risk, in that the existing socio-political context might be inimical to the theory's realization. Assuming that the reconstruction of liberalism's formal theory can bring us safely past the first two hazards, there is still need to cover the final stretch: fitting liberalism, in Anderson's words, "to new contingencies and opportunities." It is this need to unite theory to practice that is the subject of his inquiry. Drawing upon pragmatist philosophy, he reconstructs that style of practical political judgment and decision making most appropriate to the "communities of practice" operating within a liberal order. But he emphasizes that the norms defining practice as "best practice," i.e., consonant with the values of a liberal regime, are more often "corrective than anticipatory," part of a continuous reappraisal and reconstitution of the practices themselves. The vital life of liberal politics, he reminds us, is ultimately located in the very practical activities of its citizens.

* * *

Any editor depends upon the cooperation and support of his contributing authors. This is especially true in the early stages of a book such as this one. One of the first persons with whom I discussed the idea for a collection of essays on liberalism was Elaine Spitz. Her suggestions, encouragement and promise to write a contributing essay were all important to the eventual completion of this volume. Unfortunately, Elaine Spitz did not live to see this book published; she died on February 8, 1986. The author of numerous essays on liberalism and democracy, Elaine had recently published *Majority Rule,* which has quickly become required reading for anyone interested in this most important democratic practice. That Elaine cared deeply about political theory is evident in everything she wrote. One of her last essays, presented here, is a characteristically energetic defense of citizenship within liberal democracy. For that essay and her friendship, I am very grateful.

Notes

1. For representative instances, see Michael J. Sandel, *Liberalism and the Limits of Justice* (Cambridge: Cambridge University Press, 1982); Stanley I. Benn and Gerald F. Gauss, "The Liberal Conception of the Public and the Private," *Public and Private in Social Life,* ed. S. I. Benn and G. F. Gauss (New York and London: St. Martin's & Croom Helm Publishers, 1983), pp. 31–65; and Arthur L. Kalleberg and Larry M. Preston, "Liberal Paradox: Self-Interest and Respect for Political Principles," *Polity* 17 (1984): 360–77.

2. Robert Paul Wolff, *The Poverty of Liberalism* (Boston: Beacon Press, 1968); Theodore Lowi, *The End of Liberalism,* 2nd ed. (New York: Norton, 1979); Michael Freeden, *The New Liberalism* (Oxford: Clarendon Press, 1978); and David Spitz, *The Real World of Liberalism* (Chicago: University of Chicago Press, 1982).

3. Stephen Holmes, *Benjamin Constant and the Making of Modern Liberalism* (New Haven: Yale University Press, 1984), p. 78.

4. Judith N. Shklar, *Ordinary Vices* (Cambridge: Harvard University Press, 1984), p. 249.

5. This observation is a variation on points made by John Dunn in "The Future of Liberalism." See his *Rethinking Modern Political Theory* (Cambridge: Cambridge University Press, 1985), p. 155.

— I —

A Liberal Agenda for Reconstructing Liberalism

– 1 –

The Fruits of Success and the Crisis of Liberalism

RONALD J. TERCHEK

Liberalism can be understood as a political language of rights and a theory that seeks to expand the range of choices for individuals in ways that do not interfere with the legitimate choices of others. In looking at what might be called the liberal tradition, we have a history of arguments about what is and is not a proper rights-claim; about the ways in which rights-claims can be justified; and about whether, how, and to whom we should expand rights-claims. Certainly, the identification and justification of rights that began with John Locke has not remained there, and the ensuing disagreements about the meaning and practice of rights remain robust in our own time. The language of rights has been used to dismantle many ascriptive disabilities, such as race and sex, that long served to deny rights to many members of liberal society. Rights have expanded in liberal society in both their content (what is a valid rights-claim) and in their constituency (who is effectively covered by a rights-claim). Each of these changes signals important successes for liberalism, but they are successes that introduce special problems for modern liberalism.

Many reasons help to explain some of the problems now confronting liberalism. One set of reasons, and the one I want to emphasize in this essay, has to do with the way we think about the liberal tradition and our propensity to pick some parts of earlier liberal theory but not others. In particular, I want to move away from a concentration on rights-claims and how they are justified and move to a consideration of how rights are practiced. The contemporary interpretation of the liberal tradition gives little attention to the practice of rights, but important contributors to what we call the liberal tradition, writers like John Locke,[1] Adam Smith,[2] and John Stuart Mill,[3] were preoccupied with the way rights were used. They believed that rights were good in themselves and necessary for a good life, but that rights, by themselves, did not produce the good life or happiness. For Locke, Smith, and Mill, liberty was intimately tied to virtue, but this concern is largely ignored in our present reading of the liberal tradition today. And that omission has contributed to the current crisis in liberalism. Liberalism today has become a theory without clear content in which interests dominate and a concept of moderation or restraint is absent.

Before turning to the crisis of liberalism, it is necessary first to emphasize that some of the problems we face in liberal society cannot be traced to liberalism. Sexism and racism are antithetical to the basic principles of free choice and are better explained as legacies of traditional practices that plague both liberal and nonliberal societies alike. Indeed, liberalism provides many of the critics of contemporary denials of rights with their greatest theoretical justification for changing the present state of affairs. Moreover, claims that liberalism is the basis of all of our difficulties often confuse an ideology with a variety of institutions and practices that exist independent of ideology. America is not merely a liberal society; it is also a mass, complex, industrial, interdependent, and bureaucratic society. To understand our present discontents as well as our opportunities, it is necessary to ask which of our difficulties are best traced to liberalism and which are better attributed to other sources. As intriguing as it would be to sort out all of the causes of our discontents, I simply want to concentrate on a set of problems that stem from the central assumptions and the axioms of liberalism and the way we think about liberalism today.

In the first section of this essay, I examine some of the central features of liberalism, assumptions which we generally accept as essential to liberalism but which have come to contribute to the current crisis of liberalism. The reason that some of the core assumptions have introduced critical difficulties for liberal society stems from the success of liberalism as it expanded its scope about who was properly considered a rights-carrier and what was considered a proper right. In the second section, I try to show that liberalism has undergone significant changes and these changes make the practice of liberalism different today than what it once was. The next section takes up what it means to talk about a crisis in liberalism today. In the fourth section, the problems of using the conventional interpretation of the liberal tradition are explored and reasons are offered to expand our understanding of what it means to talk about a liberal tradition.

Liberalism: Axioms and Assumptions

I take liberalism to be a theory that, through the language of rights, seeks to justify and ensure the moral autonomy of men and women. From the liberal perspective, to deny human beings rights is to deny their personhood. To be sure, liberals have disagreed about some of the kinds of rights that individuals should properly carry, and this debate among liberals has been reflected in the uneven expansion of the meaning and protection of rights.

A focus on right, however, is only part of the theory of liberalism that developed with writers as diverse as John Locke, Adam Smith, and John Stuart Mill. They were also concerned about the practice of rights and what it meant to include "moral" in something like moral agency. For them, virtue represented the highest level of moral agency, and their conception of virtue required them to emphasize the moral autonomy of all human beings. From their perspective, only free men and women could become truly good. Coercion might compel good behavior, but coercion could never make people good and clearly contradicted the autonomy of men and women.

In presenting their arguments about the moral agency of individuals and the importance of virtue, Locke, Smith, and Mill tried to avoid the seamy side of the individualism implicit in liberalism. Ironically, the dangers to the best practice of rights stem from three central axioms and assumptions found not only in their work but in the writings of most other liberals. These axioms are central to liberal theory, but they had not been fully pursued and their consequences not fully felt until recently. These critical assumptions revolve around the rejection of a prior political good, acceptance of a highly individualistic psychology, and the use of a universal language to describe rights-claims.

While most of the early liberals believed that a moral standard existed—whether found in religion or in human sympathies or in a secular rendition of virtue—none was prepared to accept any standard which the state enforced on its citizens. The absence of an established prior good for politics meant, among other things, that rights could not be distributed only to those who abided by the prior good. Everyone was entitled to rights, even if that meant that some people would exercise their rights foolishly. Although J. S. Mill, for example, wanted to promote virtuous conduct, he always insisted we needed to respect the moral agency of others, including those we thought were acting foolishly. This absence of a prior political good represents one of the great achievements of liberal theory because it recognizes that the state cannot give rights to some but withhold those same rights from others. But this very absence of a moral standard serves to complicate matters later in liberal society when rights come into conflict with one another and there are no consensual standards to differentiate strong claims to rights from weaker ones.

The assumptions embedded in the psychology of liberal thinkers were also to introduce special problems for subsequent liberal theory.

Their psychological assumptions are a series of variations on the idea that desires and aversions explain the way people act. We seek to satisfy our desires and avoid pain, and each of us defines what is good or bad for him, there being no prior psychological standard that is embedded in the psyche of each person. Each of us has his own schedule of likes and dislikes, and what appeals to one person may not be attractive to another. From this perspective, reason directs us to the most efficient way of achieving our desires and avoiding pain. Rather than tell us what is good, reason becomes instrumental in helping us achieve our desires. This reading of liberal psychology has led critics like Leo Strauss to fault liberalism for fostering hedonism,[4] while Roberto Ungar criticizes liberalism for its shallowness[5] and C. B. Macpherson admonishes the liberal character for its possessiveness.[6] What has also happened along the way is that many interests in liberal society have been advanced as rights-claims.

But what also needs to be remembered is that writers like Locke, Smith, and Mill believed that some of our desires can mislead us and retard our full moral agency. The recent work on Locke,[7] Smith[8] and Mill[9] clearly demonstrates the significance that these important contributors to liberalism attached to what they considered the higher desires, or what they saw as the practice of virtue. Liberals like Locke, Smith, and Mill expected that moral education and the institutional support such an education required could lead us to more generous desires than self-gratification.

For them, moral education was the cultivation of those habits which turned us toward the practice of virtue. They believed that as men and women internalized certain moral rules, they would then make the right choices. Failure of people to develop the proper habits leads to a major problem in their psychological theories, a problem which they acknowledged. They saw a weak side of human nature always lurking in the psychic background, a side that could not abstract itself from its immediate situation of searching for sensual gratifications. In the world that Locke, Smith, and Mill saw around them, powerfully seductive temptations threatened to diminish the attractiveness of virtue.

Their vision of a more noble self distinguished Locke, Smith, and Mill from some other liberal writers, like Franklin, who looked to prudence as the most important virtue. But Locke, Smith, and Mill hoped that personality would be defined in more than a mechanistic way and that men and women would see that only by denying their immediate gratification could they approach as full a happiness as is available to humankind. In developing their theory of a higher set of desires, they relied heavily on several institutions to guide people in making the right decisions. Locke was particularly indebted to religion, Smith to the deference of the lower orders to the more successful, and Mill to a public that would at least listen to an intellectual elite.

But when the individualistic foundations of liberal psychology are stripped of concepts like higher and lower desires and moral education is missing, problems develop in the way the language of liberalism is used. Liberalism is a language of rights, not of status or a prior good, and the language of rights is not a selective or confining one. Liberalism does not and cannot claim that some people are entitled to be free but others are properly denied the same kind of freedom. To use the language of Locke, for example, is to talk about "all men," "everyone," "everybody" and "Mankind" as rights-carriers. Such language not only makes a universalistic claim for rights, but also invites people to think of themselves as rights-carriers, regardless of their station or rank.

The use of rights as the liberal political idiom contributed to the tendency in liberal society to take an extraordinary number of grievances as denials of rights and to make an extraordinary number of claims to protect or enhance some preferred values as rights-claims. Women and ethnic minorities advance claims, as do pensioners and students, as do the poor and unemployed, as do advocates for the protection of animals and rocks. However worthy each of the claims might be, surely some claims about the denial of rights and about the need for the institutional protection of those rights-claims are stronger than some of the other claims. If we live in a world where not every good cause can be simultaneously met, how do we pick and choose which to advance? Given that there are no political prior goods in liberalism, that people often see their own interests in right terms, and that many political issues become rights-issues in liberal language, liberal society becomes congested with competing rights-claims but has no way of sorting out the most worthy. To understand how liberal assumptions were to create future problems, it is helpful to consider the role of change in liberal theory and liberal society and how it affects some of the institutional features that early liberals built into their theory of rights and their expectation that the best practice of rights would tame the vulnerable parts of their application of the theory of liberty.

Liberalism and Change

Unlike some other political theories that were suspicious or even hostile to change, liberalism always expected change and welcomed it. For some liberals, change helped to banish many of the superstitions that retarded rational thought, interfered with the market, or denied rights. For others, change helped to reduce some of the old hierarchical structures that retarded individual choice; and for still others, change meant economic growth that was assumed to benefit everyone in liberal society.

But change disturbs old values and institutions. What seems natural and harmonious in one setting may be irrelevant or discordant in a radically different one. In inviting change, liberals have found themselves in a dilemma. They wanted to remove obstacles to rights, but their theory of the practice of rights usually required the continued vitality of some settled institutions and values that had long been in place in their societies.[10] For example, when they talked about rights or freedom, early liberal writers expected people to exercise their rights rationally and prudentially. However much they differed with one another about what constituted rational or prudential choice, they agreed that some choices were obviously wrong and needed to be restrained, preferably without coercion. Many of the standards of reason and prudence they favored were embedded in the existing institutions and practices of their societies. Institutions like religion and deference were to be the basis of habits that, they believed, would limit self-interest and sensual gratification.

As Hirsch and Schumpeter have argued,[11] the institutional support necessary to tame the narrow individualism implicit in liberalism has been losing its vitality, and nothing has come to take the place of the discarded or weakened institutions. The old order has become increasingly irrelevant to the practice of rights or liberty, even though the original justifications of rights and liberty rested on the assumption that rights depended on certain practices that were in place and would continue.

A second change that has occurred in liberal society concerns the extensive increase in material goods available to the members of liberal society. From its inception through the present, most liberals have promoted economic growth to move society from an economy of acute scarcity to an economy of moderate scarcity. Their belief that material security was necessary for a happy society is in no way novel. Aristotle, for one, taught that the best moral prospects in men and women came when necessity had been overcome (*Politics,* Bk. I). Escaping severe economic scarcities was considered a precondition for rational choice for most liberal writers, and many of them spent an extraordinary amount of time trying to explain why a particular economic system would produce the abundance necessary for the prudential practice of rights. Even today, liberals like John Rawls and Amy Gutmann find an absence of acute scarcity is necessary if we are to talk about a realistic practice of basic liberties.[12]

Considering that one of the central tenets of liberalism has been the protection of rights and that the state can act as a potential protector as well as a threat to the use of rights, the members of liberal society have a concrete stake in the administration of the state, and this leads to a third change in the history of liberalism. If some citizens have participatory rights but others do not, there is always the danger that the enfranchised will capture the state for their advantage and at the expense of the rights of others. Political or participatory rights selectively distributed to some of the members of a liberal society but not others compromise the universal claims and language that have always characterized liberalism. If liberalism is to be consistent, political rights needed to be expanded to include all of the adult members of the community. And the drive for the expansion of the franchise has generally advanced in the language of rights. The argument, for example, of the early suffragettes has been commonplace in liberal society in its emphasis on the primacy of rights in general and participatory rights in particular:

> We have met here today to discuss our rights and wrongs, civil and political, and not, as some have supposed, to go into the detail of social life alone.
>
> But we are here assembled to protest against a force of government existing without the consent of the governed—to declare our right to be free as man is free, to be represented in the government which we are taxed to support, . . . And, strange as it may seem to many, we now demand our right to vote according to the declaration of the government under which we live. This right no one pretends to deny.[13]

What needs to be noticed is that the participatory component of contemporary liberalism is not the participatory component that was in place when the earlier contributors to the theory were writing. We generally assume that this simply means that the equal participatory rights that were implicit in early liberalism have finally been achieved, even if imperfectly. But it may not be so simple. As the franchise has expanded, not only have more people entered the world of politics, but more interests also have been represented there, and some of these interests are not as compatible with one another as had been the case when participation was restrictive.

The removal of many of the old suspicions that retarded freedom and choice, the increasing availability of material goods to the members of liberal society, and the expansion of political rights must be counted as impressive achievements for liberalism, along with an expansion of the application of rights to more and more members in liberal society. But the fruits of this success have not all been sweet.

The Crisis of Liberalism

The cause of some of our problems today is that liberalism has become eminently successful. By successful, I do not mean that the promise of liberalism has come to be enjoyed by everyone in liberal society. I mean that people increasingly have come to measure success by the standards of contemporary liberalism; in particular, people think of themselves in rights terms. Early liberalism may have used universal language to express rights, but the practical consequence of their times was that rights were highly limited in their conception and application, and historic, cultural, and institutional factors helped both to dampen claims to rights as well as to structure choices in ways in which different rights-claims were believed to be harmonious.

Every critic of liberalism has a favorite list of indictments to lodge. Mine departs from many of those lists in its absence of any discussion of equity or distributional issues. The reason for this is that I believe that liberalism has the conceptual tools to identify certain inequities in modern society and to correct them; and the reasons those tools have not been used can be explained outside the framework of liberalism. Nor does my list include a place for dismantling debilitating gender and racial inequalities. Again, the reason is that liberalism has the theoretical ability to solve the problems of sexism and racism and, indeed, has provided those who demand an end to these practices with their most powerful intellectual and political resources in the language of equal rights.

What I want to emphasize are problems that stem from liberalism and not from cultural or political factors that are independent of liberalism. Let me begin with a conflict of good causes. With the expansion of rights from Locke's original tidy conception of rights as life, liberty, and estate to a much broader understanding of rights, and with the expansion of claimants to rights, we have the problem of respecting each of a large and diverse number of recognized claims simultaneously.

Few issues exhibit the conflict of good causes in contemporary liberalism as much as does equality of opportunity. As a simple moral proposition, equality of opportunity stands against arbitrary distinctions that prohibit some from developing their talents and exercising their energies while others are given the chance. (In this sense, equality of opportunity holds that rewards in the market place should not be based on some arbitrary standard but should reflect the talents and efforts of free agents.) Liberals have long been devoted to ending certain arbitrary barriers to equality of opportunity, whether based on favors from the king's courts, royal charters, or other traditional justifications that were tied to status or privilege. There is, of course, no clear and consistent argument among liberal thinkers as to what constitutes unjustifiable barriers: most liberal thinkers up to the time of J. S. Mill saw no problem with limiting opportunities to men, a position that would hardly qualify as liberal today. Although liberal accounts vary on what constitutes intolerable barriers, there is an underlying assumption that something like equality of opportunity is necessary for moral agency. To deny some the opportunity to make the best of themselves but to allow others to have such choices is to discount the autonomy of some while affirming it for others.

Someone might not be prompted to test his talents, invest his energy, or compete in the market for any of several reasons. Legal and cultural restrictions clearly have relegated women and ethnic minorities to a limited number of positions rather than invited their full participation in society. And tied to the issue of culture is the issue of motivation. Groups at the bottom, regardless of gender or race, are frequently socialized to accept the idea that they deserve to be where they are and fatalistically to accept their position as natural. But if impediments are removed and motivation is high and no credible opportunities to advance are available, equality of opportunity becomes a contest between those who have arrived and those who want their place. Liberalism, however, has attempted to avoid this kind of internal civil strife by relying on economic growth. As the economy expands, more new places are opened, and people who could not otherwise be accommodated peacefully can now advance, at least theoretically.

The very success in removing legal barriers to equality of opportunity and the widespread decline of fatalism in a growing economy has not led to the kinds of benefits promised by equality of opportunity. Levels of dissatisfaction abound, and many believe the process is unfair to them. Some complain that they are under siege from those who want the benefits that they gained by their own industry and talents, while others argue they are unfairly treated because they cannot advance as long as members of previously favored groups continue to occupy desirable positions. The problem, it would appear, is that growth has not occurred quickly enough or that too many people thought themselves qualified to participate too quickly. Given that we do not like the moral implications of the latter reason, that is, those denied entry should remain outside a little longer so those currently benefiting can continue to do so tranquilly, we tend to turn to the issue of growth as a means of settling our concerns.

But economic growth as a solution represents the second problem in liberalism today. While growth occupies a prominent place in virtually all contemporary liberal theory as well as in much earlier liberal thought, too much is expected from the growth solution. The problem is not only that growth cannot be generated with precision and at will in order to satisfy all new claimants in the market; growth also produces some disturbing externalities. For those who are moderately successful in the framework of equality of opportunity, satisfaction is not generally defined as simply having more and more opportunities to move further and further ahead. Satisfaction also means living in a community that is a source of identity and pleasure, of facing a secure economic future, and enjoying family and friends. Unrelenting mobility may be important in the abstract, but in the world of concrete realities, most people want their success in the work place to lead to other satisfactions as well. But economic growth, which provides opportunities to people who would have otherwise been left with less desirable or poorer paid jobs than they now have, also can become a highly destabilizing force in society. Many jobs that once seemed secure become irrelevant in the growth economy; some regions or cities may decline as others take advantage of the new opportunities and prosper; and the future seems less promising to many than it might have been. Without growth, the conflict of good causes would be more acute than it is, but in providing more opportunities, growth has created its own set of difficulties.

Economic growth plays a special role in liberal democratic thought because it acts as a surrogate for justice. In an economy of growth, we assume that all of the members of society will become better off, both those with much as well as those with little. We do not have to worry much about distributional issues that would take from some so that others might have or deny to some so that others might thrive. With economic growth, we assume that equality of opportunity will be able to achieve fair allocations without political pain exacted from anyone. When growth is sluggish, we assume that no one is really responsible for the condition of those at the bottom, and the political regime is largely absolved of responsibility for attending to their needs except to provide the basic requirements for survival and to stimulate renewed growth as soon as possible.

Another problem in contemporary liberalism concerns the way rights-claims are advanced. While many rights are institutionally protected, others are recognized only through constant appropriations in the legislative process. Claims to a right to education, indexed social security, adequate health care, or assistance to the poor and unemployed, that is, some of the kinds of claims some liberals call basic liberties,[14] have taken on the character of entitlements that can be satisfied only by continued legislative action. But in periods when the economy sharply declines or when political authorities decide to hold spending constant or to reduce appropriations, economic allocations for entitlements or rights-claims become a function of the bargaining power of interest groups.

The argument is not whether most of the new claims to rights are worthwhile. Most are. What becomes important is what happens when one set of rights-claims conflicts with another, which, in this case, means that only some rights-claims can be fully funded. In this sense, many of the new entitlement claims depart from free speech or voting rights-claims which expanded to groups previously denied protection without denying free speech or the franchise to others. The reason for the conflict of many new rights-claims is that they often require money if the claim is to be put into practice. If students have a right to quality education, if the elderly have a right to indexed pensions, if the poor have a right to a decent standard of living, then their rights-claims become recognized only when funds are allocated. But if there is not enough available to fund each of these rights-claims adequately, how do we judge which groups have the strongest rights-claims and which do not?

To raise such a question is to run the risk of pitting members of liberal society against one another. Given that the character of rights is individualistic, some rights-claimants will wonder why they should be asked to surrender their perceived entitlements while others do not. Moreover, most rights-claimants think in absolute terms regarding their own claims and are not inclined to reduce their claims in order to favor others. When people think in rights-terms in liberal democracy and see their claims endangered or ignored, politics is their logical means of defense.

But liberal democratic politics has introduced its own difficulties. With liberal democracies situated in mass, urban, bureaucratic societies characterized by high levels of cultural, economic, and social diversity, it becomes difficult for individual citizens to have a sustained, consequential effect on policies that are of interest to them. But we know that they do not act as isolated individuals; many are part of well-organized groups that attempt to protect and enhance the benefits of their members. But group politics also have recently received bad notice. Robert Dahl, Mancur Olson, and Charles Lindblom see the political system dominated by organizations that serve the interest of their members but that care little about those outside of the group.[15] As the political regime becomes captive to these groups in critical issue sectors, responsibility to a broader public declines, the chances for rigidity and inflexibility mount, those with institutionalized power tend to benefit, and the unorganized pay. In short, the behavior of interest groups in contemporary society leads to increasing inequity in society and unrepresentativeness in government—the fourth crisis in contemporary liberalism.[16]

The role of well-organized interest groups in issue sectors is only part of the problem. What has happened to the concept of political equality in liberal democracies has become increasingly disturbing.

The concept of "one man, one vote" in the electoral process is critically important in establishing political equality, and as the earlier situation in the American South demonstrated, denials of the franchise to some because of their race is a failure of political equality. But while the universal adult franchise is a necessary requirement for political equality in a liberal democracy, it is not sufficient. Those outside the network of organized interest groups do not have effective access to or influence on the democratic process. Their concerns are less likely to be heard or represented, and so, for them, the assumption of political equality is severely undermined. But the efforts to restore political equity by fostering greater mobilization of the unorganized only adds to the kinds of problems Dahl and Olson see in contemporary politics today. Knowing that the addition of new entrants into effective regime politics will intensify the problems of rigidity does not provide those who are already represented effectively with an argument that the unrepresented should remain unrepresented. But efforts to correct the present state of political inequality will lead only to an exaggeration of the problems that presently haunt pluralist politics. Any solution that seeks to address the problems of both political equality and democratic responsiveness will have to respect the necessity of maintaining pluralist institutions, but it will also have to move beyond pluralism to devise new institutions for effective democratic participation.[17]

A fifth problem in liberalism today is the dominance of materialism as the essential test of equity and fairness in contemporary society. Clearly, there is nothing wrong with expecting people to give material interests an important place in politics. People who politically behaved otherwise would be as strange to Aristotle as to Adam Smith or to many contemporary critics of liberalism. Yet wealth was not seen as an end in itself by the early liberal writers, but as necessary to the accomplishment of other ends. In their own ways, Locke, Smith, and Mill cautioned about the dangers of inordinate emphasis on wealth, Smith referring to wealth as a trinket that promised more than it could deliver, and Mill complaining about the "money getting" he saw as so pervasive in his own society. Most of the early liberals attempted to think of ways in which people could place material goods into perspective, but popular conceptions of the good life increasingly became measured in terms of income and consumption, and possessiveness and materialism increasingly became an integral part of liberal practice.

The materialism that pervades contemporary liberal society ought not to be attributed to some severe defect of character among the members of liberal society or to a narrow human selfishness. Rather it is the consequence of the success of many liberal projects as well as of economic growth. As life in liberal society has become more institutionally secure for more people, it is possible for them to turn to concerns about comfort and pleasure. What distinguishes contemporary liberal society from other societies is not an inherent liberal desire for comfort and pleasure, but the pervasiveness of materialism and possessiveness in modern liberal society.

In recognizing the importance of escaping acute scarcity, contemporary liberalism has not asked what the purpose of economic plenty might be for its citizens. When economic prosperity is coupled with the individualism that is so much a part of contemporary liberalism, possessiveness and materialism become the ways people define their primary goals.[18] In increasingly making wealth the supplier of happiness in contemporary society and imposing no limits on wealth, contemporary liberalism has come close to arguing that distribution solutions are ends in themselves. Indeed, contemporary liberalism has made material distributions—whether they come from the market or from government—not the preconditions for justice and fairness, but the test of justice and fairness and a matter of rights. And citizens of contemporary liberal society have largely assumed a similar position, as personal affluence has become the way citizens judge political leadership.[19]

The final problem on my list concerns the debasement of reason and virtue in contemporary liberalism.[20] Reason has become instrumental to interests,[21] and virtue has often been made into something individualistic and utilitarian.[22] To be sure, the reason of Aristotle and the scholastics is not a reason we can conceptually accept on their terms today. But as Hilary Putnam argued, reason can rely on standards other than immediate self-interest for its justification,[23] an argument forcefully advanced in a significantly different context by Harsanyi.[24] But the role and status of virtue have largely disappeared in contemporary liberal democratic theory.

What distinguishes the role of virtue in political philosophy from its role in theology is important to my argument about the decline of virtue. In theology as well as in political philosophy, we are presented with actions that are considered virtuous and reasons why we should practice these virtues. But in theology, emphasis is devoted to the will of a moral agent. Theological disquisitions about virtuous conduct try to teach that even when choices are hard, people ought to be virtuous. Political philosophies, however, considered virtue in a different light. Although the moral virtues they discussed often paralleled the virtues advanced by some theologians, political philosophers attempted to locate the practice of virtue in a specific social situation which enhanced the prospect of virtuous conduct. Leaving aside the intellectual virtues, writers like Aristotle did not expect people continually to transcend their situation and become virtuous only as they lived a life of *continual* self-sacrifice. Such is the life of the saint, not the citizen. Aristotle did see that difficult choices might have to be made and that the virtuous citizen would sometimes have to sacrifice some other desired goal if he were to remain virtuous. But what is also important to remember is that Aristotle expected that the virtuous citizen would not ordinarily have to make tragic choices between virtue and his own self-interest. He and other political philosophers tried to construct institutions that they thought would reduce these painful choices. Indeed, we call their philosophy "political" because it was designed to think about the kinds of institutions that enabled people to live in a society where moral choices were not expensive. To move from the choices of the lifeboat to the practice of virtue in society requires us to think carefully not only about the kinds of virtue we want to promote, that is, the kind of society we value, but also the kinds of institutions that will provide incentives and opportunities for virtuous conduct and that do not penalize virtue. These kinds of questions are largely absent in contemporary liberalism.

The Liberal Tradition Reconsidered

Many who see something inherently wrong in liberalism accept the methodological assumption that there is a coherent tradition called liberalism and that a core value, commonly identified as something like rights or individualism, is shared by authors who are called liberal. While there is some disagreement about when the tradition began (was it Hobbes or Locke?), the idea that there has been a coherent tradition for about 300 years to which several thinkers contributed has been an important concept for many social scientists and theorists alike who attempt to understand and explain the way we think and act today in countries like the United States and the United Kingdom. Our present set of institutions and many of our values, according to this reasoning, have been heavily influenced by prior thought and action; and to understand our current situation, it is necessary to understand our liberal past. If we see interests run wild, materialism dominating, the community weak, and popular control inadequate, then probably some of our discontents should be traceable to our ideological legacy, that is, to the liberal tradition. After all, if the assumptions or axioms of liberalism are defective or incomplete, then there is a pressing need to reexamine the ways we understand and act in the world, replacing what is inadequate or wrong in the tradition with something that is beneficial.

While I agree that liberalism is concerned with rights, I have problems with the idea that there is a continuity about the language and meaning of rights and liberty in several writers commonly identified as part of the liberal tradition. The way we have usually identified the liberal tradition is too narrow, the way we use the term liberal tradition today has often become a liability. By concentrating only on rights and individualism, there is the danger that we are missing some other important elements in liberalism that can better help us understand our present situation. And by emphasizing liberalism as a justification for rights–claims but finding that liberalism is defective today, there is the danger that, in repairing and correcting our problems, we will jettison the most important part of liberalism, that is, basic rights. Finally, if our understanding of liberalism is incomplete, we run the risk of suggesting remedies that are inadequate to solving our present difficulties.

Something that was once valuable in understanding rights, liberty, and choice may have been lost or misunderstood through the many generational transitions that embody the history of liberalism. What is missing is important not because it supplies contemporary liberals with the correct answers to their problems, but because it offers categories of thinking about our problems that have been disregarded in much contemporary liberal thought.

The problems involved in using a tradition have been emphasized in the works of Pocock, Gunnell, and Skinner, who invite us to be cautious about how we understand texts written generations and centuries ago.[25] They have argued that we typically read authors who are said to belong to a tradition as if the meaning of language used by several generations of authors remained constant. We frequently assume that the authors were writing to us and using our assumptions and our language when they originally presented their ideas, but such an assumption is defective. Recent research generally shows that writers like Locke, Smith, and Mill carried assumptions about rights and used a language of rights which often differed from the ways we use the language of rights.

Although many early liberals talk about the practice and ideal use of rights, such concerns are largely absent in our contemporary language of rights. Seeing that many rights have been denied or that many people have been denied rights leaves us impatient with arguments which ask how rights will or should be practiced. But that impatience, while understandable, should not make liberals indifferent toward the practice of rights. If rights are something that are necessary and best used when certain other things are in place, we need to inquire what is necessary for the ideal practice of rights. We need to ask whether earlier contributors to liberalism believed that rights were heavily dependent on the vitality of certain institutions and values and whether either of these conditions is valid today, or whether the institutional expectations of some earlier liberals are not acceptable to contemporary society.

Linking rights and virtue seems a discordant connection to us because we see a danger in imposing some standards on the practice of rights, something that is contrary to the goals and purposes of free choice. But Locke, Smith, and Mill did not believe that a theory of the good meant that the good must be imposed on unwilling men and women. They believed standards did exist, only free men and women could achieve those standards, and institutions and opinion should publicize and teach those standards. In seeking to find ways to promote virtue within the context of moral autonomy, Locke, Smith, and Mill looked to a theory of institutions that would provide incentives for moral conduct without imposing coercive restraints on individuals. Locke, for example, looked to religion to act as an inducement for virtuous behavior; Smith relied on economic growth and deference to enhance the expression of the moral sentiments; and Mill emphasized the institutions of education and participation to draw people away from self-interested behavior to a larger concern about the other members of society. But the institutional solutions of these earlier liberal writers have not survived in a secular society and democratic polity,[26] and what we have taken of the liberal legacy is not what they had intended as a theory of free moral agency. They certainly would not recognize liberalism as a justification of interest group politics or unrestrained choice or intense individualism.

Conclusions

The contemporary crisis in liberalism is not a simple or passing one. It strikes at the way liberalism is understood and practiced today and raises serious questions whether competing rights-claims can be adequately satisfied, whether the liberal democratic polity can be open and responsive, whether the members of liberal society can escape an identity closely fixed on materialism, and whether liberal language can be open to concepts and practices like virtue and justice while continuing to give a prominent place to rights.

There are many reasons for the present discontents. Some have their origins outside of liberalism, such as industrialization; some have occurred because of the very success of liberalism, such as the expansion of rights; and some are embedded in the very nature of the liberal project, such as individualism. Even though liberal theory is highly implicated in contributing to our contemporary problems, it would be a mistake to assume that liberalism is hopelessly inadequate to address some of these problems or that it cannot reconstruct itself. It would be unimaginable to expect that any solution would be satisfactory to us if it did not have a strong commitment to universal moral autonomy, something which is at the very core of liberalism.

The first step toward a solution is to acknowledge that the liberalism that we practice today is only a partial replica of earlier liberalism. While modern liberalism shares much with its predecessors, its concepts of rights and agency have expanded. Moreover, as liberalism has evolved over the generations, what seemed important to some early liberals has been abandoned by later generations who have added their own understandings of what it means to talk about liberty. However, earlier conceptions of liberalism offer some helpful ways of thinking about what we might take into account in facing the present crisis. By this, I do not mean that we should search the writings of earlier liberal writers who might provide us with the best solution, but rather that we need to see what has been lost in modern liberalism and decide whether the losses are important. What has been lost are a content for liberalism as well as ways of thinking about moral autonomy and the practices that best typify free men and women. In particular, in their discussion of the role and importance of virtue, Locke, Smith, and Mill raised important questions about a direction for liberalism, about the liberal personality, and about the practice of rights. And their work also invites us to think about the kinds of institutions that are necessary to promote moral autonomy.

In turning to those liberal writers who attempted to give a content to liberalism, it is also necessary to remember what made them liberals: their insistence that only free moral agents could reach their best and that it is not the business of the state or other groups to compel morality; only free men and women can make themselves moral. But to acknowledge such a fact does not mean that moral agents must be shorn of their institutional setting and that institutions cannot contribute to ways which, at the minimum, remove penalities to the practice of virtue and, at the optimum, introduce incentives and opportunities to the best practice of virtue. A return to the kinds of issues which were a part of the early tradition of liberalism can help us meet some problems that contribute to the current crisis of liberalism.

Notes

1. John Locke, *An Essay Concerning Human Understanding,* ed. A. C. Fraser (New York: Dover, 1959); idem, *The Reasonableness of Christianity,* in *Collected Works* (London: T. Tegg, 1823); idem, *Some Thoughts Concerning*

Education (London: Cambridge University Press, 1934); idem, *Two Treatises of Government,* ed. Peter Laslett (New York: New American Library, 1960).

2. Adam Smith, *An Inquiry into the Nature and Causes of the Wealth of Nations* (London: Dent, 1950); idem, *The Theory of Moral Sentiments,* ed. D. Raphael and A. L. Nacfie (Oxford: Oxford University Press, 1976).

3. J. S. Mill, *Civilization,* in *Collected Works,* vol. 18 (Toronto: University of Toronto Press, 1977); idem, *On Liberty,* in *Collected Works,* vol. 18; idem, *Considerations on Representative Government,* in *Collected Works,* vol. 19 (1978); idem, *Utilitarianism,* in *Collected Works,* vol. 10 (1969).

4. Leo Strauss, *Natural Right and History* (Chicago: University of Chicago Press, 1953).

5. Roberto Unger, *Knowledge and Politics* (New York: Free Press, 1975).

6. C. B. Macpherson, *The Political Theory of Possessive Individualism* (Oxford: Oxford University Press, 1962).

7. See Nathan Tarcov, *Locke's Education for Liberty* (Chicago: University of Chicago Press, 1984); John Dunn, *The Political Thought of John Locke: An Historical Account of the "Two Treatises of Government"* (Cambridge: Cambridge University Press, 1981); and Alan Ryan, *J. S. Mill* (London: Routledge and Kegan Paul, 1974).

8. See Donald Winch, *Adam Smith's Politics* (Cambridge: Cambridge University Press, 1978); D. A. Reisman, *Adam Smith's Sociological Economics* (London: Croom Helm, 1976); and John Robertson, "The Scottish Enlightenment at the Limits of the Civic Tradition," in *Wealth and Virtue,* ed. I. Hont and M. Ignatieff (Cambridge: Cambridge University Press, 1983).

9. See Bernard Semmel, *John Stuart Mill and the Pursuit of Virtue* (New Haven: Yale University Press, 1984).

10. Fred Hirsch, *Social Limits to Growth* (Cambridge: Harvard University Press, 1976).

11. Ibid.; and Joseph A. Schumpeter, *Essays of J. A. Schumpeter* (Cambridge: Addison Wesley, 1951).

12. John Rawls, *A Theory of Justice* (Cambridge: Harvard University Press, 1971); Amy Gutmann, *Liberal Equality* (New York: Cambridge University Press, 1980).

13. Elizabeth Cady Stanton, "Address Delivered at Seneca Falls and Rochester, New York," July 19 and August 2, 1848, as cited by Ross Paulson, *Women's Suffrage and Prohibition* (Glenview: Scott, Foresman & Co., 1973), pp. 37–38.

14. See Rawls, *Theory of Justice.*

15. Robert Dahl, *Dilemmas of Pluralist Democracy* (New Haven: Yale University Press, 1982); Mancur Olson, *The Rise and Decline of Nations* (New Haven: Yale University Press, 1982); and Charles E. Lindblom, *Politics and Markets* (New York: Basic Books, 1972).

16. Cf. Ronald J. Terchek, "Retrieving Pluralism," *Ethics* 94 (1984).

17. Cf. Benjamin Barber, *Strong Democracy* (Berkeley: University of California Press, 1984); and Carole Pateman, *Participation and Democratic Theory* (Cambridge: Cambridge University Press, 1970).

18. Macpherson, *Possessive Individualism.*

19. Lindblom, *Politics and Markets.*

20. See Unger, *Knowledge and Politics;* and Alasdair MacIntyre, *After Virtue* (Notre Dame: Notre Dame University Press, 1981).

21. Thomas Spragens, *The Irony of Liberal Reason* (Chicago: University of Chicago Press, 1981).

22. MacIntyre, *After Virtue.*

23. Hilary Putnam, *Reason, Truth and History* (Cambridge: Cambridge University Press, 1981).

24. John Harsanyi, "Morality and the Theory of Rational Behavior," in *Utilitarianism and Beyond,* ed. A. Sen and B. Williams (Cambridge: Cambridge University Press, 1982).

25. J. G. A. Pocock, *Politics, Language and Time: Essays in Political Thought and History* (New York: Antheneum, 1973); John Gunnell, "The Myth of Tradition," *American Political Science Review* 72 (1978): 122–34; and Quentin Skinner, "Some Problems in the Analysis of Political Action," *Political Theory* (August 1974): 277–303.

26. Cf. Schumpeter, *Essays;* and Hirsch, *Social Limits.*

– 2 –

Reconstructing Liberal Theory: Reason and Liberal Culture

THOMAS A. SPRAGENS, JR.

The past 15 years have seen a considerable renewal of interest in liberal theory—both in reexamining the ideas of classic liberal theorists such as Locke and Mill and in producing new or revised constructive theories of liberalism. It also seems clear by now that this effort has not produced and is not likely to produce some new grand theory of liberalism that commands general acceptance. What accounts for this pattern? And what lessons should we draw from it for our current efforts?

The theory of liberalism seems worth reconstructing, I would suggest, because the fundamental political orientation and values of liberalism have appeared to regain or retain their appeal at a time when other orientations have suffered. Not long ago, liberalism seemed to be on the defensive—at best shopworn, possibly obsolescent, at worst a source of destructive policies and insoluble problems. Radicals and reactionaries alike delighted in heaping scorn on poor, mundane, stumbling liberalism: it stood condemned from the left, and apparently with some justification, as an ineffectual check on repressive and imperialistic policies; and at the same time it was condemned from the right, also with some apparent justification, as at least a victim and at worst an instigator of social and cultural disintegration.

But times and circumstances change. The homely and pacific liberal virtues and practices that suffer in periods of crisis tend to regain their appeal in somewhat calmer periods. Simultaneously, the principal antagonists of liberalism find themselves more on the defensive. It is not only arch-conservatives, for example, who have wondered in recent years about the viability of socialism. Even those on the left have noted that seeming inability of socialist societies to avoid economic and cultural stagnation. And serious reformers of socialism find it hard not to borrow traditional liberal practices—such as civil liberties and the use of market mechanisms—in order to give socialism a "human face" and economic dynamism. Traditionalist and authoritarian reactions, on the other hand, seem only to demonstrate by their very unattractiveness the necessity of holding fast to representative institutions and to protections of civil rights.

The political theory of liberalism, then, seems worthy of the serious attention it had a hard time attracting earlier. But why should we be concerned with the reconstruction of liberal theory? Why not speak more simply and unproblematically of its revival? If at least some of the traditional practices of liberalism have seemed able to regain their appeal in relatively unaltered form, why cannot the same be the case for the traditional theory of liberalism? Why can't we simply restate the old arguments in exactly the same terms with renewed assurance?

The fact is that the philosophical foundations of political liberalism have always been suspect in a number of respects. In its earliest incarnations, liberal philosophy tended to be something of a problematic amalgam of largely unexamined traditional beliefs and rather simplistic metaphysical and epistemological ideas that attended the first attempts to make sense of the scientific revolution. This pattern is manifest, for example, in Locke's embrace of corpuscularism in metaphysics and empiricism in epistemology together with his fidelity to relatively traditional notions of natural law. It also appears in Condorcet's twin attachments to a conception of knowledge as applied mathematics and a conviction that such knowledge included the apprehension of human rights and the common good.

Such a combination of benign dogmatism and philosophical incoherence proved difficult to sustain over time, however, for rather obvious reasons. With changes of culture in the course of history, critics emerged who were unwilling to accept as "givens" the kinds of moral beliefs that Locke and Condorcet took for granted or that Tom Paine and Immanuel Kant assumed in their different ways to be part of "common sense." The old verities were just not so common, and they accordingly could not be construed as "simple truths," either. Doubt about the normative core of liberal beliefs was hardly assuaged, moreover, as more searching philosophical criticism uncovered the gaps and even the incompatibility between liberal values and liberal philosophy. What Carl Becker called the "chill at high noon of the Enlightenment" produced by Hume's skeptical reflections deepened as the nineteenth and twentieth centuries progressed. As the philosophical premises characteristic of modernity were refined, they tended to cannibalize the very liberal norms that earlier liberals expected them to sustain.

Liberalism was thus left, philosophically speaking, in an uncomfortably exposed position. One had to shrug off the erosion of liberalism's philosophical basis and hold fast to liberal values and practices despite their seeming theoretical groundlessness—rather like Hume himself returning to his game of backgammon. Or one had to abandon liberalism for seemingly more defensible and philosophically vital creeds—such as Marxism or existentialism. Or else one had to construe liberalism in such a way as to make it compatible with philosophical positions that could command some respect.

Those who undertook the latter task generally tried to assimilate liberal values and practices to utilitarian, empiricist, and positivist philosophical perspectives. By whittling away at parts of liberalism and by refashioning others, some successes could be achieved in this enterprise. These attempts to reconcile liberalism with acceptable schools of modern philosophy, however, have suffered from some profound liabilities. For liberalism's traditional concern with human rights is difficult to reconcile with a straightforward utilitarianism, liberalism's traditional concern for freedom is difficult to justify in conjunction with empiricist determinism, and liberalism's traditional concern for human dignity and the common good comports awkwardly at best with positivism's emotivist view of ethics.

These considerations, I think, sustain the conviction that reconstructing liberal theory is a useful enterprise. If liberal goals and liberal practices were truly irrelevant and outmoded, who would care to undertake the task? And if liberalism were a clearly articulated, coherent, and philosophically well-grounded theory of politics, no one would need to worry about rethinking its content. But neither of those states of affairs exists. Liberalism is neither obsolescent nor theoretically unproblematic. Hence the current interest in working through liberal theory once again, with an eye to both what we have learned from several centuries of the liberal project and what we have learned from contemporary philosophy.

It would be a fool's quest, however, to look for some single comprehensive theory of liberalism that could account for all liberal policies in a coherent fashion and could win the assent of all liberals. There never was *a* liberalism, only a family of liberalisms. Consider, for example, the political theories of Locke, Condorcet, Tom Paine, Bentham, Adam Smith, James Mill, John Stuart Mill, Benjamin Constant, Hobhouse, and T.H. Green. These are all liberal theorists, but they clearly represent a variety of viewpoints in their accounts of the fundamental purposes of liberal polities, in their moral theories, and in the priorities they establish among competing liberal values. What they share is a family resemblance that consists principally in their common dedication to some version of civil liberties and representative government.

We can always strive, of course, to improve somewhat on this historical record. But I think we are not likely to improve on it a great deal. We are likely to see not *the* reconstruction of liberal theory, but rather reconstruction*s* of liberal theories. Even if our best efforts are likely to produce only a family of reconstructed liberalisms, however, they are still valuable. The process of reflecting upon the beliefs and values that inform liberal institutions can accomplish several worthy ends. We can improve upon the traditional theoretical justifications for liberalism, jettisoning those accounts based upon premises we can now recognize to be untenable or contradictory. We can clarify the grounds of agreement and disagreement that bond and divide the quarrelsome family of liberals. And the internal tensions and complexities of liberalism can be illuminated considerably.

The Liberal State and Liberal Culture

One of the persistent issues of liberal theory that has generated a variety of answers, each with distinctive policy implications, concerns the appropriate relationship between the liberal state on the one hand and liberal society and culture on the other.

One of the genuinely decisive steps in the birth of liberalism, surely, was the acceptance of the idea that it was possible to discriminate between public and private realms of social life and that it was both possible and salutary to confine the scope of government authority to the limited public domain. In the context of European history, what liberalism offered was an escape from the wars of religion and other socially disintegrative consequences of the Reformation. The Act of Toleration constituted the central institutional implementation of this idea. And the best theoretical justification for it at the time was provided by Locke's *Letter Concerning Toleration.*

What Locke offered in his brief treatise was a variety of arguments—some moral, some theological, some epistemological, and some politically prudential—in favor of delimiting the authority of government to external and this-worldly matters. Public, authoritative mandates could feasibly be restricted, Locke argued, to protecting the lives, liberties, and property of the people. Decisions about the ultimate value and meaning of life, on the other hand, were intrinsically internal and voluntary—beyond the capacity of governmental coercion to determine or enforce, and hence appropriately to be left to the private domain.

A hallmark of liberalism has been the acceptance of the general logic behind this public/private distinction and the promotion of constitutional arrangements to give it effect. In this country, it is the First Amendment that gives paradigmatic expression to the central conception: it is no proper part of government's role to try to determine or constrain what the citizens believe about matters of morality and religion or to constrain their expression of these convictions in their private lives. Because our "inner" and "outer" selves and our "self-regarding" and "other-regarding" actions are not always easy to segregate, of course, problems of drawing the line in policy terms between the public and private domains are perennial and persistent. The general principle, however, remains essentially uncontroversial to the liberal mind, even if its concrete deployment is problematic.

The general conception of a liberal polity in which there is a restricted public domain of government authority and a larger realm of private society, however, has room within it for a number of significantly different conceptions of the appropriate interplay between the two domains. Different liberal theorists have offered very different conceptions of what a "liberal society" should be and how it should relate to the liberal state. What some theorists have seen as essential to a successful liberal polity others have seen as problematic, and vice versa. Clearly, although the liberal state can be "separated" in some legal and policy respects from liberal society, it cannot be isolated from it. But what type of social underpinnings are most conducive to a successful liberal regime and what social norms and practices are logically entailed by liberal values? Here the liberal consensus breaks down.

There are likely a whole range of normative models of the relationship between the liberal state and liberal society, but four seem to me to be especially important and influential. We can label these four models the neutralist, the contractualist, the traditionalist, and the radical conceptions. Each has had illustrious exponents. And some of the most significant internal debates and policy disagreements within the liberal tradition stem from disagreements over which of these conceptions is most persuasive. Any attempt to reconstruct liberal theory, as a consequence, to the degree that it strives to be somewhat comprehensive, must face up to the issues that generate these disagreements and offer a defensible response to them.

The neutralist and the contractualist models of liberal society are less substantively determinative than the other two. They share this open-endedness, perhaps, because they tend to share a basically agnostic position concerning morals; but they differ somewhat on the operational consequences of the moral neutrality principle.

For the neutralist liberal, liberal society is a pluralistic cipher. No standards or norms follow from liberal principles, according to the neutralist, for the appropriate conduct of liberal society. There is no such thing, then, as "liberal culture." The only norm is that the state be utterly and wholly neutral among the various life styles and value systems that people embrace. In some respects, at least, the core decision-rule in Bruce Ackerman's *Social Justice in the Liberal State* comes close to being paradigmatic of the neutralist position. A liberal polity should be utterly laissez-faire with regard to its surrounding culture. Its only concern is to regulate the conflicts among the different groups with their different conceptions of the good life by applying the principle of neutral discourse: no argument on behalf of any policy shall be given a hearing if that argument presumes that any one person or any one conception of the good is better than or superior to any other person or conception of the good. Because of some auxiliary hypotheses and claims, Ackerman draws some highly egalitarian conclusions from his principle of neutrality. But these conclusions are beside the point here. The crucial notion is the hardening of Locke's policy of toleration into a fundamental neutrality principle and the elevation of this principle to the preeminent constitutive norm of liberal *praxis*.

The contractualist conception of the relationship between the liberal state and liberal society shares the neutralist's insistence upon the principled indifference of a liberal regime to the values and culture of its citizens. The underlying rationale for this position tends to be somewhat different for the contractualist, however; and, as a consequence, some of the policy implications tend to be different as well. The neutralist tends to derive his neutrality principle from a combination of moral skepticism and egalitarianism: every person and his/her conception of the good is "at least as good as" all others. The contractualist derives his insistence on neutrality from a combination of moral skepticism and a devotion to individual liberty and rights. On this view, the essence of the liberal state is a contractual obligation entered into freely by individuals in pursuit of their rational self-interest. The logical distinction between liberal society and the liberal state is eroded, then. Both are governed by the principles and norms of a market society, with the state only one special instance of the mutually advantageous compacts that constitute the only legitimate cases of "collective" action. "Values" are for the individual to determine; and the liberal state must remain neutral among different conceptions of the good life not so much out of respect for the equal worth of individuals as out of respect for their inviolate right of self-determination. Because of their different axial principles, the neutralist and the contractualist tend to diverge on the implications of state neutrality for social justice: the gap between Ackerman's norm of "undominated equality" and Nozick's norm of freely acquired "entitlements" may be taken as representative of this divergence. But both of these theories of liberalism concur in their insistence that the liberal state can and should remain wholly indifferent about competing conceptions of the good life. A liberal society and culture is protean and plural. It is whatever the individuals populating it choose it to be. These choices are expected to vary. And neither the variety nor the protean quality of liberal culture and society are considered problematic to the successful functioning of the liberal state.

The traditionalist and the radical interpretations of the relationship between the liberal state and liberal society take issue with this common supposition of the neutralist and contractualist views. On both of these accounts, it would be unreasonable to expect a liberal state to remain viable and coherent in the context of any sort of culture whatever. The traditionalist and the radical do not deny that it cannot be a legitimate function of the liberal state to force a specific set of values or a specific conception of the good life or a specific set of beliefs about the ultimate meaning of the world upon its citizens. They believe in their different ways, however, that only a certain range of cultural norms and social practices are really consistent with the requisites of a healthy liberal polity. If the society diverges too greatly from this range of norms and practices, tensions or "contradictions" develop between the political and social spheres of the liberal system, and these tensions and contradictions at best inhibit the proper functioning of the liberal state and at worst undermine it altogether. The traditionalist and the radical thus share what might be called a "content specific" conception of liberal society by contrast with the open-ended conception found in the neutralist and contractualist models. Where they differ is in their views of what the content of a liberal culture should be.

By traditionalists, I simply mean those who understand the dynamics of the moral life in the general fashion of the classic tradition of moral philosophy—including the natural law tradition, the Judeo-Christian tradition, Stoicism, and the Platonic-Aristotelian tradition. What these outlooks share is the conviction that the fundamental moral task is the restraint, regulation, or sublimation of natural human selfish passions on behalf of a larger general good. This task may be characterized as the noetic harnessing of the appetites, the overcoming of *amor sui* by *amor Dei,* or conformity of the will to the demands of moral law. In each case, however, the common theme is the necessity to control and restrain selfish inclination for the sake of larger moral purposes.

Some who share this understanding of the moral life find that it—in conjunction with a bleak view of the capacity of individuals to accomplish this task of moral regulation internally—leads them beyond the liberal camp altogether into some form of political authoritarianism. If *id* cannot become *ego,* then a specific institutional *superego* may be required. As Burke phrased this logic:

> Society requires not only that the passions of individuals should be subjected, but that even in the mass and body, as well as in the individuals, the inclinations of men should frequently be thwarted, their will controlled, and their passions brought into subjection. This can only be done *by a power out of themselves*, and not, in the exercise of its function, subject to that will and to those passions which it is its office to bridle and subdue.[1]

In their various ways, Plato, Freud, and Luther could be said to have assented to these assumptions and to the general conclusion adduced from them.

What distinguishes the liberal traditionalist from the traditionalist detractors of democracy is the hopeful belief that liberal culture can find within itself the resources to accomplish the restraint on selfish passions that they agree is necessary for a viable polity. Instead of looking to a specifically political force "out of themselves" to perform this task, they hope that liberal society can morally habituate its citizens in ways sufficient to the demands of self-government. Leviathan is not necessary to prevent a slide into a war of all against all if the spontaneous moral resources of a liberal society can produce self-restrained and public-spirited individuals.

This general perspective could be said to be shared by a range of liberal theorists. Contrary to some accounts that depict him as a Herbert Spencer hiding behind pious terminology, Locke seems to have assumed that religion and education could and should create a moral community that needs state power only to remedy significant but marginal "inconveniences" and to protect against the depredations of a relative few vicious and degenerate men. John Stuart Mill cautioned that not all cultures could accommodate the demands of representative government. "Whenever the general disposition of the people is such, that each individual regards those only of his interests which are selfish, and does not dwell on, or concern himself for, his share of the general interest, in such a state of things good government is impossible."[2] But he hoped that education and moral habituation in culturally "developed" societies could permit a liberal regime to flourish. In the same category, I think, are the admonitions of James Madison in *Federalist #55* that apart from "qualities in human nature which justify a certain portion of esteem and confidence . . . the inference would be that there is not sufficient virtue among men for self-government,"[3] Walter Lippmann's assertions about the importance of "the second civilized nature" of human beings that constitutes "the moral system, indeed the psychic structure, of a civilized society,"[4] Reinhold Niebuhr's reference to a human "capacity for justice" that "makes democracy possible," and the concern of the republican tradition with "civic virtue."

The common theme among these accounts, then, in the context of our concern with the relationship between a liberal state and liberal society, is this: the belief that a liberal state cannot function successfully in any culture or society whatever, but instead requires for its viability a culture that civilizes and socializes its citizens along the lines of the traditional moral systems of mankind.

The radical view of the relationship between the liberal state and liberal society is similarly content specific, but it is informed by the notion that modern philosophy has underwritten a legitimate transvaluation of older conceptions of morality. A liberal culture, then, is a "liberated" culture. And the appropriate social setting for the liberal state is a society that produces liberated individuals. What differentiates the radical from the traditionalist is a contrasting normative anthropology—one that sees the natural human passions as benign and spontaneously constructive rather than as problematic to the mutual accommodations of civil society. The radical, therefore, sees the social and cultural "inhibition" of the passions not as a necessary task of a civilized liberal society and a stable liberal state, but rather as the antithesis of the whole liberal project. Not surprisingly, perhaps, liberal theorists of this persuasion may drift over from the libertarian wing of liberalism into the anarchistic wing of socialism—just as the traditionalist liberal may be tempted to slide toward the right when crises arise.

My sketch of this ideal type conception of liberal society may be something of a caricature, in the sense that it is hard to specify a liberal theorist who completely corresponds to the description. Nevertheless, there is a strong element in modern philosophy and liberal culture that embodies this general perspective. The romantic features of Bentham's hedonism and Rousseau's devotion to psychic authenticity, perhaps, are important components of the orientation—one that characterized some "New Left" views of democracy, to take a recent example. And, although he is not really a liberal social theorist, Marcuse's account of "the unifying and gratifying power of Eros, chained and worn out in a sick civilization"[5] provides one version of a philosophically sophisticated rationale for this perspective—one that arguably is an outgrowth of liberal optimism about human nature.

Facing Up to a Liberal Dilemma

The neutralist, contractualist, and radical models of the relationship between the liberal state and liberal society have virtues as well as drawbacks. The radical conception reminds us that the ultimate value of liberal democracy lies in its contribution to the flourishing of individual lives and not in any intrinsic value of purely procedural mechanisms. It similarly provides pointed reminders to some of the ways in which even a putatively liberal state and liberal society can remain unnecessarily repressive even as they congratulate themselves on being part of the "free world." The contractualist model alerts us to the oppressions that democratic majoritarianism may unnecessarily impose on the functioning of a liberal regime and usefully illuminates the way in which market mechanisms can protect individual autonomy and lessen political confrontation in a liberal system. The neutralist theories suggest a philosophically simple form of *entente cordiale* that respects the rights of self-determination of liberal citizens and promotes their equal opportunity to realize their varied life goals.

On the other side of the ledger, the radical view of a proper liberal society seems to lapse at times into romantic illusions and infantile dreams about a world in which everyone can be perfectly free and happy pursuing his or her own pleasures in the absence of any obligations or constraints. The contractualist model incurs the justifiable criticism that it reduces the communal relations of liberal society to a "cash nexus" and violates the fundamental moral maxim of not treating people as mere means by turning them into commodities. And the neutralist model seems to be only a second-best kind of ideal, one that surrenders much of the moral purpose of human community and one that in the process leaves its egalitarian aspirations logically shaky.

Each of these conceptions of liberal society, I would argue, also shares with the others a fundamental inability to solve or circumvent a persistent and deep-seated liberal dilemma that the traditionalist conception at least recognizes and takes seriously. This dilemma arises from the fact that some of the most essential limitations and imperatives of the liberal state prevent it from undertaking a comprehensive effort to shore up some of its enabling conditions. Specifically, it is imperative upon the liberal state to be "neutral" to its surrounding and sustaining culture in significant ways: a legitimate liberal state may not establish a religion or impose a particular set of values on its citizens. It must tolerate a wide range of beliefs and behavior among its members and must allow them to "pursue happiness" according to their own lights. Yet a liberal society cannot really be totally "neutral"—in the sense of being utterly indifferent—to the character of its citizenry. As both unsympathetic critics of democracy since Plato and sympathetic analysts of democracy such as Madison, Tocqueville, Mill, and the civic republicans have correctly noted, a "corrupt" culture can place great burdens on the viability of liberal government and can possibly undermine it altogether. A citizenry without public spirit, without self-restraint, and without intelligence accords ill with the demands of effective self-governance.

Many liberal theorists, including the contractualist, the neutralist, and the radical, seek to evade this problem by ascribing extraordinary powers to astutely crafted institutions or by embracing utopian conceptions of human nature or both. When a thoroughgoing advocate of free market contractualism such as Milton Friedman, for instance, is faced by issues posed by human bigotry or by the corruption of entrenched group power, he seems simultaneously to understate the historically demonstrable social effects of the *libido dominandi* and to overstate the power of the invisible hand to restrain and overcome these corruptions. The radical's optimism that the one imperative of a liberal culture is an absence of restraint on human desires sustains itself only through the embrace of highly questionable assumptions about the spontaneously self-corrective dynamics of these passions—as in, for instance, Marcuse's claims about "self-sublimating sexuality" and "libidinal morality." And the resolute neutralist never explains very satisfactorily how he expects groups holding radically divergent values not only to respect each other's integrity but even to consent to potentially significant redistributions of economic power from themselves to others whose values they disdain.

One of the interesting aspects of Rawls's *A Theory of Justice,* I think, is that it offers an innovative way of dealing with this latter dimension of the problem. His is a conception, one might say, of a deontologically derived liberal *homonoia.* For *homonoia* grounded in a common dedication to a shared conception of the good life he has no place. He accepts the neutralist assumption that this form of concord is precluded by our epistemological incompetence to know what is good. But he argues that the inescapable plurality of conceptions of the good life need not preclude consensus on a universally acceptable conception of justice as fairness. Part of the appeal of Rawls's view of liberal society, then, is that it offers the prospect of giving that society a basis for moral unanimity even in the midst of a plurality of systematically irreconcilable and inadjudicable conceptions of the good.

The difficulty, of course, is that Rawls is really not able to deliver on this promise. As the spirited controversy surrounding his theory indicates, it is not much easier to produce unanimity about what is just than about what is good. We can discuss distributive justice profitably, clarify the issues, and persuasively disqualify some patterns of distribution as rationally and morally indefensible. However, for some good reasons we cannot pursue here, morally serious people of good will cannot fully transcend some crucial disagreements over the appropriate criteria for allocating the resources and burdens of a liberal—or any other—society.

The Community of Discourse and the Discipline of Reason

It would be naive and misleading to suppose that some theoretically luminous and practically simple solution or set of solutions is out there waiting to be found by sufficiently assiduous analysis. The dilemma confronting a kind of society that—for good, practical, and moral reasons—eschews the forceful imposition of a particular morality, religion, or conception of the good upon its citizens but at the same time is—possibly more than any other kind of regime—dependent for its viability upon the character of these citizens is not easily resolvable. Indeed, it may not admit ultimately of any fully satisfactory answer, instead standing as an explanation of the inherent fragility of liberal regimes in an imperfect world. The best that can be hoped for is that the issue be confronted seriously by those engaged in reconstructing liberal theory and that, in the process, the various resources of a liberal society in protecting and preserving the cultural preconditions of its success be identified and encouraged. Many of the most influential recent theories of liberalism, I have argued, have essentially evaded the problem by adopting unrealistic assumptions. Recent critical examinations of liberal society adopting the traditionalist perspective, on the other hand, illuminate important dimensions of the problem but don't go far beyond exhortation or hand-wringing when it comes to making constructive suggestions.[6]

One promising contribution toward the end of identifying self-sustaining resources of a liberal society would be a new appreciation of the nature and potential social role of practical reason. At the outset of liberalism's historical career, it was a widespread assumption that the social power of rationality would be the principal propelling force behind liberal progress. It was the power of rational analysis and critique that was expected to erode the foundations of oppressive government by destroying its legitimacy. And when liberal enthusiasts looked hopefully toward the future, it was with anticipation toward a time when people would "know no master but their reason."[7]

It seems safe to say that this confident faith in the liberating and governing power of reason has fallen on hard times within the theory of liberalism. When liberal theorists speak of rationality, it is generally in the sense of "economic rationality"—a conception that, in Humean fashion, construes reason as a technical functionary enslaved to individual self-interest. Rationality in action thus carries some legitimacy as a vehicle of the free, individual wants and desires that liberalism sanctions and seeks to satisfy. But reason as the enemy of oppression, as an agent of reconciliation, and as an appropriate functional substitute for traditional authority has largely disappeared from liberal theory. Rawls and Gewirth have tried to revivify the Kantian account of moral reason to reinvest liberal theory with an ethical dimension transcending wholly "heteronomous" motivations and criteria. For the most part, however, liberalism has become a philosophy of will rather than of reason.

The sources of this transmutation and demotion of rationality within the liberal tradition are many and complex. Central to the process, however, has been the striking erosion over the last three centuries of belief in the moral competency of reason. At the outset of liberalism, it was widely believed that the sharpened powers of rational inquiry would carry into a more accurate and precise grasp of moral conceptions, such as rights, duties, obligation, and the general good. Descartes remained within the Augustinian tradition that conceived of moral wisdom as the capstone of knowledge, for example. Condorcet clearly assumed that the capacity of scientific reason to proceed via "infallible methods" to the discernment of "simple truths" extended into the domain of moral guidance. And John Stuart Mill, in the middle of the nineteenth century, still could believe (a) that the reliability of our moral knowledge was constantly on the increase; (b) that this increased reliability would produce an ever greater consensus on moral beliefs in advanced society; and (c) that this process of improvement in and concurrence about our moral knowledge was central to the dynamics of the political progress he anticipated. Mill thought it "the highest aim and best result of improved intelligence to unite mankind more and more in the acknowledgement of all-important truths"; and he inferred from his epistemological precepts the belief that "as mankind improve, the number of doctrines which are no longer disputed or doubted will be constantly on the increase."[8] These assumptions, in turn, were not peripheral adornments to his prognosis for liberal democracy, but were central to his analysis of how intellectual progress helped to solve the dilemma of the relationship between the liberal state and liberal society. For Mill conceded that "the strongest propensities of uncultivated or half-cultivated human nature (being the purely selfish ones, and those of a sympathetic character which partake most of the nature of selfishness) evidently tend in themselves to disunite mankind, not to unite them." What makes social existence possible, then, is "a disciplining of those more powerful propensities"; and this disciplining process "consists in subordinating [the selfish propensities] to a common system of opinions."[9]

In recent liberal theory, however, it is Humean skepticism that has triumphed. Whether on the left or the right wings of liberal thought, most contemporary liberal theorists have agreed in assuming the implausibility of Mill's views just cited and have inferred from this assumption that consensual moral judgments and the dynamics of practical discourse cannot play a meaningful role in a liberal system. On the "right" libertarian side of the spectrum, as in the arguments of a Milton Friedman, the moral philistinism and relativism of Adam Smith remains intact. It is in part because our moral views are basically rationally irreconcilable functions of individual taste, on this account, that each individual must properly be left to dispose of those economic assets under his or her control. And however much a Rawls or Ackerman may dissent from the account of distributive justice provided by the libertarians, they concur in assuming that rational inquiry into the nature of the good life is not a viable component of the normative conception of liberal society. Ackerman's view that the logic of liberalism begins with the postulate that no conception of the good is any better than another was noted earlier. And Rawls makes clear that any moral consensus of liberalism must center on justice rather than on goodness because "reasoned and uncoerced agreement is not to be expected"[10] on moral, philosophical, and religious issues. In terms of the dynamics of liberal order, one could say, then, that Rawls offers his theory of justice as a possible functional substitute for Mill's "common opinions" whose appearance he sees it as unwarranted to anticipate.

We have ample grounds, both logical and empirical, to agree with Rawls and other recent liberal theorists that the hopeful assumptions entertained by Mill, Condorcet, Descartes, and many other early liberals about the creation through an emergent moral science of moral unanimity in liberal society were in fact unsustainable. Without going into any detail, we can say that one of the major flaws in this conception was the failure to perceive that the mathematicizing methods whose development was central to and markedly productive within the natural sciences were not simply extendable to the concerns and issues of practical reason.

Nevertheless, those interested in reconstructing liberal theory need to consider whether the recent tendency to leave rationality on the sidelines, as it were, when it comes to specifying the fundamental norms and dynamics of a liberal society may not be carrying the political disenfranchisement of rationality too far. The accounts of the politically determinative and morally transformatory powers of reason found in early liberal theory were insufficiently thought through and raised false hopes. On the other hand, recent liberal theory may have gone too far in reacting against these earlier misconceptions. Despite their philosophical weakness, the early liberals' faith in reason had at its heart an intuitive appreciation of the civilizing and unifying effect of rational discourse and inquiry that was not unfounded. A failure to appreciate the validity of this basic intuition prevents us from recognizing the ways in which a less utopian and less simplistic conception of moral reason may be both adequately warranted and capable of making a significant contribution to the health of a liberal society. In more modest ways than they imagined, the early liberals were not wrong in thinking that the dynamics of reason could and should be helpful in preventing the centrifugal forces in a liberal society from resulting in political disintegration, corruption, and stalemate. If this supposition is correct, one of the components of an improved theory of liberalism would be a better account of the political efficacy of rationality.

Rational inquiry and discourse can make a number of significant contributions to the creation of a social order adequate to the stringent demands of a successful liberal regime. Before concluding, let me mention four of these contributions. The first two are central to the conceptions of rational *praxis* found in Weber and Hobbes. These contributions can be recognized and appreciated by even the most resolute empiricist. The other two contributions can be identified with a bit of help from theoretical observations found in Hume and Habermas and from noting practices of the Greeks. These contributions of reason to a liberal society require a postpositivist conception of practical reason as a solid theoretical basis; but even they can be appreciated at a commonsense level without awaiting accomplishment of that philosophical task.

First, as Max Weber insisted, it is the function of the rational mind to ferret out and place before resisting people what he termed "inconvenient facts." The will to believe that facts we do not like do not exist is remarkably strong. Fellow travelers denied the existence of Soviet gulags for years. "What caused the disastrous defeat of American policies" in Vietnam, Hannah Arendt wrote, was "the willful, deliberate disregard of all facts, historical, political, geographical, for more than twenty-five years."[11] And Anti-Semites often like to deny or minimize the facts of the Holocaust. The crucial task of reason in this context, then, is quite simply to establish, to verify, and to insist upon what the contingent facts of history and what the current facts of society are. In all societies it is needful that the pleasure principle be disciplined by the reality principle in this very basic fashion. For a liberal regime that legitimates and seeks to carry out the expressed policy choices of the citizenry, this task is especially important.

A second function of rationality that likewise bolsters the fragile powers of the reality principle in its perennial clash with human passions was well described by Hobbes. As Hobbes wrote, nature provides human beings with "notable multiplying glasses, that is their passions and self-love, through which every little payment appeareth a great grievance"; but they are "destitute of those prospective glasses . . . to see afar off the miseries that hang over them, and cannot without such payments be avoided."[12] Hobbes's observation makes an appropriate epigram, perhaps, for the current floundering efforts to grapple with the budget deficits in this country. Once again, human passions and wishful thinking generate a willful failure to look at the likely future consequences of present actions. Reason, of course, is incapable of making up for a failure of will—in this case or in any others. But what it can do is insist upon what the probable future will be as a result of current trends and current policies. Reason, in short, supplies the "prospective glasses" to help combat the dangers of the myopic passions in Hobbes's account. To the extent that the theoretical understanding can grasp relations of cause and effect, it can give us glimpses of the future—not precise predictions, to be sure, but at least some sense of what will occur, *ceteris paribus,* if present causes continue to operate on future events.

At times, the capabilities of reason just mentioned—taken together with the difficulties of making them operative in a liberal democracy—have led some theorists into taking a technocratic turn: politics should not be permitted to frustrate what reason knows. The factual and predictive roles of reason, however, are only a part of democratic discourse rather than a substitute for it. Facts do not by themselves determine action without some guiding will and purposes. Hence, it is also important to illuminate the role of reason in the process of formulating this will and these purposes in a liberal democracy. In this context, the insights of a Jurgen Habermas about the role of healthy practical discourse in rational will-formation need to be taken seriously by liberal theorists. Habermas may set his demands upon a "rational society" unreasonably high, and he may render some questionable critical-empirical judgments on the dynamics of contemporary society. But his insights into the importance of rationally discursive will-formation to the legitimacy and efficacy of a free society recapture in a useful way a vital part of liberalism's Enlightenment heritage.

Whether practical discourse can in fact create some consensus on the legitimate ends and purposes of society may be doubtful. Such an expectation probably fails to give sufficient weight to the irreducible diversity among the various legitimate particular interests and values within any society—and certainly within any advanced pluralistic society. On the other hand, the possibilities of producing some degree of convergence upon mutually agreeable general goals and policy directions should not be written off so completely as the assumptions behind neutralist and contractualist models of liberal society would require.

In resolutely neutralist and contractualist conceptions of liberal democracy, the discourse among citizens comes perilously close to being nothing more than a game of threat and bluff among adversaries. Citizens do not reason with each other, in the sense of engaging in rational discussion about what they should do. They simply bargain with each other. They indicate their self-interest and then either overcome or compromise with those who stand in the way.

This theoretical reduction of practical discourse to tactical signalling is partly a consequence, no doubt, of the positivist–inspired disposition to construe normative propositions as simple expressions of preference. On this account, assertions about what ought to be done are cognitively empty and fraudulent to the extent that they purport to be more than assertions of self-interest. But this reductive version of ethical "emotivism," as is now widely recognized, provides a distorted and misleading account of normative discourse. That distortion in turn undermines a proper understanding of the shape and content of a healthy "democratic conversation." And that weakness produces an unfortunately truncated conception of a liberal society.

The fundamental question of practical discourse is "what ought to be done?" The "ought" may represent either a moral imperative or prudential wisdom. In either case, an appropriate answer to the question may well conflict with unadulterated immediate preferences—even at the individual level. For example, I possibly ought to spend some time with my children, although I would prefer to play golf. Or I possibly ought to eat more fish and fiber, even if I would prefer steak and eggs. When individuals "wrestle with their conscience" on matters like these, part of what is going on is a process of internalized practical discourse.

When this practical discourse is carried on overtly among members of a group, additional pieces of data become relevant and a new element is added to the logic of discourse. Since prudential "oughts" are grounded prima facie in legitimate human needs or rights, it becomes relevant for these needs or rights to be identified and articulated. This necessity requires each party to the conversation both to ground his own claims in defensible considerations of legitimate needs or rights and to recognize the defensible needs and rights of other parties to the conversation. The logic of moral discourse, moreover, winnows out particularistic criteria of evaluation and imposes a general perspective on all speakers. As David Hume put it, anyone who wishes to engage in rational practical dialogue must use language based upon "general preferences and distinctions" rather than upon private prejudices or interests; each party to the dialogue "must affix the epithets of praise and blame in conformity to sentiments which arise from the general interests of the community."[13]

Participation in a healthy democratic dialogue about public policy, therefore, plays a significant role in counteracting those forces in a liberal society that—unchecked—tend toward anomic individualism. The logic and the conditions of participation in the discourse "discipline" those "selfish propensities" whose correction and restraint Mill rightly insisted to be important. In a genuine practical dialogue—as contrasted with a shouting match or a bargaining game—all individual desires must be set into a framework of evaluation that focuses upon general interests and concerns. Selfish propensities receive validation only to the extent they can be rendered compatible with a defensible conception of the common good. Individual motivations, of course, may well remain refractory, since mind and will are not the same. But particularistic claims lose much of their force when they stand stripped of moral legitimacy and revealed as power grabs based on naked self-interest.

Participation in practical dialogue also helps counteract the tendencies toward fragmentation within a liberal society in another way—this one psychological rather than simply logical. Dialogue itself works to create a communal relationship among its contributors. We can call this the "community of discourse." Its effects were noticeable and appreciated among students of the democratic Greek city-states, but they are not confined to that one historical setting. As Jean-Pierre Vernant observed in *The Origins of Greek Thought,* the dialogue of the *agora* worked to generate a community of moral equals. It worked on behalf of democratic fraternity. "Those who contended with words . . . became in this hierarchical society a class of equals." And the dialogue among this class of equals produced a "public domain," a community of "common interest, as opposed to private concerns, and open practices openly arrived at, as opposed to secret procedures."[14]

Centuries later, Tocqueville commented upon the same dynamics in his observations on American democracy. Citizens "who are bound to take part in public affairs," he wrote—and, we might add, who are bound to participate in rational dialogue about those public affairs—"must turn from the private interests and occasionally take a look at something other than themselves." He continued:

> As soon as common affairs are treated in common, each man notices that he is not as independent of his fellows as he used to suppose. . . . Those frigid passions that keep hearts asunder must then retreat and hide at the back of consciousness. Pride must be disguised; contempt must not be seen. Egoism is afraid of itself.[15]

This is but a sketch, of course, of some of the ways that reason is important to liberal society. Even this very cursory treatment, however, should be sufficient to make at least a prima facie case for several contentions:

1. that the problem of potential "contradictions" between the requisites of a liberal state and the dynamics of a free society remains a real one;
2. that many recent liberal theories—among them the neutralist, contractualist, and radical conceptions of the relationship between the liberal state and liberal society—either evade or give an inadequate response to these potential contradictions;
3. that the power of rational analysis and the dynamics of rational practical discourse help to mitigate these contradictions by forcing citizens of a liberal society to confront distasteful realities, to discipline their individual passions on behalf of common interests, and to respect the demands of a democratic community.

And, if these claims be warranted, it follows that those attempting to reconstruct liberal theory should not succumb too hastily to a complete skepticism about the competency of practical reason. Limiting the democratic dialogue to simple bargaining among those animated by self-interest or by putatively divergent views of the good life concerning which nothing rational can be said is neither necessary nor wise. The early advocates of liberal reform who envisioned reason as their ally may have been misled in some respects about the sway reason could exercise over politics. But they shared an intuitive sensitivity to the civilizing and moderating power of rationality that contemporary liberals should not dismiss too easily.

Notes

1. Edmund Burke, *Reflections on the Revolution in France* (1790; reprint ed., New York: Liberal Arts Press, 1955), p. 68. Emphasis in the original.

2. John Stuart Mill, *Considerations on Representative Government* (1861; reprint ed., Chicago: Henry Regnery Co., 1962), p. 31.

3. James Madison, *The Federalist Papers* (1788; reprint ed., New York: New American Library, 1961), p. 346.

4. Walter Lippman, *The Public Philosophy* (New York: New American Library, 1955), p. 64.

5. Herbert Marcuse, *Eros and Civilization* (New York: Random House, 1955), p. 39.

6. One striking feature of two of the very best recent analyses of the problematic cultural underpinnings of the liberal state, I think, is the notable contrast between their detailed and illuminating diagnoses and their relative dearth of constructive speculation about ways of mitigating the problems they identify. See Daniel Bell, *The Cultural Contradictions of Capitalism* (New York: Basic Books, 1976) and Alasdair MacIntyre, *After Virtue* (South Bend: Notre Dame Press, 1981).

7. Condorcet, *Progress of the Human Mind,* trans. June Barraclough (London: Weidenfeld and Nicolson, 1955), p. 179.

8. John Stuart Mill, *On Liberty* (1859; reprint ed., Indianapolis: Bobbs-Merrill Co., 1956), p. 53.

9. John Stuart Mill, *A System of Logic,* book six (1843: reprint ed., London: Longmans', 1959), pp. 604-5.

10. John Rawls, "Kantian Constructivism in Moral Theory," *The Journal of Philosophy* (September 1980): 542.

11. Hannah Arendt, "Lying in Politics," in *Crises of the Republic* (New York: Harcourt Brace Jovanovich, 1969), p. 32.

12. Hobbes, *Leviathan,* pt. 2, chap. 18.

13. David Hume, *An Enquiry Concerning the Principles of Morals,* sec. 5, pt. 2.

14. Jean-Pierre Vernant, *The Origins of Greek Thought* (Ithaca: Cornell University Press, 1982), pp. 46, 51.

15. Alexis de Tocqueville, *Democracy in America,* ed. J. P. Mayer, trans. George Lawrence, 12th ed. (1848; reprint ed., Garden City, New York: Doubleday and Co., 1969), p. 510.

– 3 –

Liberal Theory: Strategies of Reconstruction

JAMES S. FISHKIN

In this essay I will sketch a strategy for justifying certain values at the core of liberalism and will attempt to develop what I think is distinctive about my proposed strategy by contrasting it with what I take to be the main alternative strategies with which it might be compared. The entire presentation is informal and amounts to a prefatory sketch of an argument I develop elsewhere at greater length and in greater detail.[1]

Recent liberal theory has been distinctive for its thought experiments: transporting us to an imaginary situation or transforming our motivation so that we choose political principles under conditions in which only the morally relevant factors bear on the decision. Two kinds of imaginary devices have been employed to ensure impartiality—changes in the situation of choice and changes in the motivation (within which I include filtering requirements by which only certain motivations are selected, while the rest are prevented from bearing on the decision).[2] When the motivation for choosing principles has been altered or filtered in the interests of impartiality, I will classify it as "refined"; when people choose, or are imagined to choose, with unaltered motivation (as, realistically, we would expect to find them in actual life), I will classify those motivations as "brute." When the situation for choosing principles is the one in which those who must abide by the principles live together as an on-going enterprise, I will classify it as an "actual" choice situation. When the situation for choice is an imaginary one, held to be morally relevant, but not the situation in which those who must abide by the principles must live together as an on-going enterprise, I will term it "hypothetical."

These distinctions can be combined to produce the fourfold table pictured in Figure 3.1.

Motivations	*Situation*	
	Actual	Hypothetical
Brute	I	II
Refined	IV	III

Figure 3.1

An example of category I is offered by actual consent theory. According to this approach, if people consent in real life, they are obligated to uphold the state; if enough (whatever that means) do actually consent, then the state is held to be legitimate and, somehow, everyone is obligated.[3] Motivation and situation are as we find them. Neither is subjected to some transformation in the name of impartiality or moral relevance.

Category II transforms the situation for choice but not the motivation. Nozick's state of nature is a good example. We are to take the question of whether there should be a state at all to the "best anarchic situation one reasonably could hope for."[4] The motivations of people in this state of nature are not altered; they must be given a realistic construction. We are to assume that some would join protection associations voluntarily; others would choose to be independent. However, a major problem of Nozick's argument is whether his scenario for the minimal state is compatible with a realistic construction of people's preferences—whether, in particular, independents would be fully "compensated" in being forced to join the state.[5]

Category III transforms not only the situation, as in category II, but also the motivations for choice in that situation. In Rawls's original position, agents are to choose principles of justice so as to maximize their shares of primary goods without knowing whom, in particular, they will turn out to be. They are endowed with an abstract preference for primary goods regardless of the details of their actual life plans; they will know the latter only after the veil of ignorance is lifted.[6] In Ackerman's spaceship dialogues, entrants to a new world argue over the distribution of "manna" through a filtering device for relevant arguments (the "neutrality" assumption).[7] The perfectly sympathetic spectator of the classical utilitarians has both an imaginary vantage point (omniscience) and a postulated motivation (he reproduces in himself every pain and pleasure in the world and, hence, will prefer states of the world which maximize the net balance of pleasure over pain).

Of the possibilities in Figure 3.1, the basic difficulty with the top row categories (I and II) is that they are subject to *indoctrination* problems, while the basic difficulty with the right column categories (II and III) is that they are subject to *jurisdiction* problems. The only possibility offering the clear hope of avoiding both is category IV (the left bottom quadrant). The proposal I will suggest here is an instance of that category.

The top row possibilities are subject to indoctrination problems because they take motivations as they are without any requirements specified for how they come to be that way. If people generally consent or accept an alternative because they have been brainwashed or manipulated, that result has the same standing as when they come to their conclusions after a fair and unbiased analysis. Preferences are "brute" in categories I and II. No mechanism is built into these strategies for counteracting bias. In contemporary work this criticism applies, for example, to Tussman's use of actual consent theory[8] and to Walzer's *Spheres of Justice* (where the "shared understandings" current in the society determine the boundaries between "spheres" of life that ought not to be crossed).[9] It can also be applied to hypothetical choice scenarios involving brute motivations (category II). If people accept a regime or a distribution because of indoctrination, then the legitimacy of brute motivations as a basis for choice has been undermined.

It is because of this inadequacy of brute motivations that the main thrust of thought experiments in liberal theory has been the *purging* of bias and indoctrination—the determination of what appears in the chart as "refined" motivation. Behind Rawls's "veil of ignorance" we cannot design principles so as to endow ourselves with any special advantage. We do not even know what our actual preferences are (nor do we know any other particular facts about ourselves). However distorted our actual preferences, they are not permitted to bear on the choice of principles in the "original position." Behind the "veil of ignorance," we must consider our own interests as if they were the interests of anyone, our class interests as if we were members of any class, our personal histories as if they were the product of any particular history of socialization. A similar purging of bias occurs in Ackerman's theory of neutral dialogue. Compatible with his notion of neutrality, we cannot even use our own theories of the good in giving reasons for one distribution rather than another. Various forms of utilitarianism address the same problem, although they are generally less successful. Because the perfectly sympathetic spectator of the classical utilitarians must reproduce in himself every pleasure and pain in the world, no one's pleasure or pain gets special consideration. But this is a less adequate purging strategy. It escapes from some biases by counting all utility equally. But should the satisfaction of preferences induced by brainwashing and indoctrination count the same as those induced by autonomous reflection? Perhaps an "ideal" utilitarianism such as J. S. Mill's (which distinguishes higher and lower forms of utility) offers some response to this problem, but it does so only by positing a particular, controversial theory of the good.[10] In giving more than equal weight to some patterns of human development, Mill's strategy brings into question utilitarianism's claim to equal consideration—a claim which was, originally, at the core of its appeal.[11]

In any case, the general point is that a central motivation for the hypothetical choice strategies of category III is that they provide a remedy (but sometimes only a partial one) for the indoctrination problems characteristic of categories I and II. But when "refined" motivations are combined with "hypothetical" situations for choice, jurisdiction problems must be confronted.

The difficulty is that once we depart from actual life, we can appeal to any number of counterfactual situations. Even slightly different accounts of impartiality and slightly different notions of relevant claims or interests in these imaginary situations yield drastically different results.[12] Which imaginary court has jurisdiction when each can make precisely symmetrical claims?

Category IV offers the prospect of avoiding this problem, at least in its crucial aspects. The idea is to attempt to purge the actual ongoing society—rather than some imaginary counterpart—of bias and indoctrination bearing directly on fundamental questions of political authority. The notion of a *self-reflective political culture,* which I will suggest here, is intended to bring the self-purging dimension of liberal thought experiments home to the environment people actually live in, rather than merely to one they are asked to imagine.

This fact sharply differentiates my proposal from the purely hypothetical strategies (II and III). If the purging of indoctrination were limited to hypothetical scenarios, then the real people—namely us—who are asked to embark on one imaginary journey or thought experiment rather than another would need to question our capacity for evaluating the merits of the competing hypotheticals—each of which yields dramatically different prescriptions at the end of the journey.

Let us grant advocates of strategy III the benefit of the doubt. Strategy III (as opposed to II) clearly has the merit that it is explicitly designed to respond to bias and indoctrination. But the issue is how do we choose, in the first place, an unbiased remedy for bias and indoctrination? Unless a theory incorporates our requirement for a self-reflective political culture in the actual, on-going society, its advocacy of any given hypothetical strategy is suspect. Suppose Rawls's (or Ackerman's or an enlightened utilitarian's) theory of justice were fully instituted. Part of what Rawls means by "a well-ordered society" is that people will come to believe in the merits of his theory of justice when they live with it in its fully realized form.[13] If that well-ordered society does not continually subject its governing theory to conscientious criticism and dissent, then its members must rationally question their capacity to evaluate the governing theory (compared to its serious rivals). In Rawls's state people would learn to take the question of the basis for justice to Rawls's original position; in Ackerman's state they would learn to take the question to the imaginary process of neutral dialogue (under the perfect technology of justice); in a fully utilitarian society they might learn to take such questions to the imaginary procedure of the perfectly sympathetic spectator. But to the extent that their *actual* society—however ideal according to the theory in question—fails to incorporate the self-reflective requirements we are proposing,[14] agents in that society face an unendingly controversial choice among competing hypotheticals intended to eliminate bias. It is not enough that the Rawlsian original position (or any of its rivals) is, itself, intended to eliminate bias. The problem is how to eliminate the bias in *our* choice of, or susceptibility to, any particular thought experiment for eliminating bias rather than any other.

An agent in a self-reflective political culture is in a different situation. Unlike a person in Rawls's proposed just society (or that resulting from any of the other versions of strategy III), he has a compelling line of response to jurisdiction problems from hypothetical thought experiments—provided that they purport to bear on the question at issue (the question of whether there should be freedom of political culture in the demanding sense proposed here). First, he can respond that only *with* (or with at least) a self–reflective political culture are they (the advocates of any of the rival principles at issue) in a position to evaluate the claims of competing hypotheticals. Second, no argument from such a hypothetical can be conclusive to the point of obviating the need for continuing self-reflection on the part of the system. Advocates of rival theories who would presume to eliminate the conditions of actual evaluation within the system are foreclosing the dialogue even though they have no firm conclusions to put in its place. Hence strategy IV offers a distinctive response to jurisdiction problems—but only on the narrow question at issue, whether the conditions of evaluation (for a self-reflective political culture) need to be continually maintained.

My position is that the particular version of strategy IV suggested here is necessary for solving what we will call the "legitimacy problem." While proponents of more complete theories can reasonably disagree on a wide range of substantive conclusions, my proposed conclusion concerns only the distinctive conditions necessary for solving the legitimacy problem. The argument is on defensible ground if distinctive conditions can be linked to a general characterization of an unavoidable problem. The case is quite different with the hypothetical strategies of category III. There, the general characterization of the problem (working through the political implications of impartiality or the moral point of view) leads to no definite results whatsoever. The problem in its general characterization is compatible with numerous, slightly different precise constructions which support incompatible resultant principles. The trick is to get distinctive conclusions from a general characterization of a problem which is unavoidable—so that the resulting conclusions have a firm basis.

Primary reliance on strategy IV does not, of course, rule out supplementary uses of any of the other strategies. In fact, as suggested here, only partial prescriptions follow from strategy IV—prescriptions for liberty of political culture in a demanding sense. While these prescriptions yield distinctive conclusions, they leave many controversial questions unsettled. My hope is to place the essential core of liberal theory on a firmer footing while leaving the rest untouched.

The key to the strategy is to situate the core propositions of liberal theory—certain requirements of liberty—at a different point in the argument. They are not offered as conclusions that follow directly from a postulated process of evaluation. Rather, they are necessary conditions for *conducting* the evaluation in the appropriate manner. In that sense, they follow indirectly, rather than directly, from the explicit process of evaluation. Once this distinctive location in the argument is revealed, the requirements of liberty take on a special status—one that insulates them from further criticisms that they may be unnecessary or should be abandoned.

They are protected from such attacks because the inevitably controversial and provisional character of moral argument within liberal theory prevents any particular prescription from being directly established by a moral evaluation with the kind of finality or conclusiveness that would obviate the need for continuing reexamination and reevaluation. Hence the inconclusiveness and the indeterminacies familiar to critics of liberalism provide important support for the indirect strategy. They explicate the need to maintain the conditions for continuing, collective self-evaluation at the level of fundamental principles—regardless of the particular construction of those fundamental principles which we happen to accept at any given time.

The premise of my constructive argument is that justifications for state authority must be addressed to those who must live under that authority, those who must live with the claim, usually backed by overwhelming power, that the state's countless, pervasive effects on our daily lives are fully justified. The first question to raise about the state is not whether we have, in some sense, "consented" to it (tacitly, expressly, hypothetically, or whatever). Rather, it is whether the state has permitted us to be in a position where it is possible for *us,* in some reasonable fashion, to evaluate *it.* The state and its defenders are likely to limit what we can know about it, what we can know about the character of our relationship to it, and what we can know about the variety of possible alternatives to present policies and to the present system. All these factors cloud our ability to evaluate the authority to which we have been subjected.

The first question of political philosophy is whether the form of political culture that is tolerated or supported in a given state is one that permits those subject to its authority to evaluate it—to determine from *inside* whether the authority to which they have been subjected is justifiable. If that authority is justifiable—according to arguments which it is rational for them to accept from within the political culture—then I will say that a solution to the legitimacy problem has been achieved. My basic claim will be that the legitimacy problem can only be solved in a self-reflective political culture—one that is significantly self-undermining as a result of unmanipulated dialogue. By "consistently self-undermining," I mean that the political culture subjects its supporting rationales to widespread, conscientious criticism. Such an airing of counterarguments directed at our institutions and policies is necessary if we are to be in a reasonable position to evaluate the case in favor. In that sense, only a system that is consistently self-undermining can rationally support itself.

I specify "unmanipulated" dialogue (in the definition of a self-reflective political culture), for when the state engages in (or permits) the manipulation of its own evaluation, it becomes reasonable for us, as members, to distrust the results. When voices have been silenced, or intentionally drowned out, our capacity to evaluate the case for the state and its policies has been severely impaired. Even if we are confident in whatever propositions are shielded from criticism, we are denied the opportunity to test those propositions against counterarguments, we are denied the kind of dialogue that would give us a reasonable basis for accepting those propositions in the first place. And if we were not already confident in those propositions, we must suspect them further when dissenting voices are persecuted or forcibly silenced. It is only reasonable to suspect the motives of those in power (or their allies) if they severely distort the public process of evaluating the power they exercise. The interests they have at stake are too great, the possibilities for self-serving rationalizations too apparent, for us to assume that we can blindly entrust our fate to them without the benefit of continuing debate and counterargument.

A self-reflective political culture continually purges itself of bias in its own favor. In doing so, it guards the intellectual freedom of its members to evaluate whatever positive case there might be for the state, its institutions and its policies. The argument proceeds from (a) the general problem of political evaluation to (b) its characterization in terms of the legitimacy problem to (c) the requirements for freedom of political culture, for the intellectual liberties in the political sphere, which are necessary for solving the legitimacy problem. The basic idea is that justifications for political authority must be offered under conditions that permit those who live under that authority to arrive at some reasonable evaluation of it. Even if strong arguments were offered for the state but the conditions for evaluation were denied (for example, dissenters were persecuted, discussion was suppressed, newspapers were closed or bullied), no constructive solution to the legitimacy problem would be possible. Who could know what arguments had been silenced, what issues or protests might have arisen were it not for the chilling effects of suppression? By denying its citizens the conditions necessary for a reasonable evaluation of its own authority, such a state, no matter what its other benefits, would also deny itself the possibility of solving the legitimacy problem.

The first step in the constructive argument is merely to grant that there are significant problems in political evaluation. This step amounts to little more than admitting that political philosophy exists as a subject matter. My strategy aspires to distinctive results by taking a second step, that of placing the locus of decision for those evaluations, not in the hands of some closely guarded elite, but rather in the public arena of the general political culture, available to all those who must live within the political system whose evaluation is in question. After all, they are the ones who must live with the countless everyday effects of the state upon their lives. For the state to subject them to this power, virtually inescapable within the confines of its territory, without permitting them the conditions necessary for any reasonable appraisal of it, would be to subject them to a kind of continuing, unreflective servitude. It would relegate them to a perpetual state of political childhood.

If the state could demonstrate conclusively and without room for reasonable disagreement that it knew best, that it had, in fact, justifiably settled all the important questions virtually for all time, then there might be a case for relegating its citizenry to this kind of continuing political childhood. But the requirements for justifying this kind of extreme mass paternalism are too great. Political theories which presume to make such claims inevitably overreach. There are inevitable limitations of normative evaluation which block this absolutist route to paternalistic suppression.[15]

My argument proceeds from the mere requirements for conducting a certain kind of evaluation. It does not rely on the conclusions of that evaluation, but rather on the conditions necessary to conduct it. In that sense my strategy is indirect. The inconclusiveness is more straightforward, direct strategies—where a process of evaluation is conducted or posited and its explicit conclusions are prescribed—strengthen rather than weaken the argument. For the controversiality and incompleteness that inevitably apply to moral judgments provide part of the rationale for our having to continue the dialogue, for our having to view the direct results of political evaluation as provisional and open to reasonable disagreement. Hence any tampering with the conditions for unmanipulated political evaluation would foreclose the dialogue prematurely—leaving us completely in the dark when we could barely see our way to our earlier, merely provisional conclusions.

One might ask what good does it do to argue from a proposed necessary condition? I am claiming only that a self-reflective political culture is a necessary condition (and not a sufficient one) for solving the legitimacy problem. Suppose we had to choose between satisfying the particular necessary condition I propose and satisfying other necessary conditions, justified on other grounds. What could be special about my proposal if it is only one in a series of possible necessary conditions for solving the legitimacy problem (even under ideal conditions)?

My claim is that my proposed necessary condition, because it applies to the process of evaluation rather than to its conclusions, is strategically located in the competition with rival proposals. It is stategically located in the sense that any advocate of a rival construction of necessary (and/or sufficient conditions) should *also*, rationally, admit the claim we are putting forward. How can the proponent of a rival necessary condition claim confidence in his position unless it has also been subjected to counterargument and debate? To foreclose the dialogue is to foreclose the basis for our having confidence in those propositions in the first place. Other necessary conditions, arrived at as the conclusions of particular substantive arguments, are subject to all the controversies and reasonable disagreements that characterize direct strategies.

By contrast, our proposal rests on an indirect strategy, applying to the process of evaluation rather than to its conclusions. The very inconclusiveness we encounter in direct strategies provides, in itself, an argument against foreclosing the dialogue (as it would be foreclosed by any sacrifice in freedom of political culture) because it means that we can never presume to have settled questions of political evaluation to the point that our positions might not possibly be improved or corrected by further debate and criticism.

The inconclusiveness of direct strategies also means that there will be wide room for reasonable disagreement about other proposed necessary conditions. Our proposal is special because, when compared with any such rival, its status as a necessary condition should be granted by that rival. Whatever else is required for solving the legitimacy problem, people are not in a reasonable position to evaluate the authority to which they have been subjected without freedom of political culture. On the other hand, any particular rival, established by one of the direct strategies rather than the indirect one, cannot make a similar claim. In other words, everyone will have his own favorite list of additional conditions for completing the argument. But each of those lists can be subjected to the strategy of indirect argument that without freedom of political culture, our capacity to evaluate any such list has been seriously impaired. Because our proposed necessary condition applies to the process of evaluation rather than to its particular substantive conclusions, any advocate of a rival construction of necessary (and or sufficient) conditions should also admit the claim we are putting forward.

Notes

1. This essay is taken from a draft of my forthcoming book tentatively entitled *Reconstructing Liberal Theory.*

2. Ackerman's theory employs neutrality as a "filter" on the motivations which can bear on the choice of principles. See the discussion below and Bruce A. Ackerman, *Social Justice in the Liberal State* (New Haven and London: Yale University Press, 1980).

3. A good account of these ambiguities, along with specimen illustrations, can be found in Pitkin, "Obligation and Consent" in *Philosophy, Politics and Society,* ed. Peter Laslett and W. G. Runciman, 4th Series (Oxford: Basil Blackwell, 1972).

4. Robert Nozick, *Anarchy, State, and Utopia* (New York: Basic Books, 1974), p. 5.

5. Can they be fully compensated for the protection services they have already refused (that is, after all, why they are independents)? But if they are not fully compensated, then have no rights been violated? Nozick might, of course, hypothesize that they *all* would simply love to join the state, but this departs from the bounds of realism.

6. John Rawls, *A Theory of Justice* (Cambridge: Harvard University Press, 1971).

7. By "neutrality" Ackerman means "No reason is a good reason if it requires the powerholder to assert (a) that his conception of the good is better than that asserted by any of his fellow citizens, or (b) that regardless of his conception of the good, he is intrinsically superior to one or more of his fellow citizens" (p. 11).

8. Joseph Tussman, *Obligation and the Body Politic* (New York: Oxford University Press, 1960).

9. Michael Walzer, *Spheres of Justice: A Defense of Pluralism and Equality* (New York: Basic Books, 1983). For further criticisms along these lines, see my "Defending Equality: A View From the Cave," *Michigan Law Review* 82, no. 4 (February 1984): 755–60.

10. For a critical discussion which argues that Mill stretches utility to the point of vacuity see Isaiah Berlin, "John Stuart Mill and the Ends of Life," in *Four Essays on Liberty* (Oxford: Oxford University Press, 1969). For a more sympathetic interpretation, see Richard Wollheim, "John Stuart Mill and Isaiah Berlin: The Ends of Life and the Preliminaries of Morality" in *The Idea of Freedom,* ed. Alan Ryan (Oxford: Oxford University Press, 1979).

11. For some useful observations on the intuitive appeal of the notion of equality at the core of utilitarianism see Bernard Williams, *Ethics and the Limits of Philosophy* (Cambridge: Harvard University Press, 1985), pp. 105–6; Henry Sidgwick, *The Methods of Ethics,* 7th ed. (London: Macmillan, 1963), pp. 382, 420-21.

12. For more on the jurisdiction problem see my *Beyond Subjective Morality: Ethical Reasoning and Political Philosophy* (New Haven and London: Yale University Press, 1984), chap. 4.

13. See Rawls, "A Well-Ordered Society" in *Philosophy, Politics and Society,* ed. Laslett and Fishkin, 5th Series (Oxford: Basil Blackwell/New Haven: Yale University Press, 1979), pp. 6–21.

14. This notion of a self-reflective political culture is developed in greater detail below.

15. For further arguments along these lines, see my *Beyond Subjective Morality.*

— II —

The Philosophy of Liberalism

– 4 –

Liberalism and the Human Good of Freedom

RICHARD E. FLATHMAN

Among the complaints commonly brought against liberalism, one of the most familiar is that it accords unjustifiable importance to individual freedom. In ideological terms, socialists object that liberalism subordinates equality to freedom, conservatives that it promotes license in the name of freedom, communitarians that it destroys communal ties and engenders unresolvable conflict. In more philosophical formulations, the liberal emphasis on freedom is traced to an ahistorical metaphysical atomism and an empiricism or positivism that are at once jejeune and pernicious. Reflected in an untenable conception of freedom as "negative," as no more than the absence of the crudest obstacles and impediments to physical movement, these ill-considered commitments are said to explain the dangerous incoherence of liberal political and moral thought.

These charges are frequently overdrawn. Insofar as they are directed against the politically organized societies most frequently characterized as liberal (as "liberal democracies"), they of course exaggerate the individual freedom actually available in those societies. In part, these exaggerations consist of overlooking or underestimating interferences with freedom that are condemned (however vigorously and effectively) by the public philosophies that predominate in liberal democracies. But the critics of liberalism also describe incorrectly the place of freedom in influential versions of liberal ideology. It is true that "freedom" and its cognates are prominent in the political discourse of self-styled liberal democracies. It is also true that certain freedoms have been accorded a privileged position in the public law of a number of liberal democracies. But any moderately close examination of the influential versions of liberal ideology makes it clear that their authors and exponents are not only receptive to but anxious to promote extensive *de jure* limitations on individual freedom. As libertarians (against whom the charges I mentioned are perhaps more plausibly leveled) complain, freedom is no more than one of a number of liberal values, and liberal publicists have readily found justifications for subordinating freedom to conflicting and competing considerations.

The same observations hold concerning the more abstract and systematic formulations of political and moral philosophers who by self-designation or wide agreement are of a liberal tendency. Just as few among the critics of liberalism declare themselves against freedom properly understood and ordered, so many theorists who by self-declaration or common designation are liberals deny that they hold the views their critics attribute to them. Here again language that arouses the ire of critics is frequently enough encountered; "freedom" and "liberty" are certainly prominent in the work, say of Locke, Kant, and Constant; Mill, Green, and Hobhouse; Rawls, Dworkin, and Ackerman. But Locke's argument for religious toleration, said by Rawls to be a (if not the) decisive moment in the formulation of liberal doctrine,[1] has been shown to rely crucially on a view about faith that is out of keeping with the secularism characteristic of liberalism and in any case accords religious freedom no more than instrumental significance. Moreover, Locke's theory of political society, so far from being atomistic, privatistic, or even notably impersonal and adversarial, accords a central position to a notion of mutual trust.[2] As to Kant, while some of the charges I noted may seem justified concerning his specifically political and legal views, attention to the wider moral and epistemological theory that informs those views calls those charges into serious question.[3]

Benjamin Constant was certainly a vigorous champion of "modern" (roughly "negative") freedom against the "ancient," more communal or "positive" variety, and he may be a better object of antiliberal polemic than practitioners of that art have realized. If we leave aside the reasons for his relative neglect (at least in the anglophone literature), recent studies show him to have been a man of quite complex views and perhaps less opposed to "ancient" beliefs and values as such than to indiscriminate conflation of beliefs and values that are and should be kept distinct.[4] Again, classical utilitarianism, long treated as a form of liberalism, systematically and indeed insistently subordinates individual freedom to utility or the greatest happiness. J. S. Mill, for many the paradigmatic liberal, is famous for a spirited defense of freedom of thought and expression; but well-documented recent interpretations of his thought,[5] including accounts that absolve him of the cruder antifreedom features that have led recent liberals to disown Bentham and Mill's father, argue persuasively that Mill favored those freedoms primarily because they contribute to self-realization—an idealist or perfectionist concept whose salience in the self-announced liberalism of Green and Hobhouse has often embarrassed liberals as well as their critics.

To bring this hurried assemblage of reminders up to some present writers, we note that Ronald Dworkin insists that equality, not freedom, is the "nerve" of liberal thought and denies that there can be any right to liberty.[6] John Rawls opposes the idea that there is a "presumption in favor of something called 'liberty' " and instead argues for a short list of "basic liberties" on the ground that they are necessary to justice or "fair cooperation."[7] Bruce Ackerman's conception of "neutrality" or "neutral dialogue" leads him to insist upon a strong form of egalitarianism that would severely restrict a number of freedoms highly valued and strongly protected in self-styled liberal democracies.[8]

Whatever the merits of these particular qualifications upon freedom, it is impossible to deny that individual freedom must be limited in various ways. The most obvious reason for this conclusion is that freedoms often conflict with one another, so that as a practical matter either there will be some sort of standoff or one freedom must take precedence over another or others. Because freedom and its values will be on both or all sides of such conflicts, the conflicts cannot be resolved without appeal to considerations other than freedom itself.[9] Beliefs and values not reducible to convictions about freedom necessarily enter into thought and action about freedom. Moreover, the recurrence in our tradition of distinctions such as between freedom and license is powerful evidence that further limitations will be thought necessary. In bare principle it is not impossible that "license" and related notions could be restricted to cases in which one or more sets of freedoms are in conflict; in even barer principle it is perhaps conceivable that conflicts between and among freedoms might be resolved in terms of some notion of maximizing freedom. But the latter combination of ideas may well be incoherent,[10] and notions such as license are in fact regularly and potently invoked in the name of numerous beliefs and values other than freedom itself. In attending to these matters, liberal theorists have done what any theorist must do.

We will be better placed to accommodate freedoms to one another and to harmonize freedom with other concerns if we have a clearly formulated view of why freedom is valuable. Critics of liberalism write as if "it" already includes such a formulation. If taken to mean that there is a view that is at once well articulated and widely accepted among those of a liberal persuasion, this suggestion is manifestly false; it would perhaps be more accurate to say that freedom has often been verbally honored but seldom clearly located or effectively defended in liberal thought; it is in any case undeniable that a number of the liberal writers who have considered the matter more closely have put freedom in a subordinate, perhaps a less-than-secure, position.

We find ourselves, then, in a complex and perhaps anomalous situation. Vociferous opponents of liberalism attribute to it an uncritical and unjustifiable commitment to individual freedom, an attribution that finds some support in the rhetoric of self-styled liberal practices, ideologies, and theories, much less warrant in the details of those practices, ideologies, and theories. Thus (a) if liberalism does (or, consistent with other of its commitments, should) accord individual freedom the place its critics allege, it (b) might deserve the condemnations the latter direct against it. On the other hand, if (c) freedom deserves something akin to the place that critics allege liberals accord it, then liberals are subject, rather, to the criticism that (d) they do not clearly, or (e) clearly do not, accord freedom the place their detractors say they accord it.

Of these possibilities, I am disposed to (a) and (c), disposed against (b), and I argue accordingly in the remainder of this essay. I have already indicated my sympathy for (d) and (e), but for two reasons that are connected with one another and that influence my mode of argument concerning (a), (b), and (c), I will not offer further support for them here. First, (d) and (e) are propositions in intellectual history and in historical and contemporary political sociology. Confirming or disconfirming them would require detailed exegetical and otherwise empirical investigations well beyond the scope of this essay. Second and more important, to confirm or disconfirm (d) and (e) as propositions about *liberal* practices, ideologies, and theories would require that I abandon evasive phrases such as "self-declared" and "generally agreed" and specify the permissible range of the concepts "liberal," "liberalism," and the like. An account of the views about freedom of Bentham, or Mill, or Rawls, however well documented and convincing, would count for or against (d) and (e) only if it had also been established that they are (in the respects in question) properly regarded as liberal theorists. Even if it is in principle possible and desirable to settle this question (I have serious doubts on both but especially on the second score), it is obvious that I cannot hope to settle it here. Accordingly, I argue as best I can for a conception of the value of freedom. I call my conception "liberal" and I summon certain considerations in support of that designation and on behalf of the claim that the conception is an improvement over those offered by other self-identified liberals. But for present purposes the merits of the conception must be more important than the merits of calling it liberal.

Two further caveats before starting off. First, I throughout assume and employ a "negative" concept of "freedom" and "unfreedom." "Freedom" and "unfreedom" are predicates of human actions. Roughly, actions are taken by (and hence talk of both freedom and unfreedom presupposes) persons who are "agents," that is persons who, in the setting of a community with a shared language and the elements that Wittgenstein and others have identified as necessary to such a language, form and hold beliefs; form desires and interests, objectives and purposes that are influenced by their beliefs; frame intentions to act to satisfy their desires, interests, and so forth; and attempt to act on their intentions. Agents and actions are free insofar as their attempts to act are not prevented, impeded, or deflected from their objectives by the actions of other agents, and are unfree insofar as they are prevented, impeded, or deflected by the actions (including deliberate refusals to act) of other agents. In the absence of agency or action there is no "freedom-evaluability," nothing of which either freedom or unfreedom can be predicated. I have elsewhere defended this use of the concepts against arguments proceeding from various "positive" construals of them (and against the view that there are no significant differences between negative and positive formulations), and I can only refer readers who are sceptical on these points to that discussion.[11]

Second, the view of freedom I advance is quite general in character and therefore cannot itself dictate resolutions of particular conflicts among freedoms or between freedoms and other desiderata. If coherent and convincing, a general view of the value of freedom can influence and in some measure discipline the continuing task of arriving at circumstantial and revisable accommodations and harmonizations, but it cannot itself perform or displace that task. This feature of general theories is not infrequently overlooked or denied by theoreticians who claim that specific distributions of freedoms or of restrictions upon them are required by their theories. A subsidiary theme of this essay, connected in ways that I do not myself fully understand with my argument about the value of freedom, is that liberals (even if they can agree on few other things) ought to stand against such conceptions of the theory-practice relationship.

I

Among other things that they are, human beings are desiring, interest-pursuing, end-seeking, purposive creatures. Partly because of the character of their interests and desires, ends and purposes, and partly because of characteristics of the environment in which they live, in most cases they must take action to achieve their ends. Given these characteristics of human beings and their environment, freedom of action is a high-order human good, a condition or state of affairs on which human beings will, and in reason should, place high value. The value of freedom is not tied to a particular inventory of interests and desires, ends and purposes. The content or substance of human interests and desires varies from one person to the next and often changes substantially during the life history of a single person. Freedom is a good of great general value because it is necessary to the satisfaction of a great many interests and desires, the achievement of many ends and purposes, and contributive to the satisfaction and achievement of yet many more. Unfreedom is a serious evil because it prevents or inhibits achievements and satisfactions and produces frustration, distress, and harm.

There is a certain commonsensical quality to the foregoing remarks. If or insofar as we understand human beings in the ways I have employed, it seems obvious that a substantial freedom, a generous area of discretionary action, will be something valued by them and valuable to them. On the face of things, it is not easy to see how it could be denied that human beings have these characteristics or that, having them, freedom will be valuable to them.

In fact, however, there is nothing necessary, nothing rationally undeniable or indisputable about this reasoning or its conclusions. Empirically, we know of people who have very few desires, purposes, etc., and of others who, owing to the combination of the character of their desires (etc.) and the fact that their circumstances are especially favorable or unfavorable to satisfying them, have been understandably (if shortsightedly) indifferent to freedom. We are also familiar with thought experiments that imagine changes in human beings and their environment that would, if implemented, require us to qualify or abandon the reasoning. Finally, human beings and the human environment have features other than or additional to those on which my reasoning relies. Readers of these essays do not need to be told of the many attempts to ground normative thinking about freedom in considerations quite different from those I have urged.

It will emerge that the most important type of objection is the last one mentioned. But the more (or at least initially more) empirical objections require consideration in their own right, and examination will show that they merge into the difficulty last mentioned.

My initial response to the objection that the above reasoning misrepresents the facts on which it relies is as follows: perhaps the project of developing a general argument for freedom as opposed to particular freedoms is misbegotten. Perhaps such arguments will either be so abstract as to be vacuous or so hedged with qualifications as to be useless. But if there are to be such arguments, and if such arguments are to be based in part on facts about human beings, they will have to rest upon generalizations, not upon universal truths. The significant question about the reasoning I sketched is not whether we can identify exceptions to the generalizations I advanced about human beings and their circumstances; rather the question is whether exceptions occur so frequently as to make it clumsy and distracting to rely upon the generalizations in forming a general orientation toward or perspective concerning freedom. If we accept the reasoning I sketched, we will approach concrete issues concerning freedom with a certain set of expectations and with concepts and principles in which and with which to assess what we actually encounter. If our expectations are confuted, if our talk of the importance of freedom to satisfying desires and interests, achieving ends and purposes, regularly elicits incomprehension or hostility, what was intended to be a simplifying and facilitating move will complicate and divert our reasoning and our judging. Rather than being able to subsume particulars under agreed categories and principles, we will have to defend the generalizations on which our categories and principles depend. But if this happens only rarely or exceptionally we will (so far as the objection I am considering is concerned) be justified in taking our bearings from those generalizations so long as we remain alert to the possibility of exceptions to them.

There is every reason to believe that the reasoning I sketched would be irrelevant or distracting in numerous societies and cultures. Implicit in that reasoning is an understanding that I have elsewhere called the liberal principle (hereafter LP), namely that it is, prima facie, a good thing for individuals to form, to act upon, and more or less regularly to satisfy (their) interests and desires, their ends and purposes.[12] But this idea has or has had little or no acceptance, little or no standing, in numerous cultures and societies. Some cultures have regarded desires and interests, particularly desires and interests of individual persons, as prima facie or even categorically bad or wrong. The first, perhaps even the exclusive, concern has been to abide by the divine laws and commands, to discharge duties assigned by the collectivity, to pursue the common good, advance the mission of the church, the class, or the party. Individual interests are to be subordinated if not rooted out. If individual freedom has been valued at all in such societies (and characteristically such societies prize the authority of the collectivity over its individual members, the freedom of the collectivity vis-à-vis other collectivities), it has been not for the reasons I sketched above but because individual freedom (or the freedom of certain select types of individuals) enhances extra- or supraindividual goods and ideals. If one argued for individual freedom on the grounds I sketched, one would be arguing against—not from—the prevailing conceptions of, the prevailing beliefs about and values concerning, human beings.

The foregoing remarks underscore the underdefended character of the reasoning I presented for the value of freedom. The factual generalizations I advanced may be true of only some cultures and societies. But even if they are quite generally *true,* they will be accepted as elements in an argument for freedom only in societies in which they are positively valorized. A premise in my reasoning is axiological in character and attributes positive value to the state of affairs described by the empirical generalizations I advanced about human beings and their circumstances. LP is one possible formulation of such an axiological premise or principle: human beings do, or should, not only recognize but accept that they are desiring, interest-seeking, end-pursuing, purposive creatures whose well-being consists in important part in being able to pursue and satisfy their individual interests and desires, ends and purposes, and whose well-being is therefore enhanced by circumstances that are conducive to their doing so.

It is clear that premises of this character have been entirely rejected (or never considered) in some human societies and have been accepted only with severe qualification in numerous others. But it seems equally clear that premises of this character have been promoted to the standing of principles by persons influential in the shaping of modern Western societies and are in fact widely influential among the members of those societies. The fact that my sketch, abbreviated as it is, is intelligible and even commonsensical can perhaps be taken to testify to the correctness of these assumptions. The sketch is intelligible because it proceeds from, is a modest elaboration upon, thinking that is widely received in modern Western societies.

My sketch is nevertheless eminently disputable, disputable from within the confines of thinking widely received in the societies in question here. It can be controverted without adopting ascetical, perfectionist, or collectivist views more radical than those influential in the societies in question. One way to dispute it is to argue that it provides too weak an argument for freedom. By making the value of freedom instrumental to the good that is the pursuit and satisfaction of interests and desires, ends and purposes, it leaves freedom's value hostage to psychological and cultural contingencies. The value of freedom may be augmented by considerations such as those I have adduced, but its deeper grounding is, or should be made, more secure. Freedom is an inherent or intrinsic, not an instrumental, good. Or at least its value in human life is due to features of human beings that are less variable, less culture specific or dependent (and more noble, elevated, or at least dignified?) than "interestedness," "desirousness," and purposiveness.

"Intrinsic," "inherent" and related terms are sometimes used as epistemological concepts signaling a direct or unmediated intuition or other apprehension of truths about which evidence or argumentation other than the experience of the intuition itself are impossible or irrelevant. The deepest difficulties with this notion need not be rehearsed here. It suffices to say that, as a moral and political matter, this view engenders dogmatism and helps not at all in resolving questions about conflicts among freedoms and between freedom and various other goods.

Leaving aside arguments about freedom as opposed to determinism (metaphysical freedom) and about physical movement as distinct from action, it will nevertheless repay us to consider one further version of the idea that freedom is an intrinsic, not merely an instrumental, good. The argument in question is that both the fact of and a high regard for freedom of action is one of the deepest conventions of and, in that Wittgensteinian sense, a starting point of thought and action in our culture. It is intrinsic to our moral and political practice in the normative sense that any practice that is deeply incompatible with or generally destructive of freedom of action is therefore, without the need of further evidence or argumentation, deemed unacceptable. We do not argue for the value of freedom: our moral and political argumentation starts from, is premised on, its value. This view is consistent with dispute as to what counts as freedom and unfreedom, as to whether this or that arrangement or action serves or disserves freedom, and whether freedom in this or that respect should properly be subordinated or sacrified, here and now, to some other value or good. But arguments against freedom as such, and hence arguments for policies and practices that are categorically or even generally antifreedom, are not countenanced.

Something like this sense of freedom as an intrinsic good is involved in Stanley Benn's discussion of the principle of noninterference (PNI).[13] Insofar as we have made it a *principle* that the burden of justification falls on anyone who proposes to interfere in or with the actions of other persons, our day-to-day reasoning *begins* with the idea or belief that freedom is a high-order good. Interferences with freedom must be justified in the face of or despite the fact that they contravene or diminish that good. The fact that we entertain and accept such justifications shows that freedom is not an absolute in the sense of a good that takes precedence whenever it is involved or at issue. But it is an intrinsic good in the sense that it is a feature of our practices that must be understood in order to comprehend those practices and one that must be accepted in order to participate intelligently and defensibly or respectably in them. An observer who did not grasp what might be called the constitutive character of the good would fail to understand much of what goes on among us; the actions and arguments of participants who did not grasp the standing of that good would almost certainly—that is, apart from quite remarkable coincidences—meet with antagonism or incomprehension from other participants.

Unlike the first construal of "intrinsic" I considered, this one does not exclude the *possibility* of arguments for the value of freedom. Of course the claim that the good of freedom is intrinsic in this sense suggests that such arguments will rarely be encountered in explicit form: for the most part arguments for the good will be unnecessary in the sense that they will be redundant. It may even be difficult for participants to think of considerations, independent of the good, in terms of which to argue for its standing as such. But this difficulty is social-psychological, not logical or epistemological in character, and there are reasons for thinking that it is valuable to do what we can to overcome it.

Leaving aside reasons that hold for all of our beliefs and values (for example Socrates' view that the unexamined life is not worth living, J. S. Mill's view that people who do not know, or who have lost sight of, the reasons for their beliefs and values do not fully know *what* they believe and value), two such reasons are especially pertinent. The first is grounded in the fact that freedom of action as a high-order value is rejected in many cultures and societies. If it is true that the value is deeply embedded in modern Western societies, it is important that those who reject or challenge it understand that, and why, this is the case. It may be a kind of response to such challenges to say, "This is what we think; this is how we do things hereabouts." It may even be that disagreements about the value of freedom of action, as with differences of religious belief, run so deep that mutual understanding and accommodation is the best that, or even more than, can be hoped. But even this modest objective is furthered if the parties to the disagreements can articulate for themselves and to others the grounds on which their views rest.

The second reason is grounded in two facts. I have already mentioned the first of these, namely that we experience freedom and its value and disvalue by exercising various freedoms, and these freedoms sometimes conflict with one another and with other of our values. Conflicts among freedoms could be resolved by appeal to the value of freedom per se only if we could make sense of the notion of maximizing freedom, and in any case such an appeal would resolve conflicts with other values only if we elevated freedom to the top of a strictly hierarchical value structure (to first position on a lexically ordered list of values), i.e., only if we made freedom an absolute as well as an intrinsic value. Having more rather than less clearly delineated general reasons for valuing freedom of action will not settle, certainly it will not still, all questions about the comparative importance of freedom or of various freedoms. But it would be irrationalist or antirationalist to assume that no such reasons are available or that having such reasons will be of no use in resolving such issues (or at least in remaining civil with one another as we attempt such resolutions and as we live with our no more than partial successes). The second of these facts is that there is lively controversy in the literature of moral and political philosophy concerning why freedom should be valued and how its value should be compared with a variety of other desiderata. In addition to being intellectually engaging in its own right, this controversy reflects—albeit no doubt imperfectly—issues, positions, and arguments that are prominent outside of philosophical books and journals.

To summarize this stretch of discussion, it is plausible to treat freedom of agency as an intrinsic good in our moral and political practices in the sense that its being a good is a datum in or of those practices. If so, the fact that it is no less than a datum is vital to understanding and to participation in those practices. The fact that it is, qua *intrinsic* good, no more than a datum means that the question why freedom of agency should be valued (and hence, finally, whether and how much it should be valued) invites our reflection. Because this version of the idea that freedom is an intrinsic good is the only one that is both plausible and pertinent to our present concerns, I can summarize the discussion of that beguiling idea by restating my original contention: freedom of agency is a contingent and an instrumental good, albeit one that is contingent upon factual generalizations about human beings that are difficult to dispute and instrumental to values that are widely shared and deeply established in modern Western societies.

II

I henceforth refer to the belief-cum-principle that freedom is a high-order good as the General Presumption in Favor of Freedom, or GPF. On the reasoning I have thus far given (as distinct from my claim that something like this belief-cum-principle is a datum of our culture), GPF is an inference from (not an entailment of) the evaluations expressed by principles such as PNI or LP. If we accept these evaluations, we have reasons to endorse and to act upon GPF. For present purposes the question then becomes whether we can further strengthen the case for GPF as a general presumption or principle of thought and action.

Disposed as I am to defend GPF, I will treat this question as how best to argue for it. But of course pursuing this objective requires identifying and assessing the merits of arguments against the principle.

Continuing to work with the sketch I first set out, the chief task is further to defend LP or some principle analogous to it. I say this because the other main elements in the argument, generalizations about human beings and their circumstances and about features of our culture, are less likely to be disputed. Of course there is no shortage of objections to self-interest and its pursuit or to desires and desirousness (albeit arguments against end-seeking and purposiveness are rare, a point to which I return below). But most such objections, certainly within our culture, are to the effect that human beings *should not* do these things or *should* subordinate the doing of these things to other of their activities, other of their characteristics. People who advance such arguments typically allow that the generalizations are (all too) accurate concerning human beings as we in fact encounter them in our culture. Their contention is that these characteristics are unfortunate and that the freedom to indulge them is anything but a good thing.

The first task, accordingly, is to defend the idea that it is good for human beings to form, to act upon, and to satisfy interests and desires. If this idea can be defended, the further ideas—that freedom of action is a high–order human good and that a heavy burden of justification should fall on those who propose to limit, qualify, or interfere with it—will be easier to defend.

The most uncompromising opposition to LP comes from proponents of various forms of asceticism or self-denial. In considering this source of objections we should first note that at least some of their force is blunted by attention to the elements out of which LP is formed and to the formulation of LP itself.

Asceticism is at its apparently most potent (at least in its secularized forms) when it objects to desires and desire satisfaction, particularly when it interprets desires as passions that "well up in," "take over," and otherwise supplant or obliterate the more rational, the more disciplined, the higher human faculties. Surrendering to these passions, "wallowing in them" in the sense of letting them and their satisfaction become the sole or primary *raison d'être* of one's existence, is "de-grading"; instead of living up to one's "grade," one's capacities or potential as given by God, or nature, or the culture into which one is born, the desirous, sensual, hedonistic person sinks to or below the level of nonhuman animals. Insofar as the sensualist can be said to have an aim or project, that project is self-defeating. Desires beget desires in a "bad infinite" that may spiral down to "polymorphous perversity" and that in any case excludes the possibility of more than ephemeral, more than unsatisfying satisfactions.

This picture is implausible if desires and action on desires are properly understood.[14] Beliefs that are subject to correction and which if corrected will alter the desire, identification of objects that will satisfy the desire, choice of courses of action likely to attain those objects, all of these are features of desires and actions to satisfy them. None of this prevents desires from being unseemly, debased, or repugnant to others, and it certainly does not guarantee that the actions taken to achieve them will be acceptable to others. But the idea that forming and acting to satisfy desires is itself an abandonment of the true or higher human capacities is largely a misunderstanding. The unqualified, necessarily debased sensuality attacked by asceticisms from fourth-century anchorites to Schopenhauer is in the realm of behavior, not desires and action on desires. There may be a case for freedom of such behavior, but it is not the same case as the case for freedom of action.

The second element in LP, namely interests and attempts to serve them, is most commonly attacked not on the ascetical ground that it is degenerate, but rather that it is narrowly calculating, egoistic, and socially divisive. The "interested" person uses her capacities for discernment, judgment, and evaluation, but she does so with no more than instrumental regard for others and hence, on some formulations of antiinterest argumentation, shortsightedly from the standpoint of her own larger or longer-term interests. As the last clause reminds us, however, the objection that actions motivated by interests are selfish in antisocial or immoral ways, or even imprudent, is contingent upon the character of certain interests and certain strategies for satisfying them. Notions such as Tocqueville's "enlightened self-interest" and J. S. Mill's "permanent interests of man as a progressive being" (and of course yet wider uses of the concept such as in the philosophies of Ralph Barton Perry and Jürgen Habermas) make it clear that these objections have no application against much thought and action standardly characterized as "self-interested."

It is no part of my intention to deny that much that occurs in human affairs in the name of desires, interests, and their pursuit and satisfaction is objectionable and—albeit this is a further point—justifiably prevented. But recognizing this provides no reason for objecting to LP. LP says that it is, prima facie, a good thing for human beings to have, to act upon, and to satisfy desires and interests. If categorical objections to desires and interests (or "desirous" and "interested" conduct) are without merit, it remains open to us to adopt LP and the presumption it establishes in favor of human desires and interests and then to consider arguments that this or that desire or interest, as pursued in these or those circumstances, is nevertheless objectionable. Nor does this stance or strategy debar the conclusion that certain subclasses of desires and interests are generally objectionable and to be discouraged. If we are committed to LP we will, of course, view such reversals of the burden of proof with suspicion; but the logic of the principle itself, featuring as it does both "prima facie" and the comparative notion of "good," requires that we remain open to the possibility that they will sometimes be justified.

Aside from the last comments about LP, my remarks thus far are modest elaborations of the point that the concepts "desire" and "interest" are situated in the Wittgensteinian sense that they are part of a conceptual system governed by widely accepted conventions and rules. Although capacious in that they accommodate a wide range of beliefs and objects, they are concepts, not mere words or markers, "somethings," not "anythings." The desires and interests that we can form and pursue are restricted in ways either misunderstood or ignored by ascetical critics.

The conventions and rules that govern "desire" and "interest" are, of course, open textured and subject to change. They are part of language-games and forms of life that are internally complex and changeable and that are influenced by activities and developments more or less independent from them. I am not suggesting that there is a fixed inventory of possible interests and desires or that either the fear of declension or the hope of an ascension in their usual or predominant character are *necessarily* misplaced or misbegotten. But attention to secular tendencies in the language-games of desire and interest will further disqualify the more fervid concerns that they sometimes arouse.

According to Albert Hirschman, the concepts of interests and self-interest came into prominence in Western thought in contrast with and as means of controlling the very notions, that is "passions," to which ascetical and antiinterest writers are prone to assimilate them. Further abbreviating a complex story that Hirschman himself has severely compressed, as confidence declined that reason (and, one should add, faith and its discipline) could control the violent and destructive passions, the idea developed that interests could help to tame them, to domesticate them sufficiently to make peaceful social life possible. Denoting "an element of reflection and calculation with respect to the manner in which [human] aspirations were to be pursued,"[15] interests came to be regarded as more potent sources of motivation than abstract reason and yet less divisive and destructive than passions. "Once passion was deemed destructive and reason ineffectual, the view that human action could be exhaustively described [in their terms] meant an exceedingly somber outlook for humanity. A message of hope was . . . conveyed by the wedging of interest in between the two traditional categories. . . . Interest was seen to partake in effect of the better nature of each, as the passion of self-love upgraded and contained by reason, and as reason given direction and force by passion."[16]

On the view of interests Hirschman describes, severely ascetical forms of antiinterest argumentation are not only archaic but self-defeating in that they demean and condemn the forms of motivation-cum-reason for action most likely to prevent degeneration to the unbridled and destructive sensuality that those who advance such arguments fear and despise. Strikingly, the "element of reflection and calculation" of which Hirschman writes corresponds closely to features still "denoted" by "desire" as well as by "interest."

In an analysis that endorses but extends Hirschman's, Stephen Holmes develops further themes pertinent here. Focusing primarily on seventeenth- and eighteenth-century materials, Holmes argues that interests were distinguished from and preferred to notions of privilege and paternalism. The allegedly more-elevated character of the latter bases for and motivations to action came to be viewed as a device for giving a spurious legitimacy to social and political arrangements that were oppressive insofar as they were effective and increasingly ineffective in maintaining peace and order:

> Liberals turned a friendly eye toward self-interest to discredit the degrading ranks of prestige and chains of dependency characterizing the old regime. . . . By focusing on [desires and] interests, and by attributing paramount importance to self-preservation, Hobbes strove to put an end to the English Civil Wars. His aim was not to promote the interests of the merchant class, though that may have been a side-effect of what he did. By discrediting [for political purposes] the ideals of glory and salvation, he hoped to encourage peace.[17]

Holmes's remark about the merchant class alludes to objections to interests and interest-oriented conduct that became familiar after the period he is discussing; but the arresting feature of the contrasts he is most concerned to draw is that they are between, on the one hand, the desires and interests promoted by liberals and by Hobbes and, on the other, forms of thought and action that *in fact* are self-indulgent and self-defeating in just the ways *attributed to* desires and interests by severe critics of the latter. Holmes's liberals distinguish claims based on sharable and, in principle, mutually reconcilable desires and interests from entitlements of place and privilege that are insisted (by their holders and defenders) to be incommensurable with such desires and interests. Because the entitlements are regarded by their claimants as intrinsically superior, they can be accommodated to or harmonized with the ordinary run of desires and interests only in the weak sense that the latter might be given consideration after the superior entitlements have been fully honored. Holmes's Hobbes distinguishes desires and interests, which can be pursued and satisfied by all members of a society, from ideals of character and conduct, which their partisans at least tacitly concede, are unsharable or at least undistributable. In fact, however, the privileges the liberals attacked are self-, class-, or caste-indulgent in at least two senses: (a) they are *excessive* in demanding a gross superfluity of wealth and power, and (b) they are unjustifiably *exclusive* in that they are restricted to a small and assignable number of persons or to specific classes or castes with fixed memberships. Because of these characteristics, claims to the privileges are self-defeating: if satisfied they corrupt their beneficiaries at the same time that they harm those from whom the benefits are extracted; the corruption of the former and the oppression of the latter delegitimate the claims to them so that the claims must either be abandoned or enforced by tyrannical means that are costly in themselves and that sooner or later incite revolts that destroy the system of privileges. The ideals of character that Hobbes attacks are (again from a political standpoint) self-indulgent in the sense of having an exclusivity closely analogous to that already discussed (they are aristocratic ideals) and self-defeating because conduct in pursuit of them is incompatible with a society stable enough to allow such conduct to flourish. By comparison with both the privileges and the ideals, the *allegedly* self-indulgent and self-destructive desires and interests are sharable and are supportive of a peaceful and stable social and political order.

The particular passions, privileges, and ideals at issue in the controversies Hirschman and Holmes report play a smaller part in the debates of our own time. But in form these early defenses of desires and interests are responsive to any attempt to discredit them either as self-indulgent or self-defeating. Because such attempts remain common in our time, the defenses are pertinent to present concerns.[18] The timeliness of yet wider moral and political views that were part of the thinking Holmes discusses is evident from a further passage from his work. When asserted against views such as Maistre's that "human individuality" is a "nullity" from God's point of view, "Self-interest was a dimension of self-affirmation." Yet more broadly, it was important to the thinking of Constant and others of his time that interests "are distributed without regard to birth: they are just as independent of the social status of your family as they are of your religious beliefs. To act upon interest is to claim the status of an equal—of a masterless man."[19] Here we have much more than a defense of desires and interests against various traditional charges, much more than a claim that interests and desires do not have various unacceptable characteristics and consequences. In these formulations, developing, pursuing, and satisfying interests and desires are positive goods, are characteristics that deserve to be valued, protected, and promoted. They are made central to conceptions of individuality, of equality, and of freedom and hence are fundamental to a society suitable to human beings as liberals had come to conceive of them. We are not to apologize for our "desirousness" and "interestedness"; we are to insist upon them.

These last views are in effect arguments for LP (or at least PNI) and GPF. They say that human beings have certain pronounced characteristics, and they make connections between those characteristics and values that should be central to society. If analysis of "desires" and "interests" helps to defend these notions against certain persistent forms of attack, the linkage between them and equality and freedom not only legitimates but positively promotes them. Combining Hirschman and Holmes, we can say that the thinkers Holmes discusses were doing two things at once. They were promoting equality among and the freedom of individuals in a society that had begun to accept these values, but in which opposition to the values remained strong. In order to do so, they drew upon the emerging legitimacy of desires and interests to affirm a notion of the individual for whom equality and freedom were appropriate. By tying the two sets of notions together, they gave support to both. And the resulting combination constitutes an argument for LP and GPF.

Of course this combination and hence this argument for LP and GPF can be and has been resisted. If Rawls and others are correct that an at least implicit commitment to freedom and equality is the distinctive feature of moral and political thought and practice in modern Western societies, then one of the pairs that form the combination has been generally accepted. And while it can hardly be denied that desires and interests are widely regarded as *legitimate,* and are viewed yet more positively than this term suggests by many people in these societies, more and less vehement antidesires and antiinterests views remain familiar among us. Perhaps some who hold such views are also opposed to freedom and equality, but it is implausible to think that this is always or even commonly the case. We cannot assume that arguments for LP and GPF that depend upon the combination just discussed will be generally convincing.

Let us *reculer pour mieux sauter.* Let us assume that Hirschman is correct in his claim that desires and interests have been recognized as prominent characteristics of the members of our societies and that these characteristics have been legitimated to the extent that generalized stigma no longer attaches to them. Forming, pursuing, and satisfying desires and interests may not have attained to the standing of prima facie goods, but they have shed the disrepute that once attached to them. (Or at least let us assume that the arguments supporting generalized hostility to desires and interests have been shown to be without merit and hence that in reason generalized stigma ought not to attach to them.)

On these assumptions, a number of further arguments can be made for LP and GPF as normative principles. These arguments can be introduced by making a comparison. Consider the phenomenon of children, wives, employees, soldiers, and so forth who are told to "think for themselves," "take initiatives," "be independent," and the like, but whose every thought and initiative is disapproved and rejected. Such people quickly learn either to dismiss as insincere the advice and await the forthcoming directives (perhaps simulating thought, initiative, and independence) or to rebel against the disapprovals and rejections and pursue their chosen courses as best they can. Either way, the practical incompatibilities among the demands made upon them are a source of severe and often damaging confusion and frustration.

There is a strong and positive analogy between this phenomenon and the situation that would obtain in a society that legitimated the formation and pursuit of desires and interests but that rejected LP (or at least PNI) and GPF. Encouraging an employee to think for herself and to take initiatives does not commit superiors to agree with her every thought or to applaud the particulars of all the initiatives she takes. But doing the former in good faith creates, or rather carries with it, several presumptions. The most obvious of these are the presumptions that the superior believes that the employee is in fact capable of the kind of conduct in question (at least latently so) and that the superior genuinely encourages or perhaps authorizes her engaging in it. Taken together, these two presumptions carry a third, a guarded formulation (akin to PNI): if the superior disapproves or rejects the employee's thoughts and initiatives, she must justify doing so and must do so in terms responsive to the particulars of the thoughts and initiatives in question. We might say that the superior must present such justifications in order to avoid engendering dissonance, exasperation, and the like in the employee. But since it is only very likely and not certain that these consequences will be produced, we should first say that in practical reasoning anyone who understands the first two presumptions will also accept the third.

The parallels between the first two presumptions and my Hirschmanesque assumptions about the recognition and legitimacy of desires and interests is clear enough (a possible difference being that "legitimacy" may be a weaker term than "encourages" or even "authorizes" in the second presumption). In the guarded form in which I stated the third presumption, something like Benn's PNI is more closely parallel to it than is LP. This is because neither PNI nor the third presumption as stated imply or even suggest a disposition positively to approve, or even an expectation that one very likely will approve, the content of the thoughts and initiatives. The idea is more formalistic; having licensed or authorized the thinking or the initiative-taking, the superior is obliged to justify disapprovals and rejections of their content; having recognized and legitimated a tendency to form and pursue desires and interests, society is obliged to justify interferences with manifestations of that tendency.

The less-guarded formulation of the third presumption parallels the more positive idea expressed by LP that forming, pursuing, and satisfying desires and interests is, prima facie, a good. Having judged the employee capable of thinking for herself and of taking initiatives, and genuinely approving of her doing so, the superior is disposed to approve her thought and her initiative or at least maintains a grounded expectation that she will approve of them. Rather than a mere, perhaps even a somewhat grudging, formal authorization, the superior has wholeheartedly and out of genuine conviction encouraged the thinking and the initiating. (The more positive formulation of the third presumption goes better with "genuinely approved" than with "legitimated" in the second presumption.) Her reasons for having done so create and support a disposition or expectation to approve the actual content of the thinking or of the initiatives. Society's reasons for recognizing and genuinely approving the formation, pursuit, and satisfaction of desires and interests carry over to and inform its response to the desires and interests actually formed and pursued. "Prima facie" does not mean "initially and formally but readily subject to justified exception"; it means "for good general reasons that are expected to hold in most cases albeit subject to the possibility of justified exceptions."

My claim, then, is that the legitimation of desires and interests charted by Hirschman and Holmes itself suports an argument that goes beyond legitimation. In the weaker forms that stop at rebutting generalized objections to desires and interests, the legitimation of the latter supports PNI and GPF. It does so in the internalist sense that those who understand and accept the legitimation and the reasons for it will understand and accept PNI-GPF and also in the consequentialist sense that accepting legitimation but rejecting PNI-GPF will very likely create confusion, frustration, and conflict. In the stronger formulations involving genuine approval of desirousness and interestedness (for example, those formulations that link desires and interests closely to freedom and equality), legitimation itself supports LP in both the internalist and the consequentialist renderings of "supports." In short, to reject PNI-GPF or LP-GPF, one would have to adopt some version of the views that come to be rejected in the period studied by Hirschman and Holmes and that comport very badly with the present logic of "desires" and "interests." At a minimum we are entitled to conclude that generalized antiinterest and antidesire arguments are either confused or deeply radical in the sense of rejecting an interwoven and mutually reinforcing set of beliefs and values that is very firmly established in modern Western societies. In a society that recognizes and has legitimated desires and interests, LP is appropriate at least as a principle of mutual toleration or a weak principle of equality. In a society that genuinely respects individuality and diversity, certainly in one with a genuine enthusiasm for them, it recommends itself much more strongly. If desires and interests are in fact among our salient characteristics, and if we genuinely accept and value this fact about ourselves, we will accord one another's desires and interests the presumptions expressed in and required by LP.

III

If it is easy to list moralists who object to desires and interests, it is difficult to identify any who object to "end-seekingness" and purposiveness. Neither "end" nor "purpose" has been associated with passion, impulses, and other subjectivist or even "animal" notions that are prominent features of the literature concerning desires and interests. It is true that virtue-, duty-, and rights-oriented theorists argue that the pursuit of the ends and purposes we form should be disciplined by principles and rules of conduct that are in some sense independent of those ends and purposes. It is also true that teleological and consequentialist theories that reject or seem unable to accommodate such disciplining principles and rules have been much criticized. But virtue theorists identify the virtues they promote as qualities of character that are necessary or strongly conducive to the achievement of certain end-states judged to be suitable to human beings at their best; most deontologists have allowed that the constraints of duties and of rights, even if in some sense self-justifying, are constraints upon end-seeking, purposive activities and would have no application to creatures who do not engage in such activities.[20]

The fact that LP includes ends and purposes among the prima facie goods means that, formally or conceptually, it has room for, it can accommodate, the as-it-were positive concerns or objectives just mentioned. When combined with the foregoing arguments about desires and interests this suggests that, formally, LP should prompt few if any objections. Indeed, in respect to the more individualist of the rights-oriented deontological theories, we can make the stronger claim that something akin to LP is presupposed by them. Rights are discretionary, not mandatory; they leave it to the right-bearer to determine whether to take the class of actions that the right protects. At a minimum, this allows that agents may make these determinations on the basis of their ends and purposes as they see them. If end-seeking, purposive conduct were not at least a prima facie good, it is difficult to see how such discretion could be justified. In this perspective, decisions to establish rights are based on judgments that certain classes of ends and purposes are especially important and deserve not merely the protection afforded by LP and GPF (the protection afforded by a right in the sense of a "liberty" in Hohfeld's schema),[21] but the further protection afforded by a right (a "claim-right" or "right in the strict sense" in the Hohfeldian vocabulary).

But proponents of the doctrines just mentioned typically argue not for end-seeking or purposiveness as such, but for particular, more or less definite ends or purposes that they regard as embodying the ideals or excellences of human life. In the moderately technical language now current, proponents of these doctrines are advocates of perfectionism.[22] Accordingly, the fact that LP includes an endorsement of "ends" and "purposes" in abstract, generic terms is not likely to heighten appreciably their enthusiasm for it. Perfectionists cannot deny that LP as an axiological principle formally *encompasses* the ends and purposes they favor. Nor can they deny that an argument for freedom of action grounded in LP will provide support for freedom to pursue those ends and purposes. But they will surely object that the support it offers for those freedoms is much too weak, and they surely will also object that it offers at least initial support for freedoms that are insupportable. The axiological principles of society should *coincide with* the inventory of substantive ends and purposes that perfectionists favor (or at least the axiological principles should exclude all ends, purposes, and other reasons for action that conflict with pursuit of the ends and purposes perfectionists favor).

As a first step in assessing these objections, it will be helpful to consider the case of freedom of religious belief and practice. For people who are indifferent about religion, the religious desires and interests, ends and purposes that people in fact have and pursue are as eligible for the standing of prima facie goods as any other. Moreover, according a wide freedom for religious practice may diminish conflicts that might prevent or inhibit other activities supported by LP.

But what about people who are convinced that their beliefs, whether pro or antireligion, are true not merely in the sense that they themselves hold them, but simply or unqualifiedly? Consider the atheist who is satisfied that she has conclusive arguments against the existence of a divine being and who is also convinced that all forms of religiosity are worse than vulgar superstition. Or consider the fideist who is "morally certain" of the truth of her specifically religious beliefs and who is equally convinced that irreligiosity and religious diversity make so much as decency impossible in human society. For such people religious freedom will seem much worse than a poor thing. How can it be, even prima facie, a good thing to maintain practices that are false and harmful? How can society allow, let alone endorse as a good, ends and purposes that lead to action destructive of human well-being?

Of course atheists and fideists can accept a generous religious freedom as a lesser evil. If it has proven to be genuinely impossible to win general acceptance of the beliefs and practices that are true and good, we retreat to that arrangement to protect such truth and goodness as obtains among us, and we regretfully pay the price of tolerating beliefs and practices known by us to be false and harmful. But we do not pretend that what we know to be false is prima facie true or that what we know to be harmful is prima facie good. Indeed, we do not pretend that the arrangement that protects the false and the harmful is anything better than an unfortunate necessity, an evil that we accept because it is least among the evils with which we are confronted. (Somewhat more positively, the arrangement might be defended as a way of buying time. By protecting the good practices that exist among us we preserve the possibility that example and argument will win converts enough to permit us to advance to something better.)

Perfectionist positions in respect to moral and political questions are analogous to (albeit not necessarily fully parallel with) the position of the atheist and fideist as just discussed. There are ends and purposes that are good simply or, all things considered, not merely prima facie. There are others that are clearly wrong or harmful or evil. In the latter cases the burden of justification falls on anyone who proposes to pursue those ends and purposes, not on those who object to them. How we should go about promoting good ends and purposes, and how dispositions and attempts to pursue bad or evil ones should be discouraged or prevented, are of course further questions. But actions and arrangements that are means to achieving good ends take at least initial justification from that fact about them, and actions and arrangements that are means of preventing the pursuit or achievement of evil ends take initial justification from that fact about them. Insofar as perfectionists have concerned themselves with freedom, freedom to pursue good ends is easily justified; certainly freedom to pursue evil ends is objectionable and restrictions on such freedom are easily justified.

As with strongly convinced atheists and with religious believers in respect to freedom of religion, convinced moral and political perfectionists might accept or accommodate themselves to a view of freedom that maintains wide latitude in the pursuit of individual ends and purposes. They could accept moral and political toleration as a lesser evil or as a temporizing device. Society averts its glance, at least its organized, collective glance, from much that is undoubtedly objectionable and even harmful, reserving its collective notice and its collective, authoritative action to the most directly and seriously harmful activities of its members. Nevertheless, within the compass of their perfectionism, that is in respect to the ends and purposes that they judge to be undeniably evil or harmful, a moral and political perfectionist must regard such arrangements as no better than arrangements of toleration. They can no more cherish or delight in such arrangements and the freedoms of action they recommend than the deeply committed atheist or fideist can cherish or delight in freedom of religious belief and practice.

IV

My remarks about ends and purposes are overly schematic in respects that would have to be remedied in a full discussion. For one thing, there are numerous versions of perfectionism, and it would be wrong to suggest that they all involve the same stance toward or the same implications concerning LP and GPF. (Consider, for example, the differences among T. H. Green and Friedrich Nietzsche, Alasdair MacIntyre and Hannah Arendt. Each of these writers is plausibly regarded as a perfectionist in Rawls's sense, but their conceptions of the good or ideal to be pursued, their conceptualizations of freedom, and their assessments of the value of freedom or various freedoms to achieving the good or ideal vary widely.) For another, there are well-developed positions that reject both LP-GPF and perfectionism.

I cannot discuss these variations in detail, but I suggest that they share an objectionable feature, namely privileging certain ends or purposes so strongly as to categorically exclude the possibility of justifying actions (and hence freedom to take those actions) that conflict with the preferred ends and purposes. I conclude by developing and briefly defending this suggestion by reference to a view, that of John Rawls, that sharply challenges my argument but does so from a position that shares many of the assumptions from which I have been arguing and a number of the conclusions I have drawn.

Although allowing that his theory includes "ideal-regarding" as distinct from "want-regarding" principles,[23] Rawls rejects perfectionism in the sense of views that claim that there is a single substantive conception of the good that ought to be accepted by all persons and that should be adopted and implemented by politically organized societies.[24] But he also rejects, or rather sharply qualifies, LP and GPF, arguing against them that interests and desires that conflict with the principles of justice deserve no consideration and that freedom to pursue such interests and desires can never be justified.[25]

It is important to recognize that Rawls's principles of justice hold only in respect to the "basic structure" of politically organized society, and that outside of the ambit of that structure he endorses a position very close to the one I have presented here. As the term itself tells us, however, the basic structure includes the principles, institutions, and practices fundamental to social life, those that do more than any other to influence the thought and action, the purposes and prospects of everyone in society.[26] Seen in this light, the categorical restrictions that his theory imposes on LP and GPF are by no means marginal or inconsequential.

For reasons already discussed, we cannot treat freedom of action to pursue interests and desires, ends and purposes as a good that can never be subordinated to any other objectives or principles. Rawls's theory is not objectionable because it argues for justice-based rankings of and restrictions on freedoms. Nor, in my view, is the content of Rawls's proposed principles of justice seriously objectionable. In its abstract formulation the first of those principles is at least akin to GPF in that it is a principle of equal liberty, and Rawls's elaboration of it yields a familiar and to my mind quite eligible short list of basic liberties.[27] The second principle is more disputable (and much disputed), but it is worth noting not only that it is subordinate to the first principle, but that it is defended in part as necessary to making the first principle effective.[28]

The difficulty, rather, is that Rawls rigorously excludes the possibility of revisions in and/or circumstantially justified departures from the rankings of and restrictions upon freedoms of action that his theory proposes. The principles of justice are in lexical order, and justice itself is accorded strict, invariable priority over all other considerations. The justice-based basic liberties have the standing not merely of constitutional rights, but of pre- or extra-constitutional principles that could be revised, reconsidered, or justifiably violated only (so long as "reasonably favorable conditions" obtain) as a part of the deeply radical activity of rethinking the entire basic structure of society. We are to privilege some and restrict other freedoms not merely by accepting social and moral conventions, by adopting constitutions and promulgating laws, but in the much stronger sense of committing ourselves unqualifiedly and into the indefinite future to principles and institutions that embody them that we will thereafter regard as beyond justifiable violation and all but beyond reconsideration.

My argument for LP and GPF is of course an argument against any such commitment. If human beings and their circumstances are as I have described them, and if modern Western culture has (at the least) recognized and legitimated those characteristics and features, then Rawls's scheme presents itself as severe, uncompromising, and perhaps alien. For limited but crucial purposes openness to and celebration of the possibilities of freedom of action are replaced by unyielding rejection of large classes of interests and desires and of actions taken to serve and to satisfy them; within the realm of social justice impulses and tendencies to diversity and change are not only subject (as they must be) to disapproval and prohibition by (disputable and revisable) public judgment and by the (contestable) decisions of (replaceable) public officials, but categorically excluded by principles that are to be regarded as immune to reconsideration in or through the processes and procedures of moral, constitutional, and political discussion and debate. In its most basic respects the realm of freedom is not to be settled, unsettled, and settled and unsettled anew, it is to be settled once and for all. We are to deprive ourselves of the freedom that is arguably the most fundamental of all, the freedom to go on deliberating the scope of our freedom.

Rawls advances a number of arguments of an affirmative character for his principles of justice and for the quite extraordinary standing he assigns them. He proposes a conception of moral personality featuring two "moral powers" (a sense of justice and the capacity to form a conception of good) and two corresponding "highest-order interests" (roughly, interests in developing and using the two moral powers),[29] and he argues for a "thin" theory of the good according to which there are certain "primary" or all-purpose instrumental goods that are necessary to the satisfaction of the highest-order interests and in particular to realizing any and all conceptions of the good.[30] In this perspective, the rigorism of his position presents itself as a function of his conception of moral personality and its needs.

These affirmative arguments for the absolute weight of justice and the strict lexical ordering of the two principles of justice may or may not be vulnerable to Rawls's own strictures against perfectionist views. (As noted, Rawls allows that his theory includes ideals, but claims that it is not perfectionist because it does not advance a substantively determinate conception of the good to be adopted by everyone.) For present purposes the more important point is twofold. First, we could accept Rawls's conception of moral personality and its needs and yet reject his rigorism. Accepting the former would dispose us to the basic structure Rawls proposes, and we might in fact create and sustain a constitutional system instantiating that structure. But we would insist that the features of that structure must remain open to reconsideration both in the sense that the principles might be revised so as to better serve the needs to which the structure is instrumental and in the further sense that particular circumstances might justify refusals to act in the manner specified by the principles. (The principles would be regarded as constitutional, not pre- or extra-constitutional, and there would be a constitutional procedure for amending the constitution; civil disobedience and what I have elsewhere called "civil encroachment" on rights[31] would have an accepted place in constitutional and political theory.)

Second, Rawls acknowledges the possibility just canvassed, at least in the sense that he advances another, negative, argument for his rigorism, an argument that appeals less to the affirmative merits of his conception of moral personality and his principles of justice than to the consequences of adopting a less rigorist approach.[32] The sort of mobile, amenable, latitudinarianism proposed here, he argues, depends upon an unworkable form of "intuitionism," on the unwarranted assumption that conflicts such as those among freedoms and between freedoms and other values can be successfully resolved circumstantially, that is, by resort to the unsystematized (or less systematized) moral and political intuitions that have developed out of our socialization, acculturation, and education. Of course in Rawls's own thinking this negative argument is connected with the affirmative one just discussed; the (in Rawls's mind) predictable failure of reliance upon intuitions is objectionable first and foremost because of the effects it would have (has) on the moral powers and the highest-order interests that go with them. But the force of the negative argument need not depend upon acceptance of the affirmative one. One need not subscribe to Rawls's conception of moral personality or his theory of the good in order to object to intractable conflict, arbitrary imposition, and the other barriers to fair cooperation that, according to Rawls, are certain to attend unconstrained intuitionism. By introducing this negative argument Rawls encourages the thought that the case for rigorism is separable from the case for his principles of justice. While it is surely not his view that *any* rigorist scheme would be preferable to intuitionism, his objections to the latter constitute his most general challenge to the view I have advanced here.

The affirmative arguments for the latter view presented in sections I–III require rejection of neither Rawls's conception of moral personality nor of his principles of justice. Those arguments do require that we recognize the conception as a moral ideal, one that may or may not be judged superior to other ideals. They also require that we view the principles of justice as instrumental to the ideal and hence revisable and defeasible, even if allegiance to the ideal is general and constant. Those arguments promote an openness to possibilities not only as regards life styles and patterns of conduct outside of the basic structure, but concerning social and political structures, arrangements, and practices. Although hardly agnostic about general human characteristics and values, even in this respect they are culture-specific, not transcendental or universalist, and they otherwise express a moderate skepticism intended (among other things) to protect freedom from overweening philosophical and ideological claims, from kinds of dogmatism that issue (as my arguments themselves do) from the urge to general theory. True, they leave the question whether in other respects freedom will be adequately secured to interactions among moral and political agents taken as we find them in the settings in which they live their lives. If—as I think—this is a liberal conception of the role of political philosophy in political practice, it is indeed likely that political practices informed by it will continue to feature the disagreement and conflict that Rawls regrets and seeks to contain. But even if it is within the powers of political philosophy to institute the fuller accord and greater harmony that Rawls seeks (which is of course unlikely), it would be objectionable for it to do so.

Notes

1. John Rawls, "Justice as Fairness: Political not Metaphysical," *Philosophy and Public Affairs* 14 (1985):249.
2. John Dunn, *The Political Thought of John Locke* (Cambridge: Cambridge University Press, 1969), esp. chap. 4; *Rethinking Modern Political Theory* (Cambridge: Cambridge University Press, 1985), esp. chap. 2.
3. I am indebted here to conversations with George Armstrong Kelly and Bonnie Honig.
4. See, for example, Guy H. Dodge, *Benjamin Constant's Philosophy of Liberalism* (Chapel Hill: University of North Carolina Press, 1980); Stephen Holmes, *Benjamin Constant and the Making of Modern Liberalism* (New Haven: Yale University Press, 1984).
5. See John Gray, *Mill on Liberty: A Defence* (London: Routledge and Kegan Paul, 1983); Fred Berger, *Happiness, Justice, and Freedom: The Moral and Political Philosophy of John Stuart Mill* (Berkeley: University of California Press, 1984).
6. Ronald Dworkin, *A Matter of Principle* (Cambridge: Harvard University Press, 1985), p. 183; *Taking Rights Seriously* (Cambridge: Harvard University Press, 1977), esp. chap. 12.
7. Rawls, "Justice as Fairness," pp. 232ff. and passim.
8. Bruce Ackerman, *Social Justice in the Liberal State* (New Haven: Yale University Press, 1980).

9. See H. L. A. Hart, *Essays in Jursiprudence and Philosophy* (Oxford: Clarendon Press, 1983), esp. chaps. 9 and 10.

10. Cf. Dworkin, *A Matter of Principle,* p. 189.

11. Richard E. Flathman, *The Philosophy and Politics of Freedom,* part one (University of Chicago Press: 1986, forthcoming).

12. Richard E. Flathman, *The Practice of Rights* (Cambridge: Cambridge University Press, 1976), pp. 7–8, 44–47, 167–81.

13. Stanley Benn, "Freedom, Autonomy, and the Concept of a Person," *Proceedings of the Aristotelian Society* 76 (1976):109–30.

14. I rely here on an analysis of desires and interests presented in part one of Richard E. Flathman, *The Philosophy and Politics of Freedom.*

15. Albert Hirschman, *The Passions and the Interests* (Princeton: Princeton University Press, 1979), p. 32.

16. Ibid., p. 43.

17. Stephen Holmes, *Benjamin Constant and the Making of Modern Liberalism,* p. 253.

18. Cf. Holmes: "Even today, antiliberal attacks on self-interest express nostalgia for systems of deference, authority, and condescension." Ibid.

19. Ibid., pp. 252–53.

20. See esp. John Rawls, "The Basic Liberties and Their Priority," in *The Tanner Lectures on Human Values, III,* ed. S. M. McMurrin (Salt Lake City: University of Utah Press, 1982), p. 49; "Kantian Constructivism in Moral Theory," *The Journal of Philosophy* 77 (1980):530.

21. See Wesley N. Hohfeld, *Fundamental Legal Conceptions* (New Haven: Yale University Press, 1919).

22. I believe that the concept acquired its present prominence because of its central place in Rawls's work. See *A Theory of Justice* (Cambridge: Harvard University Press, 1971), esp. p. 25 and section 50.

23. Ibid., pp. 326-27.

24. Ibid., pp. 326ff, 414ff.

25. See ibid., p. 31 for an especially severe statement. Cf. Rawls, "The Basic Liberties and Their Priority," p. 171, and "Kantian Constructivism in Moral Theory," p. 527.

26. See Rawls, *A Theory of Justice,* pp. 7, 259.

27. See Rawls, "The Basic Liberties and Their Priority."

28. See ibid., esp. section 7.

29. Rawls, "Kantian Constructivism in Moral Theory," section 7; "Justice as Fairness," pp. 233–34.

30. Rawls, *A Theory of Justice,* section 15; "Kantian Constructivism in Moral Theory," pp. 525–27; "The Basic Liberties and Their Priority," pp. 21ff.

31. Richard E. Flathman, "Moderating Rights," *Social Philosophy & Policy* 1 (1984):149–71.

32. Rawls, *A Theory of Justice,* section 7, pp. 315 ff; idem, "The Basic Liberties and Their Priority," pp. 10, 26, 32, 74; idem, "Justice as Fairness," p. 258.

– 5 –

The Idea of a Duty to Justice in Ideal Liberal Theory

STEVEN M. DE LUE

Introduction

Ideal liberal political theory is a formal argument for a political regime built upon the expectations of free individuals for a cooperative social scheme that is committed to both equal liberty and political equality. Moreover, as an argument for how liberal societies should be organized, ideal theory provides a perspective from which to critique existing liberal societies.[1]

In this essay, I provide a general statement of what I consider to be the "neglected assumption" of ideal liberal theory, the importance of a sense of justice which, to use Rawls's terms, is a "desire to act in accordance with [principles of a just social scheme]."[2] This assumption, at the core of ideal theory, emphasizes the centrality to liberal societies of a moral culture, especially one that facilitates (and necessitates) the capacity to make judgments of the moral worth of society. I call this last essential aspect of a sense of justice (the capacity to make judgments of moral worth) a duty of justice. Critiques of existing liberal societies from the standpoint of ideal theory would recognize that the failure of those societies resides in their inability to provide a moral culture that helps persons sustain both a sense of justice and the concomitant duty of justice to judge the moral worth of society.

The Neglected Assumption

Ideal liberal theory is often accused of conceptualizing persons as detached from the social contexts essential to their identities as persons.[3] On this view, liberal theory is criticized for failing to understand that persons share a social context marked by common traditions, sentiments and even on occasion, common substantive purposes. Liberal theorists forget that understandings, choices and even self-concepts are defined inevitably in terms of these common social facts of life, so that in making choices about how to live, persons are at the same time exhibiting a commitment to a social context. But liberal theorists, say critics, must neglect the social dynamics of ordinary life. The attempt to conceptualize principles of justice that guarantee to each person those rights and (negative) freedoms that allow persons to make choices without interference from outside obstacles excludes those social facts of life that might otherwise shape outlooks and direct (and thus interfere with) choices. On this view, then, persons are nothing but mechanisms of choice and desire whose relationships are mediated by universally applicable abstract rules of exchange or contract.

But modern ideal liberal theorists, in contrast to earlier views of liberalism found, for instance, in Hobbes, are aware of this criticism, and they have attempted to rewrite liberal theory in light of it.[4] The importance of a sense of justice to support just principles and social arrangements that embody them represents, then, one aspect of this response.

My argument is that a commitment from a sense of justice to the rules of right reads back into ideal liberal theory the importance of community in two senses. First, the sense of justice presumes that free individuals are rational persons who have a desire to be a part of an environment that, in addition to facilitating personal autonomy, is known to be just and fair. Second, I contend that the desire to be a part of a fair or just environment creates for free persons a responsibility to judge the justness of their environment. And this responsibility can only be carried out in the midst of a moral culture that aids judgments of moral worth. Insofar as an environment exists to permit judgments of this sort, the sense of justice is reinforced.

In the next section, I will discuss the importance of the idea of a sense of justice in John Rawls's ideal liberal theory, and I will discuss in the remaining sections the place and manner of judgments of moral worth. My argument will be that an important dimension of the effort to make these judgments is a moral culture that sustains public support for government policies seeking to implement principles of justice of the type Rawl's theory maintains. In discussing the type of judgment associated with holding a sense of justice, I will comment only upon Rawls because he, unlike many modern theorists, provides a moral psychology that can be construed as providing a social foundation for these judgments.

The Core of Ideal Theory

The centrality of a sense of justice in ideal liberal theory stems, first, from an understanding of persons as rational agents who determine principles that all members of society could accept as the basis for establishing the social order. But equally important, this view of persons presumes they have an interest in making these principles a major part of their conduct in everyday life. Here persons would abide by the rules of a just scheme from a sense of justice. In doing so, persons do not approach the social scheme as "free riders" and thereby seek to avoid compliance while receiving benefits from the compliance of others.[5] Further, given this commitment, it is also possible to demonstrate that such persons would manifest the need to make judgments of the society's moral worth (or justness) and would expect their social environment to help provide a basis for these judgments.

As is well known, Rawls, like all ideal liberal theorists, assumes that persons are distinct and separate selves who have and who seek the capacity for agency. Here persons wish to define their own goals, develop their own talents, interests, and needs, and determine strategies for action that are effective means to attain self-determined purposes.[6] To this end, the social scheme is to provide to all persons equal liberty (defined in terms of political liberty, liberty of conscience, liberty of thought, equal liberty to have private property, freedom of speech, freedom from arbitrary arrest). Also all persons are to be provided the basic primary goods (such as rights and liberties, opportunities, self-respect, income and wealth) necessary for an agency-centered life, and the distribution of these goods is to be made in terms of a fair and just pattern. For instance, once basic liberties are assured, the distribution of basic goods is to follow the difference principle, the idea that the better-off have a right to their privileges so long as their use of them works to enhance the lives of the worst-off members of society.[7]

Once the principles are embodied in the institutions and schemes of an ideal just society, one of the main threats to its stability is the free rider. Ideal theory surmounts the free-rider problem by attributing to persons a sense of justice or desire to support just schemes.

Thus in Rawls's theory persons would, as a consequence of their sense of justice, revise and reformulate their own life plans when the latter clashed with the constraints embodied in the just social institutions of the society. Here citizens manifest the importance in their own life of the priority of justice itself.[8] In the Dewey Lectures Rawls does in fact characterize rational persons as moral persons with two important moral powers.

> The first power is the capacity for an effective sense of justice, that is, the capacity to understand, to apply and to act from (and not merely in accordance with) the principles of justice. The second moral power is the capacity to form, to revise, and rationally to pursue a conception of the good. Corresponding to the moral powers, moral persons are said

> to be moved by two highest-order interests to realize and exercise these powers.[9]

Individuals have the capacity to define their own good, and under the second moral power, they do so in terms of their own personal choices for life. The second moral power by itself is not the main feature of the moral personality. However, when it (the second moral power) is joined to a firm commitment to the principles of justice (the first moral power), the goal structure of a person reflects a desire to pursue basic goods only in conjunction with an equally strong desire to conform one's conduct to the principles of justice.

In *A Theory of Justice,* the sense of justice is the "capacity . . . that insures that the principles chosen will be respected,"[10] and the sense of justice is associated with an understanding to "act in accordance with whatever principles are finally agreed to."[11] But the sense of justice in the Dewey Lectures is assigned even more prominence and importance in the personality of free individuals than was first the case in *A Theory of Justice.* In the former, free individuals are to act "from" and not "merely in accordance" with (as in *A Theory of Justice)* the principles of justice. This means that Rawls realizes that simply having a capacity to respect these principles is not sufficient to ensure conformity with them; in addition, persons must make these principles an integral part of their personalities.

As part of what it means to make the sense of justice "integral to one's personality," it would seem characteristic of a person who is committed to nurturing both moral powers, to satisfy himself that the scheme in which one maintains these powers is basically worthy of him. Holding a sense of justice, then, always requires of persons a need to form an opinion of a regime's moral worth. To aid their judgments, persons need a social environment that encourages and facilitates citizen assessments of society's moral worth. Here, as I will claim, taking part in these judgments symbolizes not simply a need to know if the scheme is just (a need associated with a moral personality), but it would symbolize as well an effective commitment on the part of persons to move their society toward a just arrangement, and this endeavor itself would, no doubt, strengthen their sense of justice.

Thus the sense of justice presumes an additional duty on the part of moral persons: a duty to judge the moral worth of the society. But how are such judgments made? In Rawls's view (of pure procedural justice) such judgments could be simplified by virtue of the fact that persons, in ideal theory, would be committed to support the results of a fair procedure, one that operated with respect for the difference principle as it (the procedure) distributed goods and opportunities. When institutions operate from fair procedures, "the outcome is likewise correct or fair, whatever it is, provided that the procedure has been properly followed."[12] In this context fair procedures would permit inequalities in order to ensure the well-being of the "representative men." The latter are assigned various positions throughout society, and expectations are defined with respect to the basic goods and opportunities representative persons must possess as a basis for a decent life. Policies must be designed so that any inequalities benefit every representative man through society.[13]

But given the diversity of interests involved, it is likely that some persons will argue that certain policies manifest poor or wrong uses of inequalities. Disagreements over how to determine the representative man for many social positions are likely to arise. Because persons are free individuals, they will have different and potentially conflicting opinions on the best way to apportion opportunities fairly. When this situation arises, some citizens (who do not accept the results) could contend that the fair procedures have allowed certain "suspect" results to emerge. Rawls's theory, of course, would not allow these persons to claim that laws were unjust, because in a perfectly well-ordered society (one grounded in pure procedural justice) the question of "whether to comply with unjust laws would not arise."[14]

Yet even the postulate of pure procedural justice could not completely avoid the emergence in some persons of a sense that the actions of a well-ordered society bordered on injustice. No system that assumes persons are free individuals could be so perfect or pure that it would eliminate conflict over how to interpret outcomes of accepted procedures. To make the ideal theory authentic to the real character of free individuals who exist at the heart of this theory, one must presume that conflicts of this sort would always occur. Here persons could argue that the results follow from fair or just procedures and still disagree with them (the results) anyway.

Once these claims are made, assessing them is made very difficult by virtue of the fact that persons are obligated to consider all results that emerge from fair procedures as just, even ones they do not accept. What would be unjust about this turn of events (for free individuals) is not the results they object to, but the failure of society to provide a way to assess the claims people make about these results. Thus, citizens must find an approach to judge these claims outside of a strict reliance on the procedures themselves; otherwise, persons (with claims) are likely to feel that their claims have no importance to society, thus making them believe, perhaps, that society deals with them in an unfair and arbitrary manner. This uneasiness would not necessarily dissolve the sense of justice, but it would surely diminish (even in a well-ordered society) the strength of the sense of justice in persons, possibly to the point of allowing persons to think of themselves as justified, at times, in assuming the role of free rider.

The tension would be abated (as the next section will contend) only as citizens are able to assess the claims of persons who argue that the procedures produce questionable results in a variety of areas that crucially affect them. To provide a basis for such judgments that is not wholly dependent on the procedures themselves, however, persons must share an understanding of the moral purpose that the just system is to attain, and use that understanding to determine how the issues in question might advance or obstruct that purpose. Further, in the formulation of one's own opinion, one would have to approach this judgment with an understanding of how others might see a given claim as affecting the shared moral purpose. In this type of judging, the independent viewpoint for judgment is located in a sincere respect for persons, not only by ensuring that one's judgment is based on the shared moral purpose (as opposed to just one's own interest), but by including the views of others in the formulation of one's own.

Here disagreements of opinion still exist on whether a given claim is valid or not. But these differences would not threaten the desire to support a just scheme. The sense of justice is strengthened in a social context that supports persons as they assess, from the standpoint of shared objectives and with respect for the diverse opinions found in society, the claims of others. For in this setting, persons know that a society that facilitates judgments of this sort is committed to ensuring that its fair procedures are linked to its shared moral objectives. In a society that nurtures these types of judgments, persons recognize the authentic nature of society's overall commitment to publicly shared principles of right. This environment would sustain a full sense of justice, enabling persons to reject the free-rider role and diminishing the potential for conflicts of view to undermine the desire to support just arrangements.

While the activity associated with judgments of this type is not discussed in Rawls, it is possible to derive from his moral psychology a basis for understanding how judgments of this sort could be constructed.

Judgments of Moral Worth

Rawls's original position helps to define the nature of persons as moral and rational beings, and it demonstrates the principles of right such persons would choose.[15] Further, the original position becomes the basis even for an agreement as to how the principles would be applied to actual settings. "An agreement on a conception of justice is fruitless in the absence of an understanding about the application of the principles."[16] But what is not discussed fully by Rawls is the basis in terms of which persons would make judgments of the outcomes of these applications. What I do here is to construct from Rawls's theory a possible view of how citizens would approach judgments of moral worth.

On what basis are such critical judgments made in an ideal liberal society? Any judgment of moral worth depends upon the existence of shared values in terms of which a particular society's policies and practices can be assessed by the citizens. Rawls's *Theory of Justice* provides, amidst his discussion of the "ends" of citizen life, a view of the socialization process that would have to exist for citizens to develop a sense of justice. Further, embodied in his view of how citizens are socialized to uphold a sense of justice is a substantive vision of the hoped-for world that is to emerge from the rules and procedures of a just society. It is against this vision that citizens can "judge" existing and past life circumstances.

Recent critiques of Rawls argue, in effect, that no sort of vision can exist in his theory that would sustain a moral language empowering persons to make judgments about a community's worth. William Sullivan argues that genuine communities, with a moral language that facilitates critical self-reflections from a community standpoint, derive from "common understandings and practices"[17] or a "living tradition" that is a "dialogue concerning those things which matter most deeply to participants."[18] Here community teaches a "moral ecology" consisting of common symbols, derived from the shared understandings that orient thought, action, and judgment.[19]

Sullivan recognizes that Rawls seeks to locate his moral theory in a context that stresses "the historical and social dimensions of the moral vision which guides his theory."[20] But Rawls's effort to locate his theory in a shared moral vision that forms motives and basic outlooks always engenders a conflict between the psychology of liberalism's rational egoist and the sentiments of persons engaged in life from the standpoint of a vision embodied in a moral community.[21] In the former instance, persons choose principles that are neutral to any legitimate end a person might make his own, and the intent of the principles is to set up a just scheme to allow persons to pursue these legitimate ends without interference. In the latter instance of a moral community, the shared vision as embodied in a tradition is not neutral to the ends persons might chose, but as persons conform themselves to the common understandings of the community, the shared tradition *constitutes* the types of ends available to persons.

For Sullivan, character, the enduring commitment to the shared values that are the basis of moral judgment, is formed when community is constitutive of personality. "What disappears in [liberal paradigms like Rawls provides] is that defining, authoritative role of the substantive paradigm of the good society, the good person, and good life practices."[22] Rawls wants to establish a moral character in his citizens, but to do so he would have to accept the governing ethos of an authoritative paradigm. And that would conflict with the basic purpose of his thought: legitimizing neutral principles of justice. To attain successfully a society based on neutral principles, Rawls, according to Sullivan, would have to "proceed without dependence upon an ethic of character or commitments to any substantive ends of action."[23]

But Sullivan's view of Rawls fails to appreciate fully the importance to Rawls's ideal theory of the process of socialization that teaches respect for the scheme that embodies principles of justice. As we are taught to accept the rules and arrangements of a just social scheme, we are taught at the same time to appreciate the shared objective that support for this scheme implies. The shared objective is not sought for its own sake, but for the fact that persons are shown, again thanks to the process of social learning, that this objective is of essential importance to each person. And the objective is important because, as society teaches, in obtaining it persons satisfy basic, shared needs.

As persons reflect on the nature of the socialization process of liberal societies (and therefore become more self-conscious of what these processes impart), persons gain an understanding of the shared purposes that the process extols and of the scheme of life associated with obtaining this purpose. (In the case of Rawls, the main objective of the social scheme is to provide a basis for attaining the good of self-respect, and this goal is achieved by providing a just scheme that nurtures autonomy.) In fact, what emerges from this reflection is the vision of how life should and can be when the common scheme is made an integral part of the life of a community. Further, what helps to maintain the vision's usefulness for supporting Rawls's quest for equality is the existence of the capacity for judgments of moral worth, as I will argue in the next several sections. As a prelude to this concern, I first turn to a discussion of the process of socialization that teaches the shared vision that is the foundation of these judgments.

The Moral Culture of Ideal Theory

The experience of a well-ordered society teaches that the attainment of self-respect is the chief good that all free individuals seek as a consequence of their need for autonomy. And persons are taught that this good is obtainable so long as they maintain a sense of justice and thereby conform their lives to the arrangements of a just scheme. The family and the role of enlarged thinking are the main socializing agencies connecting support for a just scheme to the basic need for autonomy and the basic good of self-respect.

Family love is important for developing the capacity in persons for autonomy. Children develop an awareness of their own competence and skills within the protective atmosphere of unconditional parental love. Without the latter, the child would have neither the confidence in himself nor in his environment to "launch out and to test his maturing abilities." But with the experience of parental love, children find that others exist to nurture their own autonomy and, in such an atmosphere, they learn that they are able to "affirm [their] sense of the worth of [their] own person."[24] Attachments to others in the family do not inhibit the emergence of fellow feeling with nonfamily members. Enlarged thinking in the just scheme encourages persons to recognize that many nonfamily members help to facilitate the need for an autonomous life that, in a just scheme, is the basis for the attainment of the good of self-respect.

In a well-ordered society persons learn to "take up their [others'] point of view and to see things from their perspective." To acquire an understanding of others in this way, we must develop "the intellectual skills required to regard things from a variety of points of view and to think of these together as aspects of one system of cooperation."[25] In this way, we not only gain appreciation for the whole scheme, which contributes to our own autonomy, but we are able to see others as the particular contributors to the scheme (and thus to our autonomy). That recognition occurs when "we understand and assess their actions, intentions, and motives. Unless we can identify these leading elements, we cannot put ourselves into another's place and find out what we would do in his position."[26] And as others manifest "evident intentions [to] live up to their duties and obligations" in this scheme, we not only recognize others' contributions to our autonomy, but we can develop toward them fellow feeling and in doing so establish the basis for mutual respect and cooperation, for friendship and fellowship, and for the concomitant virtues like trust, fidelity, integrity, and impartiality.[27] Our appreciation for others grows as they contribute to the scheme that enhances our self-respect.[28]

Enlarged thinking focuses our attention on understanding others from the diverse points of view in the social scheme. At first, we think only from within the context of the particular groups that facilitate our autonomy, but as we enlarge our understanding of the society and become part of Rawls's "social union of social unions" we gain the capacity for understanding the worth of groups beyond our own and their contribution to a whole society's capacity to sustain the life of the free individual. Here we are taught to look upon others not as objects to be used solely for our own private purposes, but as fellow contributors in a just scheme. To think from an enlarged viewpoint, then, we must avoid locating our point of view in one particular interest perspective that cripples our ability to consider other views and to understand the possible life forms and contributions of others. We must, instead, be constantly looking from the standpoint of others, who, like us, are understood to contribute to a just scheme.

In a well-ordered society, enlarged thinking contributes to having a sense of justice by allowing us to understand how the activities of others in a just scheme contribute to our own agency and how we in turn contribute to the agency of others. Thus as we see others honor their duties and obligations to us, our own desire is strengthened to honor our duties and obligations to them.[29] Initially our sense of justice or desire to comply with just rules is maintained by a sense of fellow feeling that arises from an appreciation for the way others, who are a part of our group or association, contribute to our chances for autonomy. But as we expand our understanding to include the many others (beyond our group) involved in supporting the society that sustains our own autonomy, we gain an appreciation for the society as a whole and for its principles, and we see that in a well-ordered society you "and those for whom [one] cares are the beneficiaries of such arrangements [as a just scheme permits]."[30]

Here persons acknowledge that the main benefit gained from a well-ordered society is Rawls's chief primary good, the good of self-respect (or respect for persons). In this setting, where self-respect is a primary good of the highest importance, each knows that there are others "out there" who value (or who show respect for) their lives, by sustaining duties and rights that promote autonomy, and who do so in order to create an atmosphere for persons to gain a sense of self-respect or confidence in "one's ability . . . to fulfill one's intention."[31] It is within this experience that one manifests to others one's self-defined life plans, and others exist to recognize, to witness, and to facilitate one's endeavors. Rawls says,

> It normally suffices that for each person there is some association (one or more) to which he belongs and within which the activities that are rational for him are publicly affirmed by others. In this way we acquire a sense that what we do in everyday life is worthwhile.[32]

Here others are a part, with us, of a larger "social union" that works to provide spaces for persons to gain self-respect.[33] When conflict occurs among groups, persons have an interest in resolving these conflicts in a manner that maintains the principles of justice, for in doing so, the conditions for respect for human flourishing are protected.[34]

Rawls's ideal theory, then, is grounded in a vision as to what society should look like once the principles are put into force. Rawls's moral persons, who possess a sense of justice, and who in consequence comply with the duty *of* justice to judge the moral worth of their society would make the vision of the hoped-for world (in which self-respect is the preeminent reality) the focal point of such judgments. Individuals, in looking upon their society to assess its moral worth, would seek to determine not only if society was a scheme that properly embodied the principles of right in a procedural sense, but in addition, if the society provided spaces where persons could gain from others the respect and recognition that is fundamental to the development in persons of a sense of self-worth associated with the autonomy of a freely formed self. A society that distorts such spaces, in a way that excludes self-worth for some, lacks moral worth because it fails to permit all persons a chance for a sense of self-respect based on autonomy.

Indeed, then, the target of our judgments are claims made by persons (against the background of this shared focal point) that society's policies prevent persons from gaining self-worth (and autonomy). Where these claims arise (and given that society is composed of diverse interests and points of view, it is clear that they would arise), the concern of persons is to see if these claims have value: if in fact the commitment to promote self-respect and respect for persons has been undermined in a given situation and perhaps by implication for society as a whole.

Moreover, these judgments would be based in Rawls not only on the central focal point, but upon approaching judgments from this focal point in a manner that encompasses the viewpoint of enlarged thought. Persons must, as they form their own opinions, consider the views of many diverse others; one's judgment cannot be based solely upon the particular interests of oneself or of the person's interest whose claim we are assessing in light of the respect for a person's commitment.

The mental culture of an ideal society would encourage this enlarged view to assessing claims. For an ideal society requires us to be constantly open to understanding the diverse interests of others who contribute to the just scheme. Where persons refuse to look upon their own experience from the views of other contributors in the just scheme, then the scheme itself is put in jeopardy (as Rawls's scheme for socialization would emphasize). My own judgment of a claim, then, is based on whether the claimant's contention manifests a denial by society to him of the shared values of self-respect, *but* my approach to developing an opinion must, for the sake of maintaining the scheme itself and its shared value of respect for persons, include an effort on my part to consider the points of view of others (including of course the claimant's opinions) as I develop my own judgment.

Thus in judging claims made by those who argue that they are harmed by the society, persons must look upon these claims as spectators whose objective is to determine if the claim symbolizes a failure to provide spaces for the respect and recognition of persons, and thus by implication, a lack of commitment to the central aspirations of society. As a spectator, I seek out other opinions that represent different angles of perception on the question, angles which I would be cut off from if I did not think from an enlarged viewpoint. My task as a spectator is to assimilate these different views, compare and contrast them, and finally derive my own opinion as to the claim's merit. If I determine that the claim has merit and if enough people agree with my view, then (assuming a fair political system, open to citizen influence) we, together, are in a good position to place our concerns on the political agenda of society for the purpose of using politics to move society more in the direction of its own vision.

The Intersubjective Space and Equality

Judgments of moral worth in ideal theory are facilitated by the mental culture (just discussed) of liberal societies. The "good of the community," which orients this mental context, is based on sentiment or a sense of justice. Sandel, in his critique of Rawls, claims that the sentiment is "limited to communitarian aims" and this view of community does not provide a constitutive conception of the "good of community" that penetrates "the person more profoundly so as to describe not just his *feeling* but a mode of self-understanding partly constitutive of his identity, partly definitive of who he was."[35]

Sandel's complaint (not unlike Sullivan's) is that Rawls's ideal community, as a community based on sentiment, is not strong enough to foster Rawls's commitment to equality and thus to the difference principle. Sentimental communities presume persons can have benevolent motivations (and not just self-interested ones) and these motivations help sustain a commitment to justice. But a view of justice that allows a community to make claims on the assets of individuals for the sake of improving the condition of the worst-off presumes that persons in the ideal order will allow the "concept of the good" to have priority over the self's choices of what it seeks and who it is. Yet Rawls's persons seek principles that leave the self free to choose itself, independent of a "good" that forms it. On Sandel's view, for Rawls to allow the good "a hand in the constitution of the self" is to "violate the priority of the self over its ends."[36] The question then is whether, in the face of this fact, a sense of concern for others would be sufficient to justify persons accepting and conforming to the conditions of Rawls's concept of equality (especially the difference principle).

Sandel says no, but I disagree. The assumption that grounds my view is that persons with a sense of justice *have* as a duty of justice to determine the moral worth of their society. To do so, persons inevitably "form" their identities in ways that habituate themselves to make fellow feeling into a mode of life that places on government (in this case a government operating from fair and open democratic procedures) a responsibility to promote Rawls's conception of justice (and others possibly as well). Let me explain.

In making judgments of moral worth, people evaluate, from within an enlarged thought context, how well society attains its chief goal of respect for persons. Because the focal point for judgment is respect for others and because persons want to determine if others have received such respect as a result of a certain law or policy, persons constitute or habituate their self-understanding to include a concern for the claims made by others who say that social policy harms their attainment of self-respect. Consequently, in performing our duties of justice, we are always oriented to hear the expressed needs of our fellows, and to assess their validity in light of society's commitment to promote spaces where persons can attain self-respect.

Moreover, because persons approach judgments from an enlarged outlook, part of one's "identity" is arranged to make the need for a diversity of views essential to one's determination of a claim's worth. Here persons display an ability to locate their concern for the claims of persons in a context of the other opinions of the society in which the claim originates. In the process (again as part of the duty of justice), persons develop a habit or tendency to interpret the general attitude of benevolence or fellow feeling to mean a need to show respect both for others who have claims (especially the ones judged valid) and for those others whose points of view contribute to the development of one's own opinion about the validity of these claims.

As the members of the society judge in this way, they create an intersubjective space among themselves that is the basis for manifesting a common desire to rid society of those harms that threaten the society's moral worth. Just the fact, then, that a general sense of benevolence exists in Rawls's society would not necessarily function to move society toward the goals of Rawls's system. Here I agree with Sandel. But Rawls's notion of citizen concern for others, when placed into the context of the duty to make judgments of moral worth from the standpoint of the views of others, integrates benevolence into the identities of persons, and this reality would be the source for an intersubjective space or a common language of concern that helps and encourages persons to recognize the obligation to ensure that others are treated fairly and that they are accorded respect as autonomous persons. In judging the claims made by those who believe they have been harmed and in making this endeavor a main dimension of one's outlook as a citizen determining moral worth, citizens would create a set of expectations for their government to abide by. In particular, governments must treat all such claims using, in Ronald

Dworkin's words, "the same respect and concern as [given] everyone else."[37] The government must either show that claims are lacking in worth or, if these claims are indeed valid, then the government must make every effort to remedy them. Otherwise society would lack moral worth.

The capacity for citizen judgment takes on special importance in Rawls's nonideal political scheme, because here the procedures of an actual, nearly just government are "imperfect" and not pure. This means that there is no actual political process that can ensure that the "laws enacted in accordance with it will be just."[38] The public perspective associated with the judgments of moral worth would pressure government to be aware of this fact and constantly to assess the use of its own procedures by carefully addressing the claims made by others that the government acts in ways detrimental to the shared purposes of society.

Judgments of moral worth have special significance in the realms of nonideal theory, where the basis for support of principles and policies in a "nearly just," but imperfect procedural scheme is for Rawls a sense of a "natural duty to uphold just institutions."[39] A duty to justice is stronger than a sense of justice, because the former must be maintained even in settings not guaranteed to produce complete justice. But in this context the need for judgments of moral worth would be just as necessary, if not more so. Here even if society's procedures do not always provide justice, still because society provides a space in which persons would be constantly concerned to listen to and to work to remedy the claims of persons, governments would live under constant public pressure to ensure that their procedures (and the policies coming from them) comported with the shared public purpose to promote respect for persons. In this setting, the public's sense of justice (or in this case its natural duty to justice) would be strengthened and, as it is, the public's tolerance of Rawls's commitment to equality would be furthered.

In conclusion, Rawls's community would be strong enough to sustain his quest for equality. At the same time his community would not be so strong that persons would cease to be agents of their own choice. Indeed, in a social setting where others look upon us as persons seeking self-respect through the exploration of our opportunities and potential, there is a strong incentive to live as autonomous persons.

Conclusion

Persons looking upon existing liberal society from the vantage point of Rawls's ideal theory would see that the problem with these societies is not a tendency, endemic to ideal theory, to define persons as abstract preference machines, living outside of social attachments and devoid of any capacity for a moral language that can be used to judge society against its shared communitarian sentiments. Rather, the problem of these societies is the failure to make possible an intersubjective space that permits persons to make judgments of moral worth. Without the possibility of these judgments, persons cannot sustain the pressure on government to make its procedures conform with the goals of a just society. And where this public expectation is diminished, a sense of justice (or a duty to justice), so necessary to combating the free-rider mentality, cannot be sustained.

Notes

1. John Rawls, *A Theory of Justice* (Cambridge: Harvard University Press, 1971), pp. 8–9.
2. Ibid., p. 9.
3. See for instance C. B. Macpherson, *The Political Theory of Possessive Individualism: Hobbes to Locke* (Oxford: Oxford University Press, 1962), chap. 6; Michael J. Sandel, *Liberalism and the Limits of Justice* (Cambridge: Harvard University Press, 1982), chaps. 1 and 2; William Sullivan, *Reconstructing Public Philosophy* (Berkeley: University of California Press, 1982), chap. 4.
4. See Gerald F. Gaus, *The Modern Liberal Theory of Man* (New York: St. Martin's Press, 1983), for his discussion of modern liberals.
5. Rawls, *Theory of Justice,* p. 267.
6. Ibid., pp. 17–22; and Alan Gewirth, *Reason and Morality* (Chicago: University of Chicago Press, 1978), chap. 2.
7. Rawls, *Theory of Justice,* pp. 60–65.
8. John Rawls, "Kantian Constructivism in Moral Theory," *Journal of Philosophy* 77 (1980): 529–30.
9. Ibid., p. 525.
10. Rawls, *Theory of Justice,* p. 145.
11. Ibid.
12. Ibid., pp. 85–86.
13. Ibid., pp. 64–65.
14. Ibid., p. 353.
15. Ibid., pp. 17–22, 103–5.
16. Rawls, "Kantian Constructivism in Moral Theory," p. 540.
17. Sullivan, *Reconstructing Public Philosophy,* p. 115.
18. Ibid., p. 112.
19. Ibid., p. 76.
20. Ibid., p. 115.
21. Ibid.
22. Ibid., p. 112.
23. Ibid., p. 116.
24. Rawls, *Theory of Justice,* p. 464.
25. Ibid., p. 468.
26. Ibid., pp. 469, 470.
27. Ibid., pp. 468, 470, and 472.

28. Outside of this enlarged view, love and fellowship, even friendship might be simply a positive but general feeling that had no foundation in particular understandings of the real persons. In this event these feelings would lose their source of concrete inspiration. Michael Sandel (*Liberalism and the Limits of Justice,* p. 170) argues that, for Rawls, love contains this "opaque" quality because individuals are separate persons isolated one from the other. Here love and presumably fellowship, too, cannot be the basis for knowing and upholding the lives of particular others. We may love in general, but such love, just like respect for others, is a feeling that attributes love or respect to persons who have only a nonspecific general character. Loving and respecting others without being able to have particular persons in mind deprives those feelings of their practical quality and, upon reflection, makes them seem empty and vapid. Love and respect are rejuvenated as general dispositions that sustain a sense of community when they are made concrete in terms of our love or respect for particular persons, who are understood to be, with us, part of a just scheme. And it is precisely this possibility of enlarged thinking that breaks down the barriers of separation and allows us to know, to understand, and to give support to others in particular and to the entire social enterprise that exists as the basis for each person's distinctive life and sense of self-respect.

29. Rawls, *Theory of Justice,* p. 470.

30. Ibid., p. 473.

31. Ibid., p. 440.

32. Ibid., p. 441.

33. Ibid., pp. 527–30.

34. Ibid., p. 476.

35. Sandel, *Liberalism and the Limits of Justice,* p. 161.

36. Ibid., pp. 64–65, 149–50.

37. On this point, see Ronald Dworkin, *Taking Rights Seriously* (Cambridge: Harvard University Press, 1977), p. 227.

38. Rawls, *Theory of Justice,* p. 353.

39. Ibid., p. 354.

– 6 –

Goods, Virtues, and the Constitution of the Self

EMILY R. GILL

The liberal vision and its promise, according to Michael Sandel, are vitiated by the image of the self that animates this promise. Liberalism holds that what makes a society just "is not the *telos* or purpose or end at which it aims, but precisely its refusal to choose in advance among competing purposes and ends."[1] The original position of a deontological liberal like Rawls attempts to ensure the priority of the right over the good, but in so doing gives rise to the picture of an "unencumbered self, a self understood as prior to and independent of purposes and ends."[2] Only such a self, beyond the reach of experience, is free to choose its ends, because only a self not identified with its momentary aims and interests can be a free and independent agent. Such a conception of the self, then, rules out the possibility of *constitutive* ends. "No role or commitment could define me so completely that I could not understand myself without it. No project could be so essential that turning away from it would call into question the person I am."[3]

The priority of the right over the good and of the self over its ends carries two consequences. Morally, individual desires and aspirations are limited "by the principles of justice which specify the boundaries that men's systems of ends must respect."[4] The majority will is only a preferred particular conception of the good and, as such, cannot override the legitimate claims of individual rights.[5] Epistemologically, because the bounds of the self are antecedently given and beyond choice, the subject is guaranteed the capacity to choose its ends "against the vagaries of a public opinion that might one day prefer otherwise. . . . While the bounds of the self may seem an undue restriction on agency in that the self cannot participate in their constitution, they are in fact a prerequisite of agency."[6] That is, if the bounds of the self are left open, others can choose for particular selves counter to what might be those selves' self-understandings. Just as deontological liberalism needs a standard of appraisal that is not implicated in existing values, it also requires a subject whose unity is antecedently established and thus distinguishable from the contingencies of its situation. Without a distinction between the subject and the objects it possesses, we are left with a radically situated subject, indistinguishable from its experience and capable of being transformed by any contingency.

But in the end, Sandel concludes, the self of deontological liberalism is less liberated than dispossessed. Stripped of assets, which are contingent attributes rather than essential constituents of identity, the self avoids being a radically situated subject at the price of becoming a radically disembodied one.[7] "The self is disempowered because dissociated from those ends and desires which, woven gradually together into a coherent whole, provide a fixity of purpose, form a plan of life, and so account for the continuity of the self with its ends."[8] In practice, the unencumbered self is secured by a "universalizing logic of rights," removed from the vagaries of local preference and relocated at the national level, in institutions ostensibly more insulated from democratic pressures. But as the welfare state expands the promise of individual rights and entitlements, it also demands of citizens a level of mutual engagement that the unencumbered self cannot sustain. Although we picture ourselves as free individuals, without obligations prior to agreements we enter, as citizens "We find ourselves implicated willy-nilly in a formidable array of dependencies and expectations we did not choose and increasingly reject."[9] That is, our conceptions of ourselves do not allow for the sort of self-understanding that would make these obligations acceptable. Since ends cannot be constitutive of the individuated self, the collective ends of society must prevail, thus lapsing into an "ethic of the unbounded subject" of which utilitarianism is the outcome.[10]

As Sandel perceives the situation, deontological liberals like Rawls and Dworkin have only one cogent defense against the accusation that the difference principle or such a policy as affirmative action uses some individuals as means to others' ends. This defense would consist of an appeal to an intersubjective conception of the self, under which "the relevant description of the self may embrace more than a single empirically-individuated human being."[11] Under such a self-understanding, I would regard the use of "my" assets in the service of a common endeavor less as a sacrifice for others' ends than as a contribution to a community or "realization of a way of life in which I take pride and with which my identity is bound."[12] Difficulties remain, however. First, even if one could identify the relevant community across which my assets ought to be shared, that particular, arbitrarily identified community holds no greater moral claim to any particular set of endowments than does the individual who "owns" them.[13]

Second, the conception of community required for redrawing the bounds of the subject would have to be deep enough to reach beyond the self's motivations to the subject itself. That is, "Community would describe not just a *feeling* but a mode of self-understanding partly constitutive of the agent's identity,"[14] not a relationship chosen but an attachment discovered. But this conception returns us to the radically situated subject, the avoidance of which is the original aim of deontological liberalism.

> The good of community cannot reach *that* far, for to do so would be to violate the priority of the self over its ends, to deny its antecedent individuation, to reverse the priority of plurality over unity, and to allow the good a hand in the constitution of the self, which on Rawls' view is reserved to the concept of the right.[15]

For present purposes, I am willing to grant Sandel's reading of deontological liberalism. I question, however, the dichotomy he sketches between the antecedently individuated self, which is prior to its ends, and a more communitarian image of the self, which is partly constituted *by* its ends. Specifically, I wish to do two things. Examining the recent work of Alasdair MacIntyre and Michael Walzer, first I shall argue that all selves are in some sense situated subjects. Although MacIntyre denigrates the characteristic absence of a *telos* in liberal societies, his account of the evolution of goods, virtues, and notions like worth and merit is applicable to liberal as well as nonliberal societies. And Walzer's emphasis upon shared understandings as the basis for determinate principles of distribution implicitly demonstrates that, even in a liberal society, selves are situated subjects. Second, I shall argue that the individual's constitutive identity thus created not only *allows* for critical reflection and meaningful choice but is a necessary condition for reflection and choice. Such an identity reempowers the individual, supporting intrasubjective self–understandings and also the possibility of intersubjective ones. Perhaps, as Sandel suggests, true community must describe more than a feeling. But it must still *begin* with a feeling, though over time it may *become* a mode of self-understanding partly constitutive of the individual's identity.

I

As is well known, Rawls's difference principle is based upon an agreement to treat the distribution of natural talents and social circumstances as a common asset and to allow the entire community to share their benefits.[16] Individual entitlements persist, but "*These* claims honor the legitimate expectations created by institutions designed to elicit my efforts, not a primordial right or claim of desert in virtue of qualities I possess."[17] That is, I do not deserve in the traditional, preinstitutional sense the benefits to which I am entitled. First, under Rawls's conception of the person, my assets are alienable attributes rather than essential constituents of the self. Possession in the weak, contingent sense rather than in the strong, constitutive sense cannot establish desert in the strong, preinstitutional sense. Second, although I am entitled to my share of benefits as specified by the rules, "I am not entitled that *these* rules, rewarding *these* attributes, be in force rather than some others."[18] Thus I am only the guardian or repository of my assets and attributes, not their owner; I can make "no special moral claim on the fruits of their exercise."[19] Furthermore, I have no intrinsic worth, prior to or independent of what just institutions attribute to me by the valuation they place upon my attributes.[20]

Rawls's logic, suggests Sandel, "undermines desert not directly, by claiming I cannot *deserve* what is arbitrarily given, but indirectly, by showing I cannot *possess* what is arbitrarily given, that is, that 'I,' *qua* subject of possession, cannot possess it in the undistanced, constitutive sense necessary to provide a desert base."[21] But the priority of the self over its ends, which is necessary to avoid the radical situation of the subject that Rawls eschews, leaves the self barren of substantive features and characteristics, leading to the radical disembodiment of a subject whose real power to choose is now in question. Moreover, if individual ownership of assets is contingent and arbitrary from a moral point of view, is not the notion of community ownership of "my" assets equally accidental and arbitrary? If individual selves cannot possess intrinsic worth, merit, or desert antecedent to what is attributed to them by just institutions, deontological liberalism, the ethic of which is designed to protect the inviolability of the self and its rights, ironically results in a moral disempowerment so severe that virtually no self is left to protect.

For Alasdair MacIntyre, accounts of the self of moral philosophy are incomplete without some account of the human *telos*, "man-as-he-could-be-if-he-realised-his-essential-nature."[22] Critical of liberalism, he disagrees with the deontological viewpoint that moral agency requires the ability "to stand back from any and every situation in which one is involved, from any and every characteristic that one may possess, and to pass judgment on it from a purely universal and abstract point of view that is totally detached from all social particularity."[23] Any principles such a self may profess are mere preferences, prior to and thus ungoverned by any allegiance to true criterion or value. This self, then, "can have no rational history in its transitions from one state of moral commitment to another. Inner conflicts are . . . necessarily . . . the confrontation of one contingent arbitrariness by another. It is a self with no given continuities."[24] In Sandel's terms, the subject is so radically disembodied that it has no constitutive identity, merely a contingent identity, "constantly vulnerable to transformation by experience . . . rather than epistemologically guaranteed."[25]

What is needed, instead, is "a self whose unity resides in the unity of a narrative which links birth to death as narrative beginning to middle to end."[26] Such a self is admittedly situated. But for MacIntyre, it is only from within the context of the narrative of a specific human life or the tradition of a particular community that choice has meaning. As the human *telos,* the good for MacIntyre has a hand in the constitution of the self as subject of possession and is thus prior to the right. But even for a self with constitutive ends, its *objects* of possession still function initially as contingent attributes rather than as essential constituents of identity. That is, whether antecedently individuated and prior to its ends or *not,* the self cannot seem to possess intrinsic worth, merit, or desert independent of what is attributed to it by the institutions which are its context. Put differently, the self's assets are always initially contingent, in the sense that it possesses them by chance. They become constitutive of identity, however, to the extent that the self is afforded the opportunity and incentive to use and develop them. And this opportunity and incentive are in large measure a function of the social context within which the self exists. For MacIntyre *and* for deontological liberalism, concepts of worth or merit become determinate only as they are interpreted within specific communities and their traditions.

MacIntyre espouses a core conception of the virtues, which makes them a part of the human *telos* yet also allows them to function in accordance with the practices and institutions of specific communities and their traditions. The virtues function, first, to sustain practices and their internal goods. Second, they sustain the narratives of individual lives and their goods, each life having the unity of a narrative quest, at its best, for the good human life. Finally, the virtues "find their point and purpose . . . in sustaining those traditions which provide both practices and individual lives with their necessary historical context."[27] Traditions make individuals the bearers of particular social identities and give each life its own moral particularity.

The specific way in which a virtue functions, suggests MacIntyre, is dependent upon the practice, life, or tradition the goods of which it sustains. And his cardinal virtue, so to speak, lies in a grasp of the possibilities that confront one in the context of one's tradition. It appears as a "capacity for judgment which the agent possesses in knowing how to select among the relevant stack of maxims and how to apply them in particular situations."[28] Morality is always tied to the socially local and particular; the modern ideal of "a universality freed from all particularity" is illusory. We can only possess the virtues when we do so "as part of a tradition in which we inherit them and our understanding of them from a series of predecessors."[29] The virtues act, then, to sustain the goods of practices, individual lives, and traditions. But, "It is always within some particular community with its own specific institutional forms that we learn or fail to learn to exercise the virtues."[30] The human *telos* lies in the quest for the good human life, but this notion is highly indeterminate apart from its interpretation within the context of a specific community and its practices, institutions, and traditions.

The self, then, is situated. Its roles and commitments within the context of its community define the self in such a way that they are partly constitutive of the human good for that particular subject. Writing of heroic societies, MacIntyre suggests that characters in heoric epics make all choices within a given and unchosen framework of rules and precepts. The virtues are those dispositions which enable individuals to discharge their roles within this framework. But it is this role and framework which assign worth or merit to individual actions. When a warrior remembers his orchards and cornfields, the symbols of prosperity, back home, he also remembers that it is because he is among the most valiant of the warriors that he deserves these good things.[31] The notion of desert, suggests MacIntyre, "is at home only in the context of a community whose primary bond is a shared understanding both of the good for man and of the good of that community and where individuals identify their primary interests with reference to those goods."[32] The kind of desert basic to this sort of entitlement is particularistic, defined by the community through its tradition that honors and rewards the heroic virtues. It attaches to individuals on account of their roles and the actions that fulfill the expectations accompanying these roles.

These entitlements, then, are not preinstitutional claims of desert but, in Sandel's terms, instead "honor the legitimate expectations created by institutions designed to elicit my efforts."[33] The symbols of material prosperity accrue to individuals not by virtue of any sort of intrinsic worth, but rather by virtue of what institutions attribute to them by the valuation these institutions place upon individual attributes. The notion of desert may be at home only where there exists a bond of shared understandings as to the good, but in making these understandings determinate, the community is implying that there are no preinstitutional entitlements that some attributes be rewarded rather than others. In sum, worth and merit are contingent attributes, not essential constituents of identity, because it is the community and its traditions that give substance and definition—even reality—to the *notions* of worth and merit.

As MacIntyre notes, heroic societies more than some others ground conceptions of the good in social roles and in the virtues that enable individuals to discharge these roles. But his overall point is that one cannot seek the good only as an individual. "This is partly because what it is to live the good life concretely varies from circumstance to circumstance even when it is one and the same conception of the good life and one and the same set of virtues which are being embodied in a human life."[34] It is also because we are all, as we interact with our circumstances, "bearers of a particular social identity" that gives each individual life "its own moral particularity."[35] Thus, notions of worth and merit, and of the legitimate expectations that accompany their definition, will vary from community to community, along with the practices, institutions, and traditions of these communities. That is, the notions of worth and merit only become determinate for an individual within the context of that individual's social identity. In addition, although the self's attributes are initially contingent upon chance, these attributes may become constitutive of identity insofar as their development and exercise are elicited by the particular community in which that self exists. The self, then, possesses constitutive ends, and thus a constitutive identity, as a function of that self's social identity. And it appears that this conclusion would hold not only in the nonliberal societies that MacIntyre apotheosizes, but in liberal societies as well.

A related point is made by Michael Walzer in his contention that individuals can never be ideally rational contractors who, if properly constrained, would choose a single set of distributive principles which alone may be claimed to constitute justice. Social goods along with their meanings and values are historically defined within the contexts of different communities. There is no single, universally applicable route from a notion like fairness to a distribution of the social goods necessary to its realization. According to Walzer's account of the social contract, "It is an agreement to redistribute the resources of the members in accordance with some shared understanding of their needs, subject to ongoing political determination in detail. The contract is a moral bond."[36] But this bond does not bind the members of the community to engage in any particular undertakings. For example, within the sphere of welfare, Walzer believes that need ought to predominate. But "No *a priori* stipulation of what needs ought to be recognized is possible; nor is there any *a priori* way of determining appropriate levels of provision."[37] In medieval Europe the cure of bodies was private, but the cure of souls was public. "Among medieval

Christians, eternity was a socially recognized need; and every effort was made to see that it was widely and equally distributed. . . . Among modern citizens, longevity is a socially recognized need; and increasingly every effort is made to see that it is widely and equally distributed."[38] Shared understandings of need change over time and space, hence the difficulty of prior stipulation of what constitutes either need or adequate provision for its relief. Walzer concludes, "A given society is just if its substantive life is lived in a certain way—that is, in a way faithful to the shared understandings of the members."[39]

Walzer states that correct decisions in matters of distributive justice in any society are reached "not by appealing to principles external to the legal system, but by exploring the internal principles of the system itself—and of the legal and political culture in which it is embedded."[40] Because the conception and creation of goods are social processes, the same goods have different meanings in different societies.

> Men and women take on concrete identities because of the way they conceive and create, and then possess and employ social goods. . . . In fact, people already stand in a relation to a set of goods; they have a history of transactions, not only with one another but also with the moral and material world in which they live.[41]

Thus social goods and the spheres governing their distribution must be fixed partly by empirical investigation and interpretation, not by rational deliberation alone. "They have the forms they take in a particular society; there are no preordained forms."[42] Whatever the distributive principles turn out to be, Walzer's point is that they will be determined because of what certain goods mean *to us,* within the context of our particular community. This sort of determination is a necessary condition for ensuring that distributive principles are just. "Justice is rooted in the distinct understandings of places, honors, jobs, things of all sorts, that constitute a shared way of life. To override those understandings is (always) to act unjustly."[43] And institutions governed by theoretical principles of justice "are of little use unless they are inhabited by men and women who feel at home within them and are prepared to defend them."[44] The implication is that the meaning and content of notions like worth and merit, and the self's identity as it grapples with these notions in a determinate context, are also social creations; their grounding will vary from one community to another. Insofar as the internal principles of liberal societies encompass a broad range of values, there exists a broad spectrum of ways in which the individual can be a situated subject. But the subject is, nonetheless, a situated one.

By examining MacIntyre's and Walzer's notions of the ground for individual choice and judgment, I have tried to show that the self must always understand its good, and therefore also its own identity, within the context of the practices, institutions, and traditions of a particular community. Notions of worth and merit, of desert, of entitlement, are always the shared understandings that evolve in and only become determinate within such a particularistic setting. The self may possess constitutive ends and a constitutive identity, but as a function of social identity. And this description of the self should hold true both for nonliberal and liberal communities. In the next section, I will argue that the possibility of *intrasubjective* self-understandings, especially in liberalism, rescue the subject from a radical situation that would preclude meaningful choice. Such a self-understanding reempowers the subject and, ultimately, includes the possibility of the *intersubjective* self-understandings Sandel perceives as essential to a reconstituted self.

II

Sandel suggests that deontological liberalism, by defining individual assets as contingent attributes rather than as essential constituents of identity, presupposes a self incapable of true choice. The antecedently individuated self ostensibly guarantees individual choice of ends and secures rights not threatened by others' conceptions of the good. But because the self has no preinstitutional identity and is only considered the accidental repository of its assets, no one has preinstitutional entitlements. Individual rights secured are then based upon legitimate expectations as defined by the community. The collective ends of society must prevail, thereby negating individual claims to choose. And the individual is thus implicated in obligations and dependencies that he in fact did not choose and which his self-understanding does not allow him to support. I have attempted to show that the self's attributes *may* become constitutive of identity as their development and exercise are elicited by a particular community; individual identity is partly a social product. But if the self is vulnerable to transformation by experience, how, then, does the individual set his own boundaries, as it were, to avoid "drowning in a sea of circumstance"?[45]

We have seen that for Sandel, deontological liberalism of the Rawlsian sort must appeal to an intersubjective conception of the self to justify the treatment of individual attributes as common assets in whose benefits the community as a whole may share. Much less prominent in Sandel's account is the *intrasubjective* conception of the self, according to which "For certain purposes, the appropriate description of the moral subject may refer to a plurality of selves within a single, individual human being, as when we account for inner deliberation in terms of the pull of competing identities, or moments of introspection in terms of occluded self-knowledge."[46] On Sandel's interpretation, Rawls implicitly rejects this notion by assuming that every individual represents but a single system of desires. The antecedently individuated self is ill-equipped for the self-reflection necessary to make qualitative choices among desires or to form second-order desires that assess the desirability of the original desires. The "choice" among conceptions of the good is basically an assessment of existing desires and of the means available for satisfying them.[47]

Moreover, "on Rawls's account, the worth of a desire only appears in the light of a person's good, and the identity of the agent is barren of constituent traits so that no aim or desire can be essential to it."[48] That is, since the bounds of the self are antecedently given and not subject to revision, "the identity of the subject can never be at stake in moments of choice or deliberation (although its future aims and attributes may of course be affected), for the bounds that define it are beyond the reach of the agency . . . that would contribute to its transformation."[49] We have seen that because all subjects are in some sense situated, they may in fact possess constitutive ends and a constitutive identity, the substance necessary for self-reflection on Sandel's account. Reexamining MacIntyre and Walzer, I want to suggest now that this constitutive identity, rather than precluding critical self-reflection and meaningful choice, is a necessary basis for critical reflection and choice, supporting both intrasubjective self-understandings and also the possibility of intersubjective ones.

In MacIntyre's case, we have seen that the human *telos* is determinate only within the context of a particular community and its notion of the good. And the specific way in which a virtue functions is dependent upon the practice, individual life, or tradition the goods of which it sustains. Nevertheless, notions of the good *and* right do not simply mirror the culture within which they receive their definition. MacIntyre notes that the virtues as understood by an Athenian provide him with norms that allow him to question the justice of practices or policies within his community. Yet it is his very membership in the community that provides him with this sort of critical understanding.[50] That is, if the content of the good is indeterminate apart from its interpretation within a specific community, so also is a definition of the right, the standard by which notions of the good may be assessed. Although the self's moral identity is discovered through its membership in a community, this "does not entail that the self has to accept the moral *limitations* of the particularity of those forms of community. . . . It is in moving forward from such particularity that the search for the good, for the universal, consists. Yet particularity can never be simply left behind or obliterated."[51]

In other words, individuals may perceive moral limitations in a community's shared understanding of the good for individuals or for that community. They, and perhaps in time the entire community, may eventually move beyond or transcend certain manifestations of particularity. Yet their original critical perceptions *and* their possible later, more "universal" resolution of conflicting claims will still be the perceptions and the resolutions that they are within and because of the context of that particular community and its traditions. In actual debates, the question is never "What code ought *I* as rational person to adopt?" but rather "How ought *we* as members of this particular community, sharing these particular beliefs, inheriting this particular moral tradition or traditions, to resolve this issue?"[52] There *is* a right in terms of which goods may be assessed, but it is defined within a particular tradition. Or, alternatively, although it is defined within a particular tradition, there *is* still a right.

In fact, for MacIntyre, conflict plays a major role in the moral development of individuals and of traditions. For individuals, "It is often and perhaps always through conflict that the self receives its social definition,"[53] or "that we learn what our ends and purposes are."[54] Similarly,

> When an institution—a university, say, or a farm, or a hospital—is the bearer of a tradition of practice or practices, its common life will be partly, but in a centrally important way, constituted by a continuous argument as to what a university is and ought to be or what good farming is or what good medicine is. Traditions, when vital, embody continuities of conflict.[55]

Moreover, MacIntyre allows for conflict among goods, conflict for which there is no single, "right" resolution. In some crucial conflicts, "Different virtues appear as making rival and incompatible claims upon us. But our situation is tragic in that we have to recognize the authority of both claims. . . . For to choose does not exempt me from the authority of the claims which I choose to go against."[56] MacIntyre, like Plato, is assuming an objective moral order and disagrees with those like Berlin who contend that attempts to reconcile the heterogeneity of human goods within a single moral order is likely to lead to the imposition of a moral straitjacket upon the human condition. Yet, given his other assumptions, we must infer that attempts at this reconciliation take place within the context of particular communities and their traditions, thus allowing for moral particularity both in one's moral starting point and in one's conclusions about the good. Within this framework, "There may be better and worse ways for individuals to live through the tragic confrontation of good with good. . . . To know what the good life for man is may require knowing what are the better and what are the worse ways of living in and through such situations."[57]

Now if practices, the content of individual lives, institutions, and traditions, all provide the substance or occasions for conflict, individuals, I believe, play two roles within these continuities of conflict. First, they may choose among various alternatives in attempts to resolve conflicts, always choosing from within the context of the imperatives of their particular tradition(s). Second, their choices and resolutions have an impact on them so that they define themselves differently, whether singly or in/as a group, as a result of their prior choices and the experiences these choices represent, than would be the case if they had not grappled with the issues involved in these earlier conflicts.

They are, in fact, transformed in such a way that each individual, over time, represents more than a single system of desires. And individual experiences build upon each other so that they become part of the self's identity. What begin as accidental or contingent circumstances may become essential constituents of an individual's self-definition, thereby affecting and defining the scope of his future choices. May not these accounts of agency be intertwined with one another, so that the role of the individual is at some times voluntarist, that of "willing subject to objects of choice," while at other times cognitive, that of "knowing subject to objects of understanding"?[58] It is in this sense, I believe, that we may interpret MacIntyre's statements about the role of conflict in the social definition of the self as the individual interacts with others. If a situation involves conflict, the agent's judgment, then, is about the "best" way of living through and handling this conflict. The individual is making a choice, but a choice most likely based upon self-knowledge or understanding, stemming from experience, of the rival goods for the individual involved or for the community. And the choice and its consequences in the life of the individual or community may produce new self-knowledge, new self-understandings, which in turn affect future choices.

MacIntyre is harshly critical of liberalism, as we have seen, for the abstraction from social particularity that moral agency in the deontological liberal tradition ostensibly requires. George Kateb, in turn, critiques MacIntyre by suggesting a lack of appreciation by the latter "that the only honest society is precisely the one in which moral dispute is institutionalized—the liberal society he so despises." Moreover, MacIntyre claims

> that a person's moral judgments can be authenticated only by a prior conception of the kind of life he should lead, which turns out to be life

> as a member, life in common with others in something morally prior to anyone. The moral unit is thus not the person, but the group or class.[59]

Now MacIntyre, along with Sandel, fails to see that even in the liberal tradition values are shaped within the context of shared understandings that evolve in and only become determinate within a particularistic setting. The virtue of MacIntyre's account, ironically, is in its persuasive argument that individuals can *never* be completely abstracted from the practices, institutions, and traditions of their particular communities. This means that on a contextualist view, a commitment to human rights, for example, plays as constitutive a role in the identity of a liberal as the commitment to a human *telos* did in the identity of members of heroic societies. As Amy Gutmann points out, "Many of the most widely accepted practices of our society—equality of educational opportunity, careers open to talent, punishment conditional on intent—treat people as relatively autonomous moral agents. Insofar as we are committed to maintaining these practices, we are also committed to defending human rights."[60]

Kateb, on the other hand, although correct in his criticism of MacIntyre's denigration of liberal society, himself fails to appreciate the possibility in the latter's account for critical reflection and meaningful choice. As I have tried to demonstrate, these possibilities emerge even in a contextualist framework like MacIntyre's. Although the individual must make the choices that he does from within the context of the practices, institutions, and traditions of his community, this context also provides occasions for conflict, and for the development of self-knowledge or self-understanding that may result from their resolution. The context provides the material or substance, the background, as it were, without which the individual could make no choices or judgments, could develop neither constitutive ends nor a constitutive identity. A person's ends and moral judgments are indeed *elicited* by membership in a particular community; they are not "authenticated" simply by this membership, as Kateb suggests. Authentication occurs, as MacIntyre implies, through the conflict that is instrumental in learning what one's ends and purposes are, through the "continuities of conflict" that traditions embody. And in such conflict the moral unit is still the person, not the group or class.

Because liberal societies traditionally encompass a broad spectrum of values, they provide a multitude of occasions for self-defining conflict. They are thus particularly open to the development of the intrasubjective self-understandings alluded to by Sandel. Individuals' choices among conceptions of the good need not be simply an assessment of existing desires and of the means for their satisfaction. The individual may in fact form second-order desires in the course of his moral development, as MacIntyre implies is the case in situations of moral conflict. And the reflection which makes this possible is grounded in the narrative of the individual's life, in the past conflicts, choices, and occasions of self-reflection which have brought the agent to this point. As Kateb suggests, the liberal society institutionalizes moral dispute—not only among persons, but within persons, as it were. The bounds of the self are given at the outset, but its identity changes over the course of its experience and is subject to revision. Thus, *contra* Sandel, its identity *is* at stake in the course of choice and deliberation—not simply in terms of its future aims and attributes, but also in the light of reflection upon its past choices and their consequences for the agent's identity at this moment. If the liberal society promotes diversity, it also, indirectly, promotes a multiplicity of such occasions for conflict, self-reflection, and choice.

If MacIntyre's focus in his discussion of moral dispute or conflict is upon the occasions it provides for choice, Walzer's focus is upon the conditions for choice. Although Walzer does not hypothesize a formal situation like the original position as a grounding for principles of justice, he does imply that there *is* a ground from which properly constituted principles of justice must emerge. If principles of justice are based upon the shared understandings of the members of a community, an explicit conception of membership is necessary to ensure that the understandings arrived at are really shared, and shared by all who are affected by them. Early in *Spheres of Justice,* Walzer indicates his agreement with a statement by Pascal: "Tyranny is the wish to obtain by one means what can only be had by another."[61] In fact, this is the key to Walzer's separation of social goods into various spheres differentiated by various distributive principles. "To convert one good into another, when there is no intrinsic connection between the two, is to invade the sphere where another company of men and women properly rules."[62] Thus, political power ought not to command superior medical care, physical power ought not to mandate expressions of love, and so forth.

Walzer hence concludes that "No contractualist argument can justify the creation of a [permanent] caste of resident aliens."[63] Because the members of such a caste experience lives in which *all* spheres are determined and regulated by their alien status, the citizens, though perhaps democratic in their own decision-making, through their exclusive possession of political power render it into a dominant good convertible to dominance in all other spheres. That is, because the shared understandings of the community's members demarcate the various spheres and make determinate the principles of distribution within each sphere, exclusion from membership also excludes one from participation in the formation of those shared understandings. Walzer concludes with a specific principle of political justice. "The processes of self-determination through which a democratic state shapes its internal life must be open, and equally open, to all those men and women who live within its territory, work in the local economy, and are subject to local law."[64]

Walzer, then, transcends particularity on the subject of political justice as this encompasses community membership, although different communities may accord different protections and privileges to their members. It is the members themselves who decide upon protections, rights, and privileges. Walzer's conception of membership suggests that a community becomes *more* just as it extends membership and the opportunity to participate more widely to those who live in it. Social goods with their meanings and values are still historically defined within the contexts of different communities. But if, as Walzer says, "Justice is rooted in the distinct understandings . . . that constitute a shared way of life,"[65] we can infer that a way of life shared and shaped by as many as possible who are affected by it is most likely to result in distinct understandings characterized by a high degree of justice. Put differently, "The degree of development of the common life depends on its inclusiveness, that is, on the extent to which the citizens participate in the formation of the shared understandings."[66]

The development of such a common life, in fact, is instrumental to the possible emergence of an intersubjective conception of the self. Under this self-understanding, we recall, I regard the use of my assets in the service of a common endeavor as a contribution to a community or "realization of a way of life in which I take pride and with which my identity is bound."[67] Although my community might have no greater moral claim to the use of my assets than I do, my attachment in this case would, in Sandel's terms, describe more than a feeling; it would describe "a mode of self-understanding partly constitutive of" my identity.[68] For Sandel, of course, this self-understanding is impossible for an antecedently individuated self. But, on the other hand, if the self is *intrasubjectively* conceived, open to the possibility of successive self-understandings that result from past occasions for conflict, self-reflection, and choice, then this self may move *through* various, successive self-understandings to one which corresponds to the intersubjective self-understanding described by Sandel. As such subjects, we are

> constituted in part by our central aspirations and attachments, always open, indeed vulnerable, to growth and transformation in the light of revised self-understandings. And in so far as our constitutive self-understandings comprehend a wider subject than the individual alone, whether a family or tribe or city or class or nation of people, to this extent they define a community in the constitutive sense. And what marks such a community is not merely a spirit of benevolence, or the

> prevalence of communitarian values, or even certain "shared final ends" alone, but a common vocabulary of discourse and a background of implicit practices and understandings within which the opacity of the participants is reduced if never finally dissolved.[69]

Conclusion

Sandel would maintain that this move from intrasubjective to intersubjective self-understandings is problematic. Liberalism, in its concern for the autonomy of the subject, still hypothesizes a self for whom the development of intersubjective self-understandings is especially difficult; those who develop them may end up imposing them on those who have not. On the other hand, this problem manifests the importance of Walzer's point about the necessity for inclusiveness and participation in the formation of the shared understandings that are the basis for distributive principles in particular communities. Sandel remarks that community must describe more than a feeling. Ultimately, this may be true, apart from the fact that feelings are arguably a *part* of what constitutes identity. But must it not *begin* with a feeling? Benjamin Barber suggests that "In strong democratic politics, participation is a way of defining the self, just as citizenship is a way of living."[70] In a liberal society especially, participation, ideally, "must hope to compensate for the absence of positive common values with post-hoc affections of the kind that grow out of common activity . . . those who practice a common politics may come to feel ties that they never felt before they commenced their common activity."[71] Over time, then, community *is* "a background of implicit practices and understandings" and may indeed *become* a mode of self-understanding partly constitutive of an individual's identity.

Moreover, Sandel's possible objections to my interpretation draw attention once again to the virtue of MacIntyre's account. If individuals are never completely abstracted from the practices, institutions, and traditions of their particular communities, then these practices, institutions, and traditions are partly constitutive of the self-understandings that in turn are constitutive of identity. But, as we have seen, critical reflection and meaningful choice are possible within such a context, and in fact impossible without a context. MacIntyre's account serves to remind us that we need not choose between a radically disembodied or abstracted self, on the one hand, and a radically situated one, on the other. And his reminder itself influences both the feelings and the self-understandings which contribute to the constitution of our identities.

> The dispositions of the soul are in part constituted by reflexive thought about its dispositions, and are not exclusively to be perceived from some independent standpoint. As soon as the power of reflection develops, our so-called natural dispositions are modified by our beliefs about them, both about what they ought to be, and about their naturalness; and these beliefs are modified by the norms and ideals associated with a particular way of life, the one to which we are committed.[72]

Notes

1. Michael Sandel, "The Procedural Republic and the Unencumbered Self," *Political Theory* 12 (February 1984): 82.
2. Ibid.
3. Ibid., p. 86. Also see Michael Sandel, *Liberalism and the Limits of Justice* (Cambridge: Cambridge University Press, 1982), p. 62.
4. John Rawls, *A Theory of Justice* (Cambridge: Harvard University Press, 1971), p. 31.
5. Sandel, *Liberalism,* p. 155.
6. Ibid., p. 157.
7. Ibid., pp. 78–79.
8. Ibid., p. 57.
9. Sandel, "The Procedural Republic," p. 94.
10. Sandel, *Liberalism,* p. 140.
11. Ibid., p. 80.
12. Ibid., p. 143.
13. Ibid., pp. 144–46.
14. Ibid., p. 150.
15. Ibid., p. 149.
16. Rawls, *A Theory of Justice,* pp. 101–2.
17. Sandel, *Liberalism,* p. 71.
18. Ibid., p. 72.
19. Ibid., p. 70, 82.
20. Ibid., pp. 88, 138–39.
21. Ibid., p. 85.
22. Alasdair MacIntyre, *After Virtue* (Notre Dame: University of Notre Dame Press, 1981), p. 50.
23. Ibid., pp. 30, 119.
24. Ibid., p. 31.
25. Sandel, *Liberalism,* p. 85.
26. MacIntyre, *After Virtue,* p. 191.
27. Ibid., p. 207; also see pp. 178, 191, 203–5.
28. Ibid., pp. 207–8.
29. Ibid., p. 119.
30. Ibid., p. 181.
31. Ibid., p. 120.
32. Ibid., p. 233.

33. Sandel, *Liberalism,* p. 71.
34. MacIntyre, *After Virtue,* p. 204.
35. Ibid., pp. 204–5.
36. Michael Walzer, *Spheres of Justice* (New York: Basic Books, 1983), p. 82.
37. Ibid., p. 91.
38. Ibid., p. 87.
39. Ibid., p. 313.
40. Michael Walzer, " 'Spheres of Justice': An Exchange," *New York Review of Books,* 21 July 1983, 43.
41. Walzer, *Spheres,* p. 8.
42. Walzer, "An Exchange," p. 44.
43. Walzer, *Spheres,* p. 314.
44. Ibid., p. 318.
45. Sandel, *Liberalism,* p. 57.
46. Ibid., p. 63.
47. Ibid., pp. 162–63.
48. Ibid., p. 164.
49. Ibid., p. 161.
50. MacIntyre, *After Virtue,* p. 125.
51. Ibid., p. 205.
52. Alasdair MacIntyre, "Moral Rationality, Tradition, and Aristotle," *Inquiry* 26 (December 1983): 451.
53. MacIntyre, *After Virtue,* p. 30.
54. Ibid., p. 153.
55. Ibid., p. 206.
56. Ibid., p. 134.
57. Ibid., p. 208.
58. Sandel, *Liberalism,* p. 121; also see pp. 57–59, 121–22.
59. George Kateb, "Looking for Mr. Goodlife," *American Scholar* 51 (1982): 435.
60. Amy Gutmann, "Communitarian Critics of Liberalism," *Philosophy and Public Affairs,* in press, manuscript copy p. 8.
61. Walzer, *Spheres,* p. 18.
62. Ibid., p. 19.
63. Ibid., p. 55.
64. Ibid., p. 60.
65. Ibid., p. 314.
66. Lyle A. Downing and Robert B. Thigpen, "Dilemmas of Engagement and Detachment: An Exploration of *Spheres of Justice*" (paper delivered at the Annual Meeting of the American Political Science Association, Washington, D.C., August 30–September 2, 1984), pp. 10–11.
67. Sandel, *Liberalism,* p. 143.
68. Ibid., p. 150.
69. Ibid., pp. 172–73.
70. Benjamin R. Barber, *Strong Democracy* (Berkeley: University of California Press, 1984), p. 153.
71. Ibid., p. 244.
72. Stuart Hampshire, *Morality and Conflict* (Cambridge: Harvard University Press, 1983), pp. 145–46.

– 7 –

Liberalism and Public Morality

WILLIAM A. GALSTON

I

During the past generation, the view has arisen that a liberal polity must remain systematically neutral on the widest possible range of moral and religious questions. During this same period, religious fundamentalism has attained an influence not seen in the United States for more than half a century. It is my thesis that these two developments are intimately related and that, considered together, they have much to teach us about the nature of liberalism.

Early liberal theorists worked to disentangle civil society from destructive religious quarrels. But they nevertheless assumed that civil society needed morality and that publicly effective morality rested on religion. Juridical liberalism, which focused on the exercise of liberty and the limits of government, presumed a foundation of individual moral restraint. In a liberal society, however, the civil authority would not directly enforce this moral code. Rather, the private sphere—primarily the family and voluntary religious associations—would sustain the moral foundations of a decent and orderly public sphere.

This understanding of the proper relation among politics, morality, and religion dominated the American Founding. It suffuses Tocqueville's analysis. In clearly recognizable form, it survived well into the twentieth century. In the past generation, however, this understanding came under attack, and the delicate balance between juridical liberalism and its social preconditions was disrupted. Influential forces equated liberty with the absence of all restraints. The Supreme Court encouraged this tendency, and it reinterpreted the Constitution to require impartiality, not just among religious faiths, but also between religion and irreligion. Many influential philosophers argued that the essence of liberalism was public neutrality on the widest possible range of moral issues. Thus, in John Rawls's view, "the liberal state rests on a conception of equality between human beings as moral persons, as creatures having a conception of the good and capable of a sense of justice. . . . *Systems of ends are not ranked in value.*[1] And for Ronald Dworkin, the liberal state "must be neutral on . . . the question of the good life. . . . political decisions must be, so far as is possible, independent of any particular conception of the good life."[2] Early liberals maintained that, while the public sphere should eschew direct involvement in moral and religious issues, it must nonetheless draw moral sustenance from the private sphere. Contemporary liberals reply that the public institutions of liberalism do not and cannot rest on any particular conception of the good or of religion.

This new dispensation soon encountered difficulties. To begin with, it was not firmly rooted in a popular consensus. The purely juridical understanding of liberalism was accepted by some elites, but by only a relatively small fraction of ordinary citizens. Worse, actualizing the juridical understanding meant dismantling long-established practices such as school prayer and restraints on pornography, a process that understandably evoked strong passions. The counterreaction was not slow to take shape. But although it depicts itself as purely defensive, this wave of fundamentalism in fact wishes to go well beyond the status quo ante, to a commingling of religion and the civil order that threatens the centuries-old doctrine of toleration itself.

Neither juridicalism nor fundamentalism can serve as an adequate basis for a liberal society. An urgent task of liberal theory, then, is to reflect anew on the moral preconditions of liberalism and to establish, more precisely than heretofore, how these preconditions can coexist with liberalism's powerful juridical tendencies. The following remarks, a somewhat untidy amalgam of historical and theoretical analyses, are offered as a point of departure for this task.

II

Early liberal theory is sometimes described as discarding concern for moral virtue altogether in favor of an orientation toward the nonmoral goods of self-preservation, liberty, and property. This depiction is a half-truth. Early liberals do indeed reject the Aristotelian account of virtue as an intrinsic good. But they do not wholly extrude virtue from liberal theory. Rather, they redefine it as an instrumental good, essential for the attainment of the nonmoral goods that constitute the ends of liberal politics.

In this spirit, Hobbes constructs nineteen "laws of nature," the knowledge of which, he insists, is the "true moral philosophy."

> All men agree on this, that peace is good, and therefore also the way, or means of peace, which . . . are justice, gratitude, modesty, equity, mercy,

> and the rest of the laws of nature, are good. . . . But the writers of moral philosophy, though they acknowledge the same virtues and vices [do not see] wherein consisted their goodness; nor that they come to be praised as the means of peaceable, sociable, and comfortable living.[3]

Similarly, Locke supplements the juridical account of liberal government in the *Second Treatise* with his *Thoughts Concerning Education,* which spells out the virtues that support a liberal polity and society—self-denial, civility, justice, courage, humanity, industry, and truthfulness, among others. As Nathan Tarcov has argued, these virtues "are based on the same insights as his politics and serve the same goals, the preservation of oneself and others and avoidance of the injustice and contention that so disturb human life."[4] Lockean liberty is not just a fact, but rather an achievement: "Locke saw that we have to be willing to deny our desires, face our fears, endure our pains, and take pains in labor in order to preserve our equal liberty and avoid being either tyrants or slaves."[5]

While Locke defends a version of individual morality supportive of liberal politics, he also lays the foundation for what in our time has become an assault on the very concept of a public morality, carried out in the name of liberalism itself. I refer, of course, to the argument of the *Letter Concerning Toleration.*

Locke's challenge in the *Letter* was to define the appropriate relation between religion and the civil order. This was not merely a theoretical matter. In the wake of the Reformation, Europe had been wracked by a century of religious warfare. All the combatants sought to restore the unity of Christendom by imposing their version of religious truth through the coercive power of the state. In circumstances of deep diversity, these efforts ensured endless strife. Locke's doctrine of toleration (or, in our terms, state neutrality) was an attempt to reestablish the possibility of decent politics in the context of abiding disagreements about fundamental religious questions.

Setting to one side theses proceeding from Christianity itself, Locke may be said to make five arguments in favor of religious toleration or state neutrality, divided into three categories: arguments based on the nature of religious truth, on the nature of coercion, and on the nature of politics.

The first of these arguments may be called *epistemological neutrality.* For a wide range of religious disputes, Locke insists, no rational adjudication is possible among competing claims. This does not (necessarily) mean that there is no religious truth. But it does mean that no judge "on earth" is competent to determine it.[6] Locke's religious epistemology thus denies the basic premise through which public religious coercion is customarily justified.

Locke does not, however, rest his case on the elusiveness of religious truth. Even if religious truth could be intersubjectively established, he argues, the coercive weapons at the disposal of civil society could not possibly achieve their purported end—the inculcation of true belief or faith. "True and saving religion," Locke observes, "consists in the inward persuasion of the Mind, without which nothing is acceptable to God. And such is the nature of the understanding, that it cannot be compelled to the belief of any thing by outward force."[7] This argument I will call *ontological neutrality*.

Locke's third argument, *character-based neutrality*, also revolves around the nature of coercion, but from a moral rather than ontological standpoint. Those who use the power of the state to suppress religious dissent regularly invoke as their motive their love of truth and the desire to save souls. In fact, Locke contends, these self-appointed guardians of orthodoxy are moved by cruelty and lust for power.[8]

The remaining two arguments focus on the nature of politics. *Rights-based neutrality* rests on Locke's concept of limited government. Human beings enter into civil society to attain and protect nonmoral goods: goods of the body and external possessions. To secure these goods, the civil magistrate is created and invested with coercive power. It follows, Locke insists, that the sovereign's legitimate sway extends no further than this initial grant: "the whole jurisdiction of the Magistrate reaches only to these Civil Concernments [and] neither can nor ought in any manner to be extended to the salvation of souls."[9]

Even if it were proper for the magistrate to intervene in the religious practices of the citizenry, it would not be wise to do so. Locke's final argument, *prudential neutrality*, draws important conclusions from the fact of religious differences. In circumstances of deep diversity, Locke contends, the consequences of trying to impose uniformity are worse than the consequences of accepting the existence of controversial opinions—even deeply implausible opinions. History shows that religious coercion yields not agreement and civil concord, but rather discord, destruction, and war. The sovereign once invested with the power to enforce truth can turn that power against the truth. And finally, the suppression of diversity is in no way necessary to the peace and good order of civil society. Diversity is a threat to peace only if the magistrate is repressive.[10]

Locke's thesis may be summarized in three propositions. Because religious truth cannot be known with certainty, efforts to impose truth through coercion lack rational warrant. Even if religious truth could be established, faith cannot be imposed through coercion. And even if coercion could succeed, it would be wrong to employ it.

Locke's argument is less sweeping than the contemporary doctrine of state neutrality in two respects. To begin with, Locke distinguishes between coercion and persuasion. The fact that the sovereign cannot legitimately command a specific religious belief does not mean that civil authority cannot make arguments on behalf of that belief.[11] Second, Locke insists that in cases of conflict, civil authority takes precedence over religious faith. The key criterion is the maintenance of civil order. Opinions that threaten the peace of society need not be tolerated. So, for example, Locke declares that "No Opinion contrary to human society, or to those moral Rules which are necessary to the preservation of Civil Society, are to be tolerated by the Magistrate."[12] (Locke has no doubt that such a core morality *is* politically essential.) Nor should magistrates tolerate religions that diminish their legitimate sovereignty, such as those faiths that preach or imply allegiance to a foreign sovereign. Finally, the magistrate cannot tolerate those "who deny the Being of a God" because "Promises, Covenants, and Oaths, which are the bond of Humane Society, can have no hold upon an Atheist. The taking away of God, tho but even in thought, dissolves all."[13]

The flip-side of Locke's strictures against atheism is the remarkable convergence he discerns among all forms of religious faith, not just Christianity or even monotheism: "Neither Pagan, nor Mahumetan, nor Jew, ought to be excluded from the Civil Rights of the Commonwealth, because of his religion. . . . the Commonwealth, which embraces indifferently all Men that are honest, peaceable, and industrious, requires it not."[14] In short, Locke suggests, civil society rests on certain opinions and moral rules, and religion *as such* tends to be consistent with, and supportive of, these prerequisites for a decent society. (The one exception is those religions whose teaching dilutes or divides civil sovereignty.) It follows that the sovereign should encourage all faiths without regard to doctrinal distinctions. To be sure, civil authority may legitimately indicate a preference for certain doctrines over others, but not in a manner that impedes the free exercise of competing doctrines.

For Locke, then, the fact that religious doctrinal conflicts cannot be rationally resolved does not suggest that moral virtues and rules are equally unknowable. On the contrary: our rational knowledge of morality undergirds both the critique of religious intolerance and the principles governing the relations between religion and public order.

III

This Lockean understanding was the orthodox view among the American Founders. Thomas Jefferson became famous (in some quarters notorious) for declaring in his *Notes on the State of Virginia* that "it does me no injury for my neighbor to say that there are twenty gods, or no God. It neither picks my pocket nor breaks my leg." But in that same work he asks (rhetorically), "Can the liberties of a nation be thought secure when we have removed their only firm basis, a conviction in the minds of the people that these liberties are of the gift of God?" Five years earlier, Jefferson's Declaration of Independence had traced human equality and human rights to "the Creator." Forty years later, on the threshold of death, Jefferson argued that the beliefs that there is "only one God, and he all perfect" and that there is "a future state of rewards and punishments" would, if generally shared, be conducive to decent politics. Religion, he once wrote, is "a supplement to law in the government of men" and "the alpha and omega of the moral law."[15]

The thesis underlying Jefferson's disparate remarks was perhaps best articulated by George Washington in his Farewell Address:

> Of all the dispositions and habits which lead to political prosperity, religion and morality are indispensable supports. . . . The mere politician, equally with the pious man, ought to respect and cherish them. . . . And let us with caution indulge the supposition that morality can be maintained without religion. Whatever may be conceded to the influence of refined education on minds of peculiar structure, reason and experience both forbid us to expect that national morality can prevail in exclusion of religious principles.

Washington's argument is not that religion provides premises essential to the validity of liberal arguments. It is rather that only a relatively small number of citizens can be expected to understand and embrace liberal principles on the basis of purely philosophic considerations. For most citizens, religion provides both the *reasons* for believing that liberal principles are correct and the *incentives* for honoring them in practice.

Forty years later, Tocqueville provided sociological support for Washington's thesis. America, he observed, is the place where religion has the greatest real power, and it is also the most enlightened and freest country on earth. This conjunction is not accidental:

> Despotism may be able to do without faith, but freedom cannot. . . . How could society escape destruction if, when political ties are relaxed, moral ties are not tightened? And what can be done with a people master of itself if it is not subject to God?

While there is "an innumerable multitude of sects in the United States . . . all different in the worship they owe to the Creator," they nevertheless "all agree concerning the duties of men [and] all preach the same morality." In particular, religion places strict limits on the means that can legitimately be employed in pursuit of political ends. It thereby checks the ruthlessness and cruelty that would otherwise characterize a society based on abstract philosophical principles of liberty, individualism, and revolution. "Religion, which never intervenes directly in the government of American society, should therefore be considered as the first of their political institutions, for although it did not give them the taste for liberty, it singularly facilitates their use thereof." Thus, Tocqueville concludes,

> I do not know if all Americans have faith in their religion—for who can read the secrets of the heart?—but I am sure that they think it necessary to the maintenance of republican institutions. That is not the view of one class or party among the citizens, but of the whole nation.[16]

Thus far I have spoken of American religion in the most general of terms. This is consistent with the practices of many of the Founders. Washington, for example, employed studiously nondenominational, even non-Christian language when referring to the deity in public utterances. And he argued vigorously that Jews should enjoy full religious freedom and the equal rights of citizenship. Nothing could have been farther from Washington's understanding than the notion of America as a "Christian commonwealth." In general, the Founders believed that religion supported secular liberties only up to a point. They were certainly not of the view that politics based on a literal interpretation of the Bible would be supportive of a liberal polity. When they spoke in favor of religion, they had in mind not sectarian particularity, but rather what all revealed religions were thought to have in common: the concepts of divine creation, order, and judgment; and a compact list of fundamental moral commandments.

Yet matters were not so simple. Against this juridical concept of equal religious liberty was counterposed the sociological fact that America *was* a Christian nation, of a special kind. Tocqueville himself affirmed that "all the sects in the United States belong to the great unity of Christendom." And he noted that America's Catholics had conformed in many respects to a political and social understanding characteristic of Protestantism. As George Kelly has observed, "few who have lived their lives in the United States would doubt that dissenting Protestantism is the wellspring of our ethos."[17] This orientation was only reinforced by the public schools, which from their institution in the mid-nineteenth century until well into the twentieth promulgated a nondenominational Protestantism memorably summarized for generations of schoolchildren in the "Readers" of the Ohio Protestant minister, William McGuffey. Indeed, Catholics established private "parochial schools" in large measure as a protest against this Protestant domination of the public schools.[18]

Protestantism was, of course, more than a religious orientation. It was the focal point of a set of social practices and understandings that forged the identity of the dominant social group and constituted the standard of conduct and demeanor for all others. I shall henceforth refer to this socio-religious Protestant nexus as "traditional morality."

By Tocqueville's time, then, a distinctively American political culture had been forged. Its major elements were three: the essentially secular principles of democratic liberalism, the moral maxims derived from Christianity, and the mores of Protestant Americans—in particular, white Anglo-Saxon males.

This amalgam proved remarkably enduring. At the turn of the century, Lord Bryce nicely captured its delicate balance between liberal and religious tendencies.

> It is accepted as an axiom by all Americans that the civil power ought to be not only neutral and impartial as between different forms of faith, but ought to leave these matters entirely on one side. [Nevertheless,] the national government, and the state governments do give Christianity [and by that he meant Protestant Christianity] a species of recognition inconsistent with the view that civil government should be absolutely neutral in religious matters.[19]

IV

This unstable combination was still intact and clearly recognizable as late as the early 1950s. In 1952, Justice William O. Douglas, no foe of civil liberties, was able to begin a Supreme Court decision with the assertion that "The First Amendment does not say that in every and all respects there shall be a separation of church and state" and end with the affirmation that "We are a religious people whose institutions presuppose a Supreme Being."[20] At that time, Catholics and Jews were still somewhat marginal members of American society. Blacks were thoroughly subordinated. Popular culture faithfully represented the white, Anglo-Saxon, Protestant ethos. And most important, a traditional morality was dominant and effective. A male-governed family structure that largely excluded women from the world of work and commerce, norms of personal conduct that emphasized self-reliance and self-restraint, respect for economic and political authority, unquestioning patriotism based on the conviction of unsullied American rectitude, pervasive expressions of religious faith—these were the main strands of that traditional morality. Today, this cultural consensus is gone, replaced by pitched battles on numerous fronts. The critical event in this transformation was, I believe, the civil rights movement.

This movement had two important elements that are germane to our inquiry. First, it represented a clear collision between the juridical-liberal principles of our polity and the concrete practices of our society. Black leaders presented themselves not as revolutionaries, but as conservatives, calling on white America to recall and revitalize its founding principles. These principles proved to be highly potent, stunning sober observers who believed in strict limits to the capacity of law to effect social transformation.

But the civil rights movement was more than an appeal to the moral equality of human beings and the political equality of citizens. It was also the legitimation of social differences. Black Americans, after all, had a distinctive group identity, forged in the crucible of slavery and discrimination. This identity was in no way incompatible with American principles. But it was very far from the dominant white culture. Black Americans argued that they could not rightly be asked to surrender their distinctiveness as the price of full admission into our society. What makes us a nation, they argued, was voluntary adherence to shared political and moral principles—not forced assimilation to the mores of any social group. This argument, too, carried the day, and many long-suppressed elements of the black experience began to enter the mainstream of American culture.

The civil rights movement was pivotal, I suggest, not just because it so altered the condition of black Americans, but also because it became an inspirational metaphor for other aggrieved groups. In ensuing years, the subordination of women to men, of youth to age, of deviant sexuality to traditional families, of nonbelief to religion—all these hierarchies and more were challenged in the name of freedom, equality, and the recognition of legitimate differences.

This assault on traditional morality was pushed forward by two other forces.

It is a commonplace to stress the individualism of American culture. But, as Robert Bellah and his coauthors have recently reminded us, from the outset there has been a tension between Benjamin Franklin's utilitarian individualism (a lineal descendent of Lockean morality) and the expressive individualism of Emerson and Whitman. Each places the individual at the center of the moral universe. But while utilitarian individualism teaches that personal goals can be achieved in society only through adherence to moral and prudential maxims of self-restraint, expressive individualism argues that the fullness of being, craved by each individual, stands in opposition to the constraints of morality and society.[21] During the 1960s, this ancestral tension within the individualist tradition resurfaced in the form of generational warfare. Unlimited self-expression was held to be not only good in itself, but fully compatible with—indeed, mandated by—the classic liberal distinction between the public and private spheres.

The assault on traditional morality was also spurred on by the Supreme Court. Key decisions on school prayer, pornography, criminal justice, and abortion sharpened the line between public and private, widened individual freedom, and emphasized the requirement of state neutrality in areas previously seen as the legitimate arena for collective moral judgment.

In short, during the past generation, the longstanding balance between juridical liberal principles and a complex of traditional moral beliefs, many of which rested on religious foundations, was disrupted, with liberalism in the ascendency and tradition in retreat. From the unquestionable fact that many traditional practices, chief among them racial discrimination, violated liberal principles was inferred the dubious conclusion that traditionalism *as a whole* was opposed to the actualization of those principles.

Not surprisingly, these developments were received variously in different sectors of society. Among groups constrained or aggrieved by traditional practices, the rise of the secular, putatively neutral state was interpreted as the civil rights movement writ large—that is, as the long-overdue decision to live up to our founding principles. Among the partisans of what I am calling the tradition, the response was quite different. They wondered how school prayer could be unconstitutional if it had been part of our national life under the constitution for more than a century and a half. They wondered how legislation that assisted all schools could possibly be seen as an unconstitutional establishment of religion. They wondered how abortion could be transformed from a state issue to a national question, let alone a constitutional right. From their standpoint, the new assertion of strict state neutrality on matters of morals and religion was anything but neutral. Indeed, the defenders of the tradition saw it as an assault on the very foundations of public order.

It was not long before this conflict began to dominate American party politics. By the early 1980s, religious fundamentalists and other partisans of traditional morality were among the most politically active groups in the country. And during 1984, a debate erupted between the two candidates for the presidency about the proper role of religion in our society. At a prayer breakfast the morning after the Republican convention, Mr. Reagan defended a constitutional amendment favoring school prayer and denounced its opponents as intolerant of religion. In a series of statements, he went on to charge that the Democratic party had come to support an extreme doctrine of separation between church and state antithetical to both our history and our principles—as he put it, "freedom *from* religion" rather than freedom *of* religion. This error was particularly grave, Mr. Reagan asserted, because America rests on a public morality of which religion is the indispensable foundation.

In response, Walter Mondale restated his understanding of church-state relations in a liberal polity:

> I believe in an America that honors what Thomas Jefferson first called the "wall of separation between church and state." That freedom has made our faith unadulterated and unintimidated. It has made Americans the most religious people on earth.
>
> I believe in an America where government is not permitted to dictate the religious life of our people; where religion is a private matter between individuals and God, between families and their churches and synagogues, with no room for politicians in between.
>
> To ask the state to enforce the religious life of our people is to betray a telling cynicism about the American people.
>
> Moreover, history teaches us that if that force is unleashed, it will corrupt our faith, divide our nation, and embitter our people.[22]

On the surface, this is a familiar argument. But note a complication. The doctrine of the wall between church and state is defended as essential, not only to politics, but also to religion. To intermingle them, at least in the manner proposed by the fundamentalists, would be *both* to endanger liberty and to corrupt piety.

This point has deep roots in our history. Thomas Jefferson viewed the wall of separation between church and state primarily as protection for individual intellectual and political freedom against clerical or sectarian oppression. But as Mark DeWolfe Howe has observed, the first American known to have used the wall of separation metaphor was not Thomas Jefferson, but rather the seventeenth-century clergyman Roger Williams. Williams argued that the purity of the Christian faith had always depended on its removal from what he called "the wilderness of the world" and that any effort by Christian churches to dominate rather than abstain from politics would lead Christians into temptation, not deliver the world from evil.[23]

As late as 1965, this was the view of the best–known contemporary Baptist, Jerry Falwell. "Believing in the Bible as I do," Falwell declared, "I would find it impossible to stop preaching the pure, saving Gospel of Jesus Christ, and begin doing anything else—including fighting communism. . . . Preachers are not called to be politicians but to be soul winners."[24] As late as 1975, this was the view of most Americans who regard themselves as evangelical Christians. But by 1980, both Mr. Falwell and his followers had reversed course and plunged headlong into the world.

The impetus for this new activism was the clash between juridical liberalism and the moral tradition—a clash that thoughtful opponents of the traditionalists were compelled to ponder. Here, for example, is what Walter Mondale said:

> Over the last generation, waves of change have swept our nation. No institution has been untouched. Religion, marriage, business, government, education—each has been questioned, and each has struggled toward new foundations and new rules.
>
> By and large, it has been healthy for us. . . . But change is not easy. Many Americans have been upset to see traditions questioned. They have watched durable values give way to emptiness. And too often they have seen that void filled recklessly or self-indulgently. . . .
>
> From the turbulence and unease, a great yearning has been born in America in recent years. It is a quest for stable values. It is a search for deeper faith. And it deserves welcome and respect. . . .
>
> But the yearning for traditional values is not a simple tide. It has undertows. And in the hands of those who would exploit it, this legitimate search for moral strength can become a force of social divisiveness and a threat to individual freedom.
>
> The truth is, the answer to a weaker family is not a stronger state. It is stronger values. The answer to lax morals is not legislated morals. It is deeper faith, greater discipline, and personal excellence.[25]

This argument rests on two key premises. First, the changes that have swept through our society in the past generation are on balance not only consistent with, but actually enrich, our basic principles. Second, to the extent that these changes have a darker underside, the remedy lies not in state action, but rather in individual moral responsibility.

One need not be a partisan of moral traditionalism—let alone religious fundamentalism—to question these premises. On the issue of whether the cultural revolution of the past generation has left the United States better or worse off, a strong case can be made for both sides. While the civil rights movement is widely acknowledged to have righted ancient wrongs, epidemics of crime, pornography, and teenage pregnancy have exacted a fearful toll. And on the issue of whether the remedy for these ills appropriately lies in the private or the public sphere, a case can be made that because public action has contributed to the problem, countervailing public action must be part of the solution. If the state, hiding behind a veil of neutrality, has acted anything but neutrally in tearing down traditional barriers against immoral behavior, then it would seem to follow that calls for a public change of course are not on their face implausible or improper.

V

To some extent, this disagreement revolves around differing interpretations of "neutrality." Juridical liberals typically argue as follows: Toward every action, the public authority may take one of three stances. It may command the performance of the action; it may prohibit the action; or it may promulgate neither commands nor prohibitions, in which case individuals may choose for themselves. In this last case, the state is said to be neutral, because it offers no authoritative judgment. Thus the state commands draft registration, prohibits murder, and permits—but takes no stand on—abortion.

Traditionalists do not accept this as an adequate account of neutrality. To permit a certain class of actions, they argue, is to make the public judgment that those actions are not wrong. No one denies that the state should prohibit murder. To permit abortion is therefore to determine (at least implicitly) that abortion is not murder. But this is precisely the issue between proponents and opponents of abortion. Permitting abortion cannot be construed as neutrality, because it rests on a substantive moral judgment that is anything but neutral.

At this juncture in the argument, liberal theorists typically advert to history. The Lockean doctrine of toleration was an effort to reestablish the possibility of decent politics in the context of insoluble disagreements about fundamental religious questions. The contemporary doctrine of state neutrality, liberals argue, arises as a necessary generalization of religious toleration. In a complex, diverse modern society, agreement on a wide range of moral questions simply cannot be expected. When—as in the case of abortion—warring views cannot be reconciled, neither side can rightly use the coercive power of the state to enforce its views. The state is declaring neither that abortion is murder nor that it is not murder. Rather, the state is announcing that it is incompetent to make such a judgment. There is, liberal theorists insist, a vast difference between the proposition that "abortion is not murder" and the proposition that "we do not and cannot know whether or not abortion is murder." The latter proposition, an instance of what I earlier called epistemological neutrality, is all that permission really entails. Thus, liberals conclude, the traditionalists are wrong. In permitting abortion, the state is not denying traditionalist premises but only refusing to endorse them.

But traditionalists have some history of their own to fall back upon. From their perspective, abortion is like slavery—an issue that deeply divides the community, but about which one party to the dispute can be known to be right and the other wrong. The agnostic thesis underlying state neutrality is thus parallel to the position Judge Douglas upheld in his famous debates with Abraham Lincoln—and just as mistaken. We cannot be indifferent to fundamental (and decidable) questions of right and wrong, and we violate no one's rights by putting public authority in the service of what is right. Yes, doing this in circumstances of deep moral disagreement risks discord and even violence. But how many Americans believe that the Civil War was too high a price to pay for the abolition of slavery?

We may translate this traditionalist critique into somewhat more theoretical language. Liberals, contend the traditionalists, are preoccupied with the *fact* of moral disagreement and give short shrift to the *content* of disagreement. This tendency flows from the liberal decision to give pride of place to two key goals: avoiding oppression and preserving civil tranquility. Oppression is minimized when the state refrains from endorsing any faction's moral claims. Tranquility is maximized when all parties within a society have fair (though not unlimited) scope to lead their lives as they see fit. This, say the traditionalists, is a public morality of sorts, but it is an inadequate morality. Tranquility is an important good, but not the highest good. And it is not oppression when right conduct is commanded and wrongful acts prohibited. There can be, after all, no right to do wrong.

We can place this controversy within the matrix, earlier analyzed, of Locke's case for toleration. Traditionalists argue that the reach of *epistemological neutrality* is narrower than commonly supposed, because a range of controversial moral propositions can be rationally established. They deny the relevance of *ontological neutrality,* in part because many current controversies involve action, which is subject to coercion, rather than belief, which is not; in part because in matters of belief there is an alternative to the extremes of coercion and indifference—public education backed by the moral authority of political leaders. Traditionalists are at pains to deny the charges embedded in *character-based neutrality.* Their aim is to correct, not to dominate. Besides, how can they be guilty of lust for power when they seek only to defend themselves against the aggression of juridical liberals? *Rights-based neutrality,* they contend, goes too far when it debars the state from prohibiting conduct that can be known to be wrong. And *prudential neutrality* accords too high a value to public order and civil peace at the expense of the moral substance of society.

This analysis raises the question of whether the controversy between traditionalists and juridical liberals is a quarrel *within* liberalism, or rather *between* liberalism and an opposing understanding of politics. Is it possible to challenge the high priority of civil tranquility and the strict limits to governmental power in moral issues without abandoning liberalism altogether?

These questions call our attention to a significant ambiguity in the contemporary traditionalist attack on juridical liberalism. One version of this critique maintains that in seeking to separate religion and religiously grounded values from the cognizance of the state, modern liberals are promoting a public life empty of moral meaning, a kind of collective nihilism that serves as the breeding ground for despotism. This Tocquevillian thesis is advanced, for example, by Richard John

Neuhaus, who suggests that liberal democracy properly understood cannot do without religion.

The other version of the traditionalist critique is quite different. According to this argument, liberalism is not a moral vacuum, but rests rather on a specific kind of public morality—secular humanism. The problem with this morality is that it is excessively permissive. It gives priority to untrammeled choice over normative constraints and to rights over duties. And it gives rise to a society in which piety is on the defensive against a hostile public authority. Far from needing religion, this thesis concludes, liberalism is at war with religion. The contemporary cultural conflict reflects liberalism not run amok, but rather putting into practice what was from the start inherent in its principles. Liberalism can see no arguments against equal rights for homosexuals; a Scripture-based politics must view this possibility as an abomination. And compromise is impossible.

On its face, the evidence would seem to support the latter version of the traditionalist critique. As was suggested earlier, the concept of the state as the tamer of conflict rests on a substantive judgment about the worth of civil tranquility relative to the worth of the positions of any of the contending parties. One may reach this conclusion by denying that moral and religious beliefs are matters of intersubjective knowledge as opposed to subjective conviction. Or one may reach it by arguing that the evils of coercion override the benefits of publicly promoting even rationally justified claims about virtue or the good life. But to give coercion pride of place as the *summum malum* is already to advance a nonvacuous thesis about the human good. More generally (and here I summarize the results of a detailed analysis), every contemporary liberal theory that begins by promising to do without a substantive theory of the good ends by betraying that promise. Indeed, all of them covertly rely on the same triadic theory of the good, which assumes, first, the worth of human existence; second, the worth of human purposiveness and of the fulfillment of human purposes; and finally, the worth of rationality as the chief constraint on social principles and actions. If we may call the belief in the worth of human existence and purposiveness the root assumption of humanism, then the liberal theory of the good is the theory of rationalist humanism.[26]

From this liberal theory of the good, moreover, there follows a canon of liberal virtues. The worth of human existence implies restraints on actions that terminate human life or diminish its quality—prohibitions, that is, against bloodthirstiness and cruelty. The worth of human purposiveness implies, first, the inappropriateness of denigrating worldly existence in light of the world to come; and second, the imperative of honoring a wide range of diverse human ends, a virtue we have come to call tolerance. The worth of rationality implies the virtues of civility and self-restraint in the conduct of both private and public life.

If this account is correct, then liberalism, far from embracing a thoroughgoing neutrality concerning human ends and human conduct, in fact requires a commitment to a specific account of the virtues and of the good. Some contemporary liberal theorists are aware of this. Judith Shklar, for example, argues that liberalism rests on a decision to regard cruelty as the "first vice," which must be avoided above all. But the prohibition against cruelty is not the same as full neutrality among competing doctrines and ways of life. Rather, it is itself a specific doctrine, and it creates a political order that tolerates actions and doctrines only to the extent that they do not undermine this highest value. While it is certainly the case that "as a matter of liberal policy we must learn to endure enormous differences in the relative importance that various individuals and groups attach to the vices," our endurance is circumscribed by our prior decision to give a specific account of the vices pride of place.[27]

It is important to be clear about what this argument does and does not prove. I am not suggesting that the scope for diversity in liberal societies is no greater than in closed or theocratic communities. But I am suggesting that liberalism has a characteristic tendency, imparted to the members of liberal societies both directly (through systems of education and training) and indirectly (through the tacit norms conveyed by political and social practices). And I am also suggesting that the moral commitments of liberalism influence—and in some cases circumscribe—the ability of individuals within a liberal society to engage fully in particular ways of life. If, to be wholly effective, a religious doctrine requires control over the totality of individual life, including the formative social and political environment, then the classic liberal demand that religion be practiced "privately" amounts to a substantive restriction on the free exercise of that religion. The manifold blessings of liberal social orders come at a price, and we should not be surprised when those who are asked to pay grow restive.

This line of argument would appear to support the thesis that the relation between traditionalism and liberalism is one of opposition rather than mutual support. But on the other side stands the evidence presented earlier, that this was not the view of America's Founders. Supporting this evidence are the historical studies of such scholars as Michael Malbin and Mark DeWolfe Howe, who show that the contemporary interpretation of the First Amendment is at variance with the manner in which the founders understood it. As Howe puts it,

> The American ideal of absolute equality between all religious opinions and sects indicated the government's official sympathy for the total religious undertaking. The neutrality . . . was not the neutrality of indifference but the neutrality that condemns favoritism among friends. . . . There is not, so far as I am aware, any indication that when the concept of neutrality in matters of religion first appeared in American decisions the judges conceived of the concept as one requiring an equality between religious and antireligious interests. . . . Now, however, the equality demanded is between religion, on the one hand, and nonreligion, on the other. The government's earlier neutrality was between competing faiths; today's is between belief and doubt.[28]

The thesis that religion supports a liberal political order is bolstered by contemporary evidence as well. A recent followup to the classic "Middletown" study of the 1920s indicates that the people of Muncie, Indiana, are dramatically more religious than they were sixty years ago—and dramatically more tolerant: "We cannot turn up a group whose religious chauvinism comes anywhere near the level that was normal in 1924 . . . . In a liberal perspective, these findings are almost too good to be true."[29] Today, as when Tocqueville wrote, the level of religious commitment among Americans is demonstrably higher than is the case for all other Western countries.[30] It is difficult to believe that this fact is unrelated to the extraordinary stability of republican values and institutions in the United States.

VI

These conflicting theses—that traditionalism and liberalism are opposed, and that they are mutually supportive—can be reconciled. My suggestion is that there is a substantial area of overlap between these two forces, as well as significant areas of conflict.

The relationship of mutual support obtains as long as both focus on what they share. It is supplanted by antagonism when one—or both—choose to emphasize what divides them. Pushed to the limit, the principles and practices of a liberal society tend inevitably to corrode moralities that rest either on traditional forms of social organization or on the stern requirements of revealed religion. Pushed to the limit, tradition and religion can end by denying the diversity—and the freedoms—at the heart of liberal society.

So, for example, the Moral Majority pushes its concern for the moral foundations of our institutions too far. As Harvey Mansfield, Jr. has written,

> The Moral Majority . . . is concerned above all with the souls of Americans, but it has difficulty in finding a universal definition of the

> healthy individual suitable for a free, secular society. . . . The Moral Majority seems to want to abolish the distinction between state and society.[31]

But equally, liberal theorists (and activists) who deny the existence of legitimate public involvement in matters such as family stability, sexual conduct, moral education, and religion are unwittingly undermining the values and institutions they seek to support.

Liberal politics is in part the maintenance of proper balance between these tendencies—avoiding the extremes of moral intrusion that unduly restricts diversity and of moral abdication that gives illiberal tendencies full scope for development. Somewhere between the Moral Majority and the American Civil Liberties Union lies the art of liberal statemanship.

Notes

1. *A Theory of Justice* (Cambridge: Harvard University Press, 1971), p. 19; emphasis added.
2. "Liberalism," in *Public and Private Morality,* ed. Stuart Hampshire (Cambridge: Cambridge University Press, 1978), p. 127.
3. *Leviathan,* chap. 15.
4. *Locke's Education for Liberty* (Chicago: University of Chicago Press, 1984), p. 183.
5. Ibid., pp. 210-11.
6. James H. Tully, ed., *A Letter Concerning Toleration* (Indianapolis: Hackett, 1983), p. 32.
7. Ibid., p. 27.
8. Ibid., pp. 23-24, 34-35.
9. Ibid., pp. 26, 43-44, 46-48.
10. Ibid., pp. 33, 42, 52-53.
11. Ibid., p. 27.
12. Ibid., p. 49.
13. Ibid., p. 51.
14. Ibid., p. 54.
15. For these quotations (and much else) I am indebted to Walter Berns, *The First Amendment and the Future of American Democracy* (Chicago: Gateway, 1985), chap. 1; and A. James Reichley, *Religion in American Public Life* (Washington, D.C.: The Brookings Institution, 1985), chap. 3.
16. These quotations are drawn from *Democracy in America,* vol. 1, pt. 2, chap. 9.
17. "Faith, Freedom, and Disenchantment: Politics and the American Religious Consciousness," *Daedalus* 3, no. 1 (1982), p. 127.
18. Berns, *The First Amendment,* p. 67.
19. *The American Commonwealth,* quoted in Philip B. Kurland, *Religion and the Law: Of Church and State and the Supreme Court* (Chicago: University of Chicago Press, 1978), pp. 18, 26.
20. Quoted in Mark Dewolfe Howe, *The Garden and the Wilderness: Religion*

and Government in American Constitutional History (Chicago: University of Chicago Press, 1965), p. 13.

21. Robert N. Bellah, Richard Madsen, William M. Sullivan, Ann Swidler, and Steven M. Tipton, *Habits of the Heart: Individualism and Commitment in American Life* (Berkeley: University of California Press, 1985), pp. 32-35.

22. Speech to the B'nai B'rith International Convention, Washington, D.C., September 6, 1984.

23. *The Garden and the Wilderness,* chap. 1.

24. Quoted in Richard John Neuhaus, *The Naked Public Square: Religion and Democracy in America* (Grand Rapids, Mich.: William B. Eerdmans, 1984), p. 10.

25. Speech to the B'nai B'rith.

26. William A. Galston, "Defending Liberalism," *American Political Science Review* 76, no. 3: 621-29.

27. *Ordinary Vices* (Cambridge: Harvard University Press, 1984), pp. 4-5.

28. *The Garden in the Wilderness,* pp. 151-52, 153, 155. See also Michael J. Malbin, *Religion and Politics: The Intentions of the Authors of the First Amendment* (Washington, D.C.: American Enterprise Institute for Public Policy Research, 1978).

29. Quoted and discussed in Richard John Neuhaus, "What the Fundamentalists Want," *Commentary* 79, no. 5: 41-46.

30. David Martin, "Revised Dogma and New Cult," *Daedalus* (1982), pp. 53-71.

31. Harvey C. Mansfield, Jr., "The American Election: Entitlements Versus Opportunity," *Government and Opposition* 20, no. 1: 17.

— III —

The Politics of Liberalism

– 8 –

Liberal Individualism Reconsidered

DEBORAH BAUMGOLD

Far too much has been made of the individualism of liberal political thought.[1] Political individualism, meaning the translation of political issues into questions about the motivation, rights, and duties of abstract individuals, is something different from a philosophy of political value. We commonly identify liberal philosophy with the principles of liberty, equality, and consent, and liberal sensibility with a concern for the protection of individuals from government.[2] However obvious it has seemed to link these liberal values to a style of thought, the equation restricts and biases the agenda for liberal political theorizing.

Nowhere is this more evident than in the treatment of the illiberal political philosophy of Thomas Hobbes. Hobbism is commonly taken to exemplify individualistic political reasoning. According to Lukes, for instance, "This abstract way of conceiving the individual is most clear in Hobbes, for whom Leviathan, or the sovereign power, is an artificial contrivance constructed to satisfy the requirements (chief among them survival and security) of the component elements of society."[3] Correspondingly, Hobbes commentaries customarily treat his political arguments as applications of the psychological and moral premises essayed in the prior section of the theory, "Of Man."[4] More particularly, they are treated, in the classic fashion of individualistic political reasoning, as generalizations from first principles of individual self-interest and natural right. Hence the theory provides a model illustration of that characteristic problem of political individualism, public goods and the free rider. Collective goods (e.g., elections, or a clean environment) require civic cooperation, but each individual is best off being a free rider. *Leviathan*'s stipulation of an unalienated natural right of self-defense generates a narrow range of cooperation problems, notably concerning the obligation to fight for the state. Hobbes's psychological premise of ubiquitous selfishness generates the broader question of why individuals should cooperate at all.

The central issues surrounding Hobbism, thus construed, are those of a liberal-individualist theory of politics—namely, the nature of the abstract individual who is the subject of the theory, the possibility of giving an adequate account of civic duty on individualist premises, and hence the possibility of just political society.[5] This is not the agenda of Hobbes's *political* theory, however, nor need it be the agenda of liberal political theory. The present discussion focuses on Hobbes's political arguments, to the point of showing that he reasons about public-goods issues in a structural and political fashion. Far from generalizing political conclusions from some portrait of the individual in the abstract—whether self-interested man or the bearer of natural right or the subject of natural law—Hobbes treats cooperation dilemmas in terms of political roles and governmental policy. Instead of offering another reconstruction of Hobbes's theory of obligation, in short, the present argument is a revisionist interpretation of his very understanding of politics. As Hobbism has been taken as a model for a liberal style of thought, so *Leviathan* can be the model of a revisionist liberal political analysis.

I

Leviathan's "Introduction" describes a political division of labor, in which roles and functions are the unit of analysis.

> For by Art is created that great LEVIATHAN called a COMMONWEALTH, OR STATE, . . . in which, the *Soveraignty* is an Artificiall *Soul,* as giving life and motion to the whole body; The *Magistrates,* and other *Officers* of Judicature and Execution, artificiall *Joynts; Reward* and *Punishment* (by which fastned to the seate of the Soveraignty, every joint and member is moved to performe his duty) are the *Nerves,* that do the same in the Body Naturall; . . . *Counsellors,* by whom all things needful for it to know, are suggested unto it, are the *Memory; Equity* and *Lawes,* an artificiall *Reason* and *Will.*[6]

To this structural-functional picture of the state corresponds a political analysis focusing on roles and on government's part in encouraging the performance of civic duties. By virtue of Hobbes's commitment to philosophical nominalism (the view that only individuals, particular things, exist)[7] and his statement of a "resolutive-compositive" method (meaning the resolution of society into constituent parts and subsequent derivation of normative political principles), readers have taken for granted that the unit of Hobbesian political analysis is the abstract individual. Regarding his intentions, the textual evidence is ambiguous. *Leviathan*'s structural description of the state contrasts with methodological-individualist statements in the earlier *De Cive* and in a later treatise on method, *De Corpore.*[8] But *Leviathan*'s analytic picture is the more accurate to the political theory Hobbes actually wrote. It is not inconsistent to hold that political analysis ought to focus on structural roles and the state and also to subscribe to philosophical nominalism, the latter being an ontological rather than an analytic position.[9] As well, a structural analysis, fully as much as individualistic political reasoning, is entitled to claim foundation in "the known Naturall Inclinations of Mankind."[10] Whereas individualistic analyses generalize political conclusions from assumptions about human nature, psychological as well as moral premises figure in a structural analysis in the context of roles and institutions.

Reading Hobbes through the prism of generalizing individualism, commentators have assumed his premises of self-interest and an unalienated right of self-defense undermine any obligation to fight for the state. Walzer, e.g., comments:

> One man's cowardice kills society, and yet, by virtue of the instinct for self-preservation and the fundamental law of nature, all men have a right to be cowards. The very existence of the state seems to require some limit upon the right of self-preservation, and yet the state is nothing more than an instrument designed to fulfill that right.[11]

Hobbes's reasoning, in chapter twenty-one of *Leviathan,* has a different character.[12] To start, he stipulates that subjects' obligations derive either from the "words" of the political covenant or from the "End of the Institution of Soveraignty."[13] Hence, where rights casuistry would imply the absence of an obligation to fight for the state, Hobbes rather explains that the right of self-defense does not apply to dangerous, but important, duties. Precisely in virtue of the unalienated right of self-defense, such duties must rather be considered in consequentialist terms:

> No man is bound by the words themselves, either to kill himselfe, or any other man; And consequently, that the Obligation a man may sometimes have, upon the Command of the Soveraign to execute any dangerous, or dishonourable Office, dependeth not on the Words of our Submission; but on the Intention; which is to be understood by the End thereof. When therefore our refusall to obey, frustrates the End for which the Soveraignty was ordained; then there is no Liberty to refuse: otherwise there is.[14]

The substitution of consequentialist for rights reasoning obviously entails a weaker concept of natural rights than our familiar idea of them, to use Dworkin's well-known metaphor, as "trumps" against the interference of the state.[15] To allow consequentialist considerations to govern recognition of rights-claims implies viewing the latter not as first principles, constitutive of a good society, but rather merely as liberties permissible within a well-constituted society.[16]

Not only does Hobbes fail to generalize from the right of self-preservation; more significantly, he treats the obligation of fighting in terms of roles, as opposed to the duties of individuals in the abstract. Applying the stated consequentialist principle, he grants ordinary subjects a series of excuses from the duty. A subject may furnish a substitute, "for in this case he deserteth not the service of the Common-wealth."[17] Subjects may run from battle if afraid; indeed, "for the same reason, to avoyd battell, is not Injustice, but Cowardise." Only when the defense of the state "requireth at once the help of all that are able to bear Arms"—presumably strictly in extremity—is everyone obliged to fight: "because otherwise the Institution of the Common-wealth . . . was in vain." Nevertheless, these excuses are specifically unavailable to soldiers: "he that inrowleth himselfe a Souldier, or taketh imprest mony, taketh away the excuse of a timorous nature; and is obliged, not onely to go to the battell, but also not to run from it, without his Captaines leave."[18]

The distinction between the role obligations of subjects and soldiers extends beyond the battlefield. The former may submit to a conqueror "when the means of his life is within the Guards and Garrisons of the Enemy."[19] "But if a man, besides the obligation of a Subject, hath taken upon him a new obligation of a Souldier, then he hath not the liberty to submit to a new Power, as long as the old one keeps the field, and giveth him means of subsistence, either in his Armies, or Garrisons."[20] Whereas ordinary subjects may submit when their lives are in jeopardy, soldiers' obligations hinge on their army's condition. Only when the organization fails do the obligations of the role end. When an army no longer keeps the field or supplies its soldiers, "a Souldier also may seek his Protection wheresoever he has most hope to have it; and may lawfully submit himself to his new Master."[21]

Hobbes does not ask individuals to consider the collective consequences of free riding, as in the universalizing question "What if everyone did that?"[22] They are only asked to be impressed with their own duties. Ordinary subjects have a merely prima facie, weak obligation to fight for the state. It is a law of nature, according to *Leviathan*'s "Review and Conclusion": *"That every man is bound . . ., as much as in him lieth, to protect in Warre, the Authority, by which he is himself protected in time of Peace."*[23] Nonetheless, in light of chapter twenty-one's generous account of excuses, the caveat would seem to outweigh the law—i.e., the duty never "lieth" heavily on ordinary subjects. They have a strong obligation to serve only "when the Defence of the Common-wealth, requireth at once the help of all that are able to bear Arms"—circumstances, that is to say, in which everyone has instrumental reason to fight, and in which it is not appropriate for anyone to free ride. (In similar vein, in chapter twenty-eight, discussing salaried public offices, Hobbes specifies: "For though men have no lawfull remedy, when they be commanded to quit their private businesse, to serve the publique, without Reward, or Salary; yet they are not bound thereto, by the Law of Nature, nor by the Institution of the Common-wealth, *unlesse the service cannot otherwise be done.*")[24] The problem of obligation narrowly attaches to the role of the soldier, undertaken by enlistment or acceptance of "imprest mony." In general, in Hobbes's view, salaried public offices entail strong obligations: "he that receiveth [a salary] is bound in Justice to performe his office."[25] Whereas ordinary subjects have instrumental reason to fight, in the circumstances in which they actually are obliged to do so, soldiers have a stronger moral reason to perform their more strenuous obligations. At least it is a commonplace—and quintessentially liberal—moral view that obligations may properly be more strenuous, the more expressly voluntarily they are undertaken.

In short, the problems of a generalizing individualist analysis—namely everyman's motivation and obligation to contribute to public goods and abjure free riding—are not the questions of *Leviathan*'s account of fighting for the state. Nor is *Leviathan*'s structural role analysis exceptional in classical liberal theory. Recall, e.g., the well-known Lockean statement, that read through individualist eyes only evinces a bias toward property:

> Yet we see, that neither the Serjeant, that could command a Souldier to march up to the mouth of a Cannon, or stand in a Breach, where he is almost sure to perish, can command that Soldier to give him one penny of his Money; nor the *General,* that can condemn him to Death for deserting his Post, or for not obeying the most desperate Orders, can yet with all his absolute Power of Life and Death, dispose of one Farthing of that Soldiers Estate, or seize one jot of his Goods; whom yet he can command any thing, and hang for the least Disobedience.[26]

The statement directly parallels Hobbes's discussion. Where the latter is concerned to distinguish the obligations attaching to various roles, Locke's complementary topic is the scope of role obligations. The purpose of military service, he explains, demarcates commanders' authority and soldiers' duties: "such a blind Obedience is necessary to that end for which the Commander has his Power, *viz.* the preservation of the rest; but the disposing of his Goods has nothing to do with it."[27] "Throughout his work," Dunn has observed, "Locke is concerned with the legitimacy of the claims which men levy on each other in terms of the moral resources of [the] social structures" within which individual lives are led.[28]

A structural analysis sets a different agenda for political theorizing. In the first instance, it is the point of these discussions of fighting to situate questions of obligation and motivation, and the principle of consent, in the context of roles. To modern, specially to modern liberal eyes, roles ought ideally to be assumed on the basis of consent. In point, Hobbes attempted just such a distributive argument, i.e., the argument that consent is the foundation of all authority relationships.[29] On its face, the effort is counterintuitive (e.g., most especially, the claim that parental dominion is consensual in origin)[30]—perhaps, indeed, more rationalization than a normative analysis. A more sympathetic, and suggestive, reading would focus on his applications of the principle of consent to various authority relationships; these offer a series of reflections on subtleties of consent, beyond the distinction between express and tacit varieties. His explanation of the roles of master, servant, and slave emphasizes masters' power. It is the master's decision, whether to allow corporal liberty to conquered subjects, that assigns them (with their tacit consent) to their respective roles. "Every one that is taken in the War . . . is not suppos'd to have Contracted with his *Lord;* for every one is not trusted with . . . his naturall liberty." Only those so trusted are servants, and the others, slaves.[31] Consequences of consent beyond the immediate relationship are a feature of the discussion of children. When grown, Hobbes specifies, "gratitude requireth . . . they acknowledge the benefit of their education, by externall signes of honour."[32] Whether he would agree, the stipulation resembles a retrospective criterion for consent itself (that is, sometimes it is by our present actions that we indicate the character of a relationship in the past). These analyses of consent to social roles can be seen as an effort to map the territory, the problems and considerations relevant to structural, normative liberal thinking about distributive justice. The former discussion, of "household" authorities, addresses the ready objection that consent accounts of structural authority relationships ignore the matter of power. In circumstances of dependence, Hobbes recognizes, subjects' choices hinge on the prior and more consequential decisions of authorities. As well, the realities of dependence require an appreciation for the subtlety of assessing the subordinates' consent.

Second, a structural analysis directs attention to roles themselves and their legitimacy. In Hobbesian theory, the question narrowly pertains to political roles.[33] *Leviathan,* first and foremost, is a defense of a particular constitution of political society, namely, of course, an absolutist constitution in which sovereignty is unconditional and unified.[34] It is one of the contentious issues of Hobbes interpretation, outside the scope of the present essay, whether the defense is primarily analytic or prescriptive in nature—that is, an argument about the necessary character of sovereignty or the prescription that absolutism is the desirable political constitution.[35] What is certain is that social utility figures as a major ground of the defense. As between the principal alternatives, justifying structural relationships as good or fair and justifying them as socially useful, Hobbes characteristically reasons in the latter vein (e.g., the political covenant, creating an absolute sovereign, is "the only way to erect such a Common Power, as may be able to defend them from the invasion of Forraigners, and the injuries of one another").[36] Liberals are rightly mistrustful of appeals to social utility because of the implications for the treatment of individuals. But for present purposes I want to call attention, rather, to two further features of Hobbes's thinking—his political argument for absolutism and his recognition of the plasticity of political roles.

In contrast to the abstraction of individualistic political reasoning (viz., the deduction of political conclusions from premises about abstract individuals), *Leviathan*'s consequentialist defense of absolutism rests on a practical judgment about political possibility and danger in the concrete. Accurately, Hobbes's brief emphasizes the disutility of the alternative, divided sovereignty. He has the immediate political crisis specifically in mind:

> *[A] Kingdome divided in it selfe cannot stand:* For unlesse this division precede, division into opposite Armies can never happen. If there had not first been an opinion received of the greatest part of *England,* that these Powers were divided between the King, and the Lords, and the House of Commons, the people had never been divided, and fallen into this Civill Warre.[37]

To divide sovereignty, "were to erect two Soveraigns; . . . that by opposing one another, must needs divide that Power, which (if men will live in Peace) is indivisible; and thereby reduce the Multitude into the condition of Warre, contrary to the end for which all Soveraignty is instituted."[38] Hobbes has in mind a dynamic from a mixed constitution to civil war: divided sovereignty encourages elite conflict; and that in turn tends to spread into civil war as elites mobilize the people to fight their battles.

Theorizing in this prudential vein invites contention of the sort specifically appropriate to a political treatise—contention about the soundness of political judgments (as opposed to the aptness of characterizations of self-interested rationality).[39] To the extent, furthermore, that political possibility and danger are themselves variable, prudential theory is likely to have a local character, to be more acute for some sorts of political circumstance than for others. Which is not to say that prudential reasoning and a consistent philosophy of political value are inimical, though it does mean granting that values are not isomorphic with institutions. To wit: Hobbes's prudential defense of absolutism appeals, finally, to a very "liberal" concern—for the protection of victims. He wrote *De Cive* to persuade readers "no longer [to] suffer ambitious men through the streames of your blood to wade to their owne power."[40] The point is not to claim Hobbes's political theory, from yet another angle, for the liberal tradition.[41] Hobbesian absolutism and liberal constitutionalism, the doctrine of limited government, are opposing theories about political institutions. Still, taken seriously, at least as a judgment accurate to some political circumstances, Hobbes's view that common people are most in danger from elite conflict calls into question any easy, abstract identification of liberal values with a particular set of political institutions.

Last, *Leviathan*'s treatment of military service evinces a recognition of the plasticity, the malleability, of political roles. The role of the soldier, and the distinction between the role obligations of subjects and soldiers, is a new argument in *Leviathan,* which does not appear in the two previous versions of the political theory.[42] Perhaps the addition reflects a prudential estimation, born of the Civil War, of the greater reliability of a professional army as compared to armies raised on feudal lines.[43] But by implication, the addition spells the recognition that civic virtue and instrumental rationality are not the sole relevant considerations in thinking about public-goods problems. They can also be tackled through the manipulation of roles. (The parallel normative issue, whether a political division of labor is consistent with the vision of liberal democracy, is the concluding question of this essay.) By analogy, Hobbes's creativity in providing for the defense of the *Leviathan*-state introduces, next, consideration of public-goods problems as problems of policy.

II

The formal structure of Hobbesian absolutism has such provocative implications that readers commonly discount his advice on the conduct of government. Chapter thirty of *Leviathan,* on the "office" of the sovereign, commends fair and lawful rule, directed to the common good. *Contra* the Machiavellian thesis that arbitrariness serves rulers' power (because it is better to be unpredictable and feared than to be known and loved),[44] it is Hobbes's view that good rule, according to law, enhances sovereign power. Right makes might.[45] His arguments cover positive and negative "politic" considerations, both the positive prerequisites of power and means to deter rebellion. It is as a problem of policy that that second, major, political public-goods problem, taxation, arises for treatment in the political theory.

In the first version of the political theory, *The Elements of Law,* Hobbes observed that burdensome and inequitable taxation is one of the chief causes of rebellion;

> in the time of Henry VII. the seditions of the Cornish men that refused to pay a subsidy, and, under the conduct of the Lord Audley, gave the King battle upon Blackheath; and that of the northern people, who in the same king's time, for demanding a subsidy granted in parliament, murdered the Earl of Northumberland in his house.[46]

As well, rulers have a stake in their nations' prosperity, and for this second reason ought not to bankrupt their subjects. According to *De Cive,*

> if the Ruler levie such a summe of vast monies from his subjects, as they are not able to maintain themselves, and their families, nor conserve their bodily strength, and vigour, the disadvantage is as much his, as theirs, who with never so great a stock, or measure of riches, is not able to keep his authority or his riches without the bodies of his subjects; but if he raise no more than is sufficient for the due administration of his power, that is a benefit equall to himselfe and his subjects, tending to a Common Peace, and defence.[47]

Social prosperity is the foundation of a strong state (or in the well-known phrase of James I, before Parliament, "If you be rich I cannot be poor").[48]

In the same work, Hobbes remarks on the nature of the problem of taxation in terms now familiar in theories of rational action: "that which to all together is but a light weight, if many withdraw themselves, it wil be very heavy, nay, even intollerable to the rest."[49] He attacks the problem, as Dudley Jackson has observed, partly as a matter of prudential policy and partly as an obligation issue.[50] That is, he simultaneously explains to rulers that equal taxation serves their interest, and explains to subjects why they are obliged not to free ride. To the one, prudence dictates a policy of equal taxation, because "neither are men wont so much to grieve at the burthen it self, as at the inequality."[51] To subjects, Hobbes explains the fairness of equal taxation: "Seeing then the benefit that every one receiveth thereby, is the enjoyment of life, which is equally dear to poor, and rich; the debt which a poor man oweth them that defend his life, is the same which a rich man oweth for the defence of his."[52] What he actually has in mind is taxing consumption, a policy both fair and socially useful, for encouraging work and thrift:

> The Equality of Imposition, consisteth rather in the Equality of that which is consumed, than of the riches of the persons that consume the same. For what reason is there, that he which laboureth much, and sparing the fruits of his labour, consumeth little, should be more charged, then he that living idlely, getteth little, and spendeth all he gets; seeing the one hath no more protection from the Commonwealth, then the other? But when the Impositions, are layd upon those

> things which men consume, every man payeth Equally for what he useth: Nor is the Common-wealth defrauded, by the luxurious waste of private men.[53]

Last, Hobbes claims his consumption tax policy "seemeth not only most equal, but also . . . least to trouble the mind of them that pay."[54] In short, equal taxation serves rulers' interest by deterring rebellion; taxing consumption serves the public interest; and last, *pace* this observation in *The Elements of Law,* the policy conduces to citizen cooperation. Readings drawing political conclusions from Hobbes's estimation of the selfishness of most men miss his recognition of government's part in encouraging citizen cooperation and discouraging *incivisme.*[55] Subjects, Hobbes knows, do not calculate about cooperation in a vacuum or in the abstract, but in a context framed by governmental policy. Hence governments bear some measure of (informal) responsibility for their citizens' "virtue." (In this vein, rebellion is characterized, in *Leviathan,* as the "Naturall Punishment" of negligent government.)[56]

The problem of taxation does not lend itself to solution in terms of a political division of labor. Otherwise Hobbes's argument, to subjects, is consistent with *Leviathan*'s explanation of the duty of fighting. Incipient free riders are answered in the same way in both instances. Throughout Hobbes avoids the unrealistic, even puzzling, demand of universalizing reasoning. (Why should individuals, even those impressed with their own moral duties, reckon in terms of what would happen if others—if everyone—acted as they propose to act?)[57] His arguments solely concern the specific duties of the individual (role occupant). A subject must fight when his service, in specific, is required; similarly, fighting is a universal obligation of soldiers; and paying taxes is a universal obligation of subjection, because each and every subject is indebted to the state for providing him security.

III

Hobbes has in mind a different state from that presupposed by generalizing individualistic readings. His prudential argument for absolutism (i.e., the view that ordinary lives are more in danger from elite conflict than from tyrannous government) is framed in the context of an early-modern state, characteristically weak and possessed of few resources with which to interfere in individuals' lives. Hobbes observed the point, in connection with monarchy, in particular, in *De Cive:*

> Wherefore some *Nero* or *Caligula* reigning, no men can undeservedly suffer, but such as are known to him, namely Courtiers, and such as are

> remarkable for some eminent Charge; . . . Whosoever therefore in a *Monarchy* will lead a retired life, let him be what he will that Reignes, he is out of danger: for the ambitious onely suffer, the rest are protected from the injuries of the more potent.[58]

Consistent with the weak state he has in mind, Hobbes identifies few public goods, notably the essentials of supply and a military. But the ways in which these are treated in *Leviathan,* and the underlying image of political relationships, are realistic to the frame of our own political thinking. When political ties are impersonal, and government a distant organization, as Hobbes imagines these to be, political and structural solutions to collective goods problems are not only more practical than psychological, including moral, solutions;[59] they are also more consonant with everyday political experience. Neither requires of individuals the sort of communal identification and concern appropriate to a small and close-knit association, but foreign to the experience of citizenship in a large nation-state.[60] Liberals surely should be the first to recognize the obfuscation in transferring appeals to civic virtue (including, e.g., the principle of universalization) to the latter context.

Still, the argument for separating liberalism from political individualism faces one last and fundamental question. Is a theory tying obligations to roles (political and, more generally, social roles) consistent with the liberal democratic principle of equality? On the one hand, it can be claimed for structural moral thinking that the social consciousness required of individuals is limited, and appropriate to the contours of a complex society. *Pace* Hobbes on subjects' and soldiers' military obligations, what is required is cognizance of one's role obligations. A similar insight can be detected in recent revisionist utilitarian efforts to specify the obligations of classes of persons. In *Reasons and Persons,* for instance, Parfit asks us to act on the recognition that our acts form part of a larger class of acts, an appeal that can be seen as a less determinate version of Hobbes's analysis of role obligations. "It is not enough to ask," according to Parfit, " 'Will my act harm other people?' Even if the answer is No, my act may still be wrong, *because* of its effects on other people. I should ask, 'Will my act be one of a set of acts that will *together* harm other people?' "[61] It can be claimed, second, that tying obligations to roles is a route by which the principle of consent can be made effectual in the setting of a large, complex, and distant nation-state. The idea has been essayed by Walzer, who suggests distinguishing the obligations of "alienated residents," whose nonparticipation tokens refusal of express consent, from those of the politically active; the former may be seen to have social obligations, but only the latter have incurred the ultimate obligation to fight and possibly die for the state.[62] But Walzer also observes that the impulse to distinguish between the obligations of classes of citizens is fundamentally in tension with the principle of equality: "The whole tendency of modern legislation and of contemporary social struggle, however, is to establish a single class of citizens with precisely equal rights and obligations."[63] To his mind, the objection speaks against conscription altogether and for reliance on a voluntary army; but even this (Hobbes's) solution still represents an inegalitarian political division of labor. If moral reasoning in terms of specialized roles (or more vaguely, participation in classes of acts) is more realistic to political and social experience in the contemporary world, perhaps the time has come for liberal theorists to reconsider the meaning of equality in a complex society.

Notes

1. This essay is based on parts of a larger work, *Hobbes's Political Theory*. Manuscript submitted for publication.

2. Cf., e.g., Ronald Dworkin's emphasis on the principle of equality in "Liberalism" in *Public and Private Morality*, ed. Stuart Hampshire (Cambridge: Cambridge University Press, 1978), pp. 113-43; and Judith Shklar's concern for the protection of victims in *Ordinary Vices* (Cambridge: Harvard University Press, 1984).

3. Steven Lukes, *Individualism* (Oxford: Basil Blackwell, 1973), pp. 76-77. For the identification of liberalism with political individualism see, generally, chap. 12.

4. E.g., Howard Warrender, *The Political Philosophy of Hobbes: His Theory of Obligation* (Oxford: Clarendon Press, 1957), p. 11: "The case is here presented for the view that there is a single and consistent theory of obligation connecting the duties of man, considered apart from civil society, with those of the citizen. In other words, Part II [of Warrender's own study] will be concerned with a particular application of the theory of obligation presented in Part I."

5. See, e.g., Michael J. Sandel, *Liberalism and the Limits of Justice* (Cambridge: Cambridge University Press, 1982).

6. Thomas Hobbes, "The Introduction," *Leviathan*, ed. C. B. Macpherson (Harmondsworth: Penguin/Pelican Books, 1968), p. 81.

7. E.g., ibid., chap. 4, p. 102: "there being nothing in the world Universall but Names; for the things named, are every one of them Individuall and Singular."

8. Thomas Hobbes, "The Authors Preface to the Reader," *De Cive: The English Version, entitled in the first edition Philosophicall Rudiments Concerning Government and Society*, ed. Howard Warrender (Oxford: Clarendon Press, 1983), p. 32 (emphasis omitted): "Concerning my Method, . . . every thing is best understood by its constitutive causes; for as in a watch, or some such small engine, the matter, figure, and motion of the wheeles, cannot well be known, except it be taken in sunder, and viewed in parts; so to make a more

curious search into the rights of States, and duties of Subjects, it is necessary, (I say not to take them in sunder, but yet that) they be so considered, as if they were dissolved, (i.e.) that we rightly understand what the quality of humane nature is, in what matters it is, in what not fit to make up a civill government, and how men must be agreed among themselves, that intend to grow up into a well-grounded State." See also VIII, sec. 1, p.117; and *Elements of Philosophy. The First Section, Concerning Body,* in *The English Works of Thomas Hobbes,* vol. 1, ed. Sir William Molesworth (London: John Bohn, 1839), pp. 73-75.

9. I am not claiming, in other words (as it would be wrong to claim), that Hobbes attributes ontological reality to social units, independent of the individuals composing them. Rather, the combination of an analytic emphasis on roles with a nominalist ontology implies a weak version of "methodological individualism," i.e., the position that statements about social units ought to permit translation into statements about individuals. For a further consideration of these issues, see my *Hobbes's Political Theory,* chap. 1.

10. Thomas Hobbes, "A Review and Conclusion," *Leviathan,* p. 725; see, also, *The Elements of Law: Natural and Politic,* ed. Ferdinand Tonnies (Cambridge: Cambridge University Press, 1928), Part I, chap. 1, p. 1.

11. Michael Walzer, "The Obligation to Die for the State," in *Obligations: Essays on Disobedience, War, and Citizenship* (Cambridge: Harvard University Press, 1970), p. 87.

12. The only specific discussion of the issue in the earlier versions of the theory appears in *De Cive,* XII.2, p. 147. There, Hobbes labels private judgment about the justness of a war, and therefore about fighting, a "sin." (Cf. *The Elements of Law,* II.8.4-5, pp. 135-36.)

13. Thomas Hobbes, *Leviathan,* 21, p. 268.

14. Ibid., p. 269.

15. Ronald Dworkin, *Taking Rights Seriously* (Cambridge: Harvard University Press, 1977), p. xi.

16. Cf. Howard Warrender, *The Political Philosophy of Hobbes,* pp. 188-99; and Deborah Baumgold, *Hobbes's Political Theory,* pp. 52-55.

17. Thomas Hobbes, *Leviathan,* 21, p. 269.

18. Ibid., p. 270.

19. Ibid., "A Review and Conclusion," p. 719.

20. Ibid., p. 720.

21. Ibid. See also 20, p. 257.

22. The question is the title of Colin Strang's analysis of the principle of universalization, "What If Everyone Did That?," in *Ethics,* ed. Judith J. Thomson and Gerald Dworkind (New York: Harper and Row, 1968), pp. 151-62.

23. Thomas Hobbes, "A Review and Conclusion," *Leviathan,* pp. 718-19.

24. Ibid., 28, p. 361 (emphasis mine).

25. Ibid. The passage continues: "otherwise, he is bound onely in honour, to acknowledgement, and an endeavour of requitall."

26. John Locke, *The Second Treatise of Government,* in *Two Treatises of Government,* rev. ed., ed. Peter Laslett (New York: New American Library, 1963), sec. 139, pp. 407-8.

27. Ibid., p. 408.

28. John Dunn, *The Political Thought of John Locke: An Historical Account of the "Two Treatises of Government"* (Cambridge: Cambridge University Press,

1969), p. 236. On the structural character of Locke's thought, see also James Tully, *A Discourse on Property: John Locke and His Adversaries,* paperback ed. (Cambridge: Cambridge University Press, 1982), pp. 11, 24.

29. Thomas Hobbes, *The Elements of Law,* II.3-4, pp. 99-107; *De Cive,* VIII-IX, pp. 117-28; *Leviathan,* 20, pp. 251-61.

30. Thomas Hobbes, *Leviathan,* 20, p. 253: "Paternall" dominion "is not . . . derived from the Generation, as if therefore the Parent had Dominion over his Child because he begat him; but from the Childs Consent, either expresse, or by other sufficient arguments declared." Cf. *The Elements of Law,* II.4.3, pp. 103-4; and *De Cive,* IX.I-II, pp. 121-22.

31. The quotation is from Thomas Hobbes, *De Cive,* VIII.II, p. 118. See also VIII.III, p. 118; *The Elements of Law,* II.3.2-3, pp. 99-100; and *Leviathan,* 20, pp. 255-56.

32. Thomas Hobbes, *Leviathan,* 30, p. 382; see *De Cive,* IX.VIII, pp. 124-25.

33. The preceding discussions of social roles do not have a justificatory point; they rather illustrate and elaborate a claim about the nature of authority in general. See, e.g., Thomas Hobbes, *Leviathan,* 20, pp. 256-57.

34. As defined in *De Cive* (VI.XIII, pp. 97-98), absolutism is simultaneously a doctrine about sovereigns' rights and about the role of subjects. An absolute sovereign *"can, unpunisht, doe any thing, make Lawes, judge Controversies, set Penalties."* As well, "there is so much obedience joyn'd to this absolute Right of the Chief Ruler, as is necessarily requir'd for the Government of the City, that is to say, so much as that Right of his may not be granted in vaine." See also *The Elements of Law,* II.1.5, pp. 85-86; and *Leviathan,* chap. 18. James Daly, "The Idea of Absolute Monarchy in Seventeenth-Century England," *The Historical Journal* 21 (1978): 235, notes that such translation of absolutism into a statement about subjection was typical in the period.

35. Cf. M. M. Goldsmith, "Hobbes's 'Mortall God': Is There a Fallacy in Hobbes's Theory of Sovereignty?" *History of Political Thought* 1 (1980): 33-50 (the analytic view); and Deborah Baumgold, *Hobbes's Political Theory,* chap. 4 (the prescriptive view).

36. Thomas Hobbes, *Leviathan,* 17, p. 227.

37. Ibid., 18, pp. 236-37.

38. Ibid., 19, p. 240. On the consequences of divided sovereignty, cf. *The Elements of Law,* II.1.14, p. 88; and *De Cive,* XII.V, p. 150.

39. E.g., John Plamenatz, "Hobbes," *Man and Society,* vol. 1 (New York: McGraw-Hill, 1963), p. 153: "He took it for granted that, where there is no such [sole final] authority, there will inevitably arise disputes that cannot be settled except by war. He could not see that, where there are several final authorities, each in a different field, there may yet be a settled procedure for deciding any dispute that may arise."

40. Thomas Hobbes, *De Cive,* "The Authors Preface to the Reader," p. 36 (emphasis omitted).

41. Cf. Michael Oakeshott, "Introduction to *Leviathan,*" in *Hobbes on Civil Association* (Berkeley: University of California Press, 1975), p. 63.

42. See note 12 above.

43. Parliament's Militia Ordinance and Charles I's Commissions of Array, the formal instruments by which the armies were raised, are discussed by J. S. Morrill, *The Revolt of the Provinces: Conservatives and Radicals in the English Civil*

War, 1630–1650 (London: Allen and Unwin, 1976), pp. 39-40. See also Ronald Hutton, *The Royalist War Effort 1642–46* (London: Longman, 1982); and Mark A. Kishlansky, *The Rise of the New Model Army* (Cambridge: Cambridge University Press, 1979).

44. Niccolo Machiavelli, *The Prince,* trans. George Bull (Harmondsworth: Penguin, 1961), chap. 17.

45. Why lawful rule conduces to powerful government is the principal topic in chap. 5, on Hobbes's "art of government," of my *Hobbes's Political Theory.*

46. Thomas Hobbes, *The Elements of Law,* II.8.2, p. 134. See II.9.5, p. 144; and *De Cive,* XII.IX and XIII.X, pp. 152, 161.

47. Thomas Hobbes, *De Cive,* X.II, p. 130. See also X.XVIII, p. 140; *The Elements of Law,* II.5.1, p. 108; and *Leviathan,* 19, pp. 241-42.

48. The statement is quoted in J. A. W. Gunn, *Politics and the Public Interest in the Seventeenth Century* (London: Routledge and Kegan Paul), p. 68.

49. Thomas Hobbes, *De Cive,* XIII.X, p. 161.

50. Dudley Jackson, "Thomas Hobbes's Theory of Taxation," *Political Studies* 21 (1973): 175-82.

51. Thomas Hobbes, *De Cive,* XIII.X, p. 161. The passage continues: "To remove . . . all just complaint, its the interest of the publique quiet, and by consequence it concernes the duty of the Magistrate, to see that the publique burthens be equally born."

52. Thomas Hobbes, *Leviathan,* 30, p. 386. Alternately, taxes are "the Wages, due to them that hold the publique Sword, to defend private men in the exercise of severall Trades, and Callings" (ibid.).

53. Ibid., pp. 386-87. See *De Cive,* XIII.XI, p. 162. Aaron Levy, "Economic Views of Thomas Hobbes," *Journal of the History of Ideas* 15 (1954): 589-95, emphasizes the political orientation of Hobbes's economic arguments.

54. Thomas Hobbes, *The Elements of Law,* II.9.5, p. 144.

55. The figure of the "Defaulter," in Strang's "What if Everyone Did That?" announces (pp. 155-56): "If anyone is to blame it is the person whose job it is to circumvent evasion. If too few people vote, then it should be made illegal not to vote. If too few people volunteer, then you must introduce conscription. If too many people evade taxes, then you must tighten up your system of enforcement. My answer to your 'If everyone did that' is 'Then someone had jolly well better see to it that they don't." Strang subsequently argues that ruler and ruled share responsibility for public goods (pp. 159-60).

56. Thomas Hobbes, *Leviathan,* 31, pp. 406-7. See Deborah Baumgold, *Hobbes's Political Theory,* pp. 176-79.

57. A. C. Ewing, "What Would Happen if Everybody Acted Like Me?," *Philosophy* 28 (1953): 17, poses the utilitarian version of the question, "Why on earth should I be debarred from doing something, not because my doing it produces bad consequences, but because, if everybody did it, which I know will not be the case, the consequences *would* be bad?"

58. Thomas Hobbes, *De Cive,* X.VII, p. 134. The passage continues with this invidious comparison with popular government: "But in a *popular Dominion* there may be as many *Nero's,* as there are Oratours who sooth the *People.*" For an illustrative discussion of the difficulties of early modern rulers, see Howell A. Lloyd, *The Rouen Campaign 1590-1592: Politics, Warfare and the Early-Modern State* (Oxford: Clarendon Press, 1973), esp. pp. 196-97.

59. Cf. Derek Parfit, *Reasons and Persons* (Oxford: Clarendon Press, 1984), pp. 62-64.

60. See Michael Walzer, "The Obligation to Live for the State," in *Obligations,* pp. 169-89.

61. Derek Parfit, *Reasons and Persons,* p. 86. Parfit defends this sort of moral reasoning as specifically appropriate to large-scale modern society (pp. 85-86). A second of his arguments, it might be noted, also bears some resemblance to the Hobbesian arguments surveyed in this essay—namely, his argument for recognizing imperceptible harms and benefits (sec. 29, pp. 78-82). Doing so assigns responsibility to each and every individual, i.e., avoids appeal to the principle of universalization in a manner reminiscent of Hobbesian reasoning to subjects and soldiers on fighting and taxation. Of the two lines of argument, Parfit thinks the former—the appeal to the effects of classes of acts—is likely to be more widely persuasive (p. 82).

62. Michael Walzer, "Political Alienation and Military Service," in *Obligations,* esp. pp. 109-19.

63. Ibid., p. 116; see, in general, pp. 116-19.

– 9 –

The Democratic Consequences of Liberalism

ALFONSO J. DAMICO

Ruling and Being Ruled

Politics, Aristotle taught us to say, is the activity of ruling and being ruled. His description of citizens as those who "possess the knowledge and the capacity requisite for ruling as well as for being ruled" pictures these activities as complementary parts of a unified experience. But for citizens living in a modern liberal society, the experience of being ruled far outweighs the experience of ruling—at least in the sense meant by Aristotle. The increase in the number of citizens, the size of the state, the extensive division of labor, the absence of close ties among people who must nevertheless cooperate, all contribute to the imbalance between ruling and being ruled. In short, there are two experiences here, and their relationship is now problematic. Neither their unity nor how one completes the other is self-evident.

Setting out to assess the democratic consequences of liberalism concedes, at the outset, that liberalism and democracy vary in the relative attention and significance they attach to the experiences of being ruled and ruling. Historically preceding democracy and arising against a background of religious civil wars, liberalism has always ranked the problems of misrule and legitimate authority ahead of the various values that might attend ruling itself. In a bit of useful hyperbole, Judith Shklar notes that liberalism often assumes that "the power to govern is the power to inflict fear and cruelty and that no amount of benevolence can ever suffice to protect an unarmed population against them."[1] And while democracy followed and often expanded liberalism (e.g., the extension of the suffrage, the greater value attached to popular rule), the meaning of that expansion remains controversial. For example, Giovanni Sartori in *Democratic Theory* initially summarizes this history by arguing that "liberalism is above all else the technique of limiting the State's power, whereas democracy is the insertion of popular power into the State." But his explanation of this formula concludes by stating that political democracy is simply "another name" for the liberal-constitutional state.[2] In contrast, Benjamin Barber has recently argued that democracy's expansion has been stalled or blocked by an "excess of liberalism."[3] The liberal preoccupation with misrule, Barber argues, has obscured the ways in which ruling itself, when it draws on the communal nature of political life, displaces fear with mutuality and cruelty with empathy. While Barber argues that "strong democracy" fills out or complements liberalism, it is clear that it does so mainly by superceding it.

Sartori and Barber present us with contrasting instances of the attempt to knit together the experiences of "ruling and being ruled" as twin aspects of some larger experience. Sartori does it by conflating the meaning of liberalism and democracy; Barber, by accentuating their differences. For Sartori, democratic rule does not differ significantly from those liberal guarantees meant to protect us from being misruled, i.e., the constitutional state, juridical defense, and individual freedom. What has been termed Sartori's "democratic elitism," i.e., his downgrading of popular participation, is a result of his ranking these guarantees against misrule far ahead of whatever benefits might be claimed for popular participation in the experience of ruling. For most citizens, democratic rule means being ruled well; the meaning of the former is located in the experience of the latter. In contrast, for Barber the possible meaning of being ruled democratically is located in ruling itself. "In strong democracy," he writes, "politics is something done by, not to citizens."[4] Again one experience is subsumed by the other; in "strong democracy" being ruled well is what happens when ruling is self-legislation, i.e., participatory democracy.

I will canvass a middle ground somewhere between Sartori's dismissal of more participatory conceptions of democracy and Barber's exaggerated claims on behalf of such conceptions. On the one hand, the democratic consequences of liberalism are, I think, deeper than just guarantees against misrule. And, on the other, Barber's reintroduction of those guarantees, however *en passant,* as part of "strong democracy" narrows the alleged distance separating it from liberalism. To put this somewhat differently, the types of values or goods that liberalism seeks to establish by limiting all forms of rule encourage valuing democratic rule as well. But just as liberalism generates pressure for its own democratic expansion, "strong democracy" ends up being self-limiting in a liberal direction.

Throughout, the discussion endorses the liberal sense that, given the asymmetry between notions of the self-governing community and the operations of the modern state, striking some balance between liberal fears of misrule and democratic demands for popular rule is, quite probably, the only ground available. But I do not want just to argue that liberal values and democratic ones must be deployed as counterweights so that an increase in one presupposes a decrease in the other. That would concede too much to those critics of liberalism who argue that more democracy means less liberalism. In contrast, the balance between ruling and being ruled sought by democratic liberalism is one where the fear of misrule and the demand for popular rule intersect and support each other.

The Democratic Meaning of Liberal Values

Democracy is often described as popular rule, as though, to repeat Barber's language, ruling is something "done by, not to citizens." But that imagines a sovereign without subjects, authority without power, rulers without anyone to rule. Even Rousseau, who tried to dissolve these relationships by arguing that, under conditions of social solidarity, "whoso gives himself to all gives himself to none," continued to characterize ruling itself as the issuing of "commands," the making of "demands," and the use of "force."[5] If ruling and being ruled are problematic, they are not made less so by the advent of popular rule. "It was now perceived," Mill writes in *On Liberty,* "that such phrases as 'self-government,' and the 'power of the people over themselves,' do not express the true state of the case. The 'people' who exercise power are not always the same people with those over whom it is exercised; and the 'self-government' spoken of is not the government of each by himself, but of each by all the rest."[6]

Given Mill's concern in *On Liberty* with the type of reasons that might justify overriding individual freedom, this statement is hardly surprising. What the liberal principle does best, perhaps, is to argue that neither the good realized in ruling nor the good secured by guarantees against misrule can be fully identified without comparing one to the other. This posture always makes liberalism vulnerable to the complaint of half-heartedness on behalf of democracy, that it is, as Barber labels it, a theory of "thin democracy." To that complaint, liberalism has two reasonable responses. The first is to narrow the gap between liberalism and democracy by following the lead provided by those liberals who understand that "limited government and self-government sustain one another."[7] (For a demonstration of the interdependency between the characteristic features of liberal democracies and self-government, see the essay by Elaine Spitz in this volume.) The second is to cede to "strong" democrats those more commanding conceptual heights to which ruling can be elevated by excluding the threat of misrule.

The most general way to identify those values or that good which liberalism endorses can begin with what Richard Flathman has termed the liberal principle. That principle states that "it is a prima facie good for individuals to have and be in a position to act upon and satisfy their interests and desires, objectives and purposes."[8] While liberalism is not the only "individualistic" political theory, it does attach special importance to the concept of the free subject or agent as someone who makes his own choices, pursues his particular interests, and subjects institutional arrangements and practices to the judgment of his own will. This individualism can, of course, be expressed in a variety of idioms, including utility, rights, and social contract reasoning. While there is a large literature dealing with how one's idiom of choice affects the meaning of liberal individualism, I hope to bypass most of those issues. Whether individuals are viewed as bearers of rights or, more broadly, as equally capable of acquiring and acting upon their own interests as free agents, liberalism starts with the twin assumptions that it is good for individuals to be free from interference and for them to have, develop and pursue their interests. At issue are the sort of characteristically democratic doctrines that can be fitted to this "individualism."

Once we commit ourselves to the notion that interests, however acquired, form an important part of an individual's identity, we start out with a presumptive case *against* power and rule. However constituted, authority always includes the ability to overrule another's choices, limiting their range of action. Entering into such a relationship places both our interests and our dignity at some risk.

> To be prevented from doing what one is inclined to, or from acting according to one's own judgment of what is desirable, is not only always irksome, but always tends, *pro tanto,* to starve the development of some portion of the bodily or mental faculties, either sensitive or active; and unless the conscience of the individual goes freely with the legal restraint, it partakes, either in great or in a small degree, of the degradation of slavery.[9]

Typically, Mill does not take much care here to distinguish between self-respect and self-development, between freedom and individuality. But this can, I think, be seen less as carelessness on his part than as evidence of his belief that liberalism's "freedom from interference claim" and its "developmental claim" are complementary. "If a person possesses any tolerable amount of common sense and experience," Mill writes, "his own mode of laying down his existence is the best, not because it is best in itself, but because it is his own mode." But to this "freedom from interference" claim, Mill was always quick to add that only through the act of choosing for themselves could individuals develop their reason, refine and enlarge their sensibilities, and discover new ends. Mill, then, repeated this link between the freedom from interference and developmental claims in arguing that there is a natural affinity between "self-help and self-government." Such links argue against any simple dichotomy between liberal warnings about misrule and demands for popular rule. Before presuming that we need to reconcile liberal and democratic doctrines, we might first ask how much each already adds to the other.

The most natural democratic expression of liberalism's fear of misrule is, perhaps, something like Mill's addition of a "self-protection" principle to the liberal principle: "Men, as well as women, do not need political rights in order that they may govern, but in order that they may not be misgoverned." For some, this is as much as can be said for the "protective" version of liberal democracy. But even if we set aside the ironic understatement of that phrase "as much," more is involved here than just the institutionalization of liberal misanthropy.

Liberal guarantees against misrule, i.e., those institutional arrangements that unite the liberal principle to its self-protection principle, are partly a straightforward attempt to tame power:

> We need not suppose that when power resides in an exclusive class, that class will knowingly and deliberately sacrifice the other classes to themselves: it suffices that, in the absence of its natural defenders, the interest of the excluded is always in danger of being overlooked; and, when looked at, is seen with very different eyes from those of the persons whom it directly concerns.[10]

This is not primarily an utilitarian argument. That is, Mill's case for "protective democracy" does not depend on the claim that representative institutions best satisfy the interests of subjects considered as agents of wants and interests that they seek to satisfy as fully as possible. Nor is it mainly, in Judith Shklar's memorable phrase, a "liberalism of fear" that seeks to protect "potential victims" from their "inevitable aggressors." Both considerations of utility and vulnerability play a part in Mill's argument, but the accent is elsewhere:

> it is a great additional stimulus to any one's self-help and self-reliance when he starts from even ground, and has not to feel that his success depends on the impression he can make upon sentiments and dispositions of a body of whom he is not one. It is a great discouragement to an individual, and a still greater one to a class, to be left out of the constitution; to be reduced to plead from outside the door to the arbiters of their destiny, not taken into consultation within.[11]

There is a strong practical connection between the liberal principle's respect for each person as a source of claims and its general valuation of "purposiveness," on the one side, and "membership" as the primary good of protective democracy, on the other. Representative institutions, freedom of discussion, the universal franchise and other democratic arrangements are called for in part so that individuals can be self-protecting. But they are also institutional confirmation of what Mill describes as an individual's dignity and what Michael Walzer has more recently termed "recognition."

> The democratic revolution doesn't so much redistribute as reconceptualize self-respect, tying it, as Tocqueville suggests, to a single set of norms. . . . The experience of citizenship requires the prior acknowledgment that everyone is a citizen—a public form of simple recognition.[12]

"Public recognition" is the more positive expression of liberalism's fear of misrule. And given what is at risk from misrule—one's dignity and the ability to have and pursue projects of one's own making—it is both misleading and miserly to deride this side of liberal democracy as merely negative or as "thin."

In any case, the democratic consequences of liberalism are not limited to protective democracy. The consequences start there but, *passe'* both Sartori and Barber, they do not end there. In drawing lines between state and society, public and private spheres, liberalism is often accused of privileging nonpolitical relationships and undervaluing the life of citizenship. But that accusation, while fairly accurate as a criticism of such liberals as Hobbes and Locke, underestimates how this liberal "art of separation" serves the democratization of liberalism. When, for example, Mill distinguishes between state and society, it is not their independence but their interdependency that is stressed.

> It is therefore of supreme importance that all classes of the community, down to the lowest, should have much to do for themselves; that as great a demand should be made upon their intelligence and virtue as it is in any respect equal to; that the government should not only leave as far as possible to their own faculties the conduct of whatever concerns themselves alone, but should suffer them, or rather encourage them, to manage as many as possible of their joint concerns by voluntary cooperation; since this discussion and management of collective interests is the great school of that public spirit and the great source of that intelligence of public affairs which are always regarded as the distinctive character of the public of free countries.[13]

Mill makes no invidious comparison here between the free individual and the citizen. Rather, the guaranteed private life enriches public life. The sentiments, "habits of the heart"[14] necessary to democratic citizenship, presuppose individuals used to managing their own affairs. And that sort of experience is often a function of social relationships more direct and near than those possible within the political sphere. Free to communicate their beliefs and allowed a large space for cooperating to achieve their aims, individuals are more, not less, likely to succeed as citizens. Liberalism's project involves more than protecting individuals from interference. Equally important are the new demands and possibilities that accompany this "art of separation."

> He who chooses his plan for himself, employs all his faculties. He must use observation to see, reasoning and judgment to foresee, activity to gather materials for decision, discrimination to decide, and when he has decided firmness and self-control to hold to his deliberate decision. And these qualities he requires and exercises exactly in proportion as the part of his conduct which he determines according to his own judgment and feelings is a large one.[15]

Admittedly, a language of radical individual autonomy can prevent individuals from understanding or experiencing more public commitments. But neither the liberal principle nor Mill's deployment of the public/private distinction forecasts a politics of socially isolated individuals. Border crossings are as critical to liberal democracy as are the borders drawn between state and society: "Between subjection to the will of others, and the virtues of self-help and self-government, there is a natural incompatibility." Mill defended political participation both for the rights it secures and for the fuller or richer standards of conduct that are exhibited in the activity itself. Giving the individual "something to do for the public" is important to the development of attitudes that are a chief safeguard against misrule, adds to the "moral instruction" of the individual, and reveals new possibilities and opportunities that are partially constitutive of freedom. Popular rule, attractive on its own terms, serves liberal freedom by combating an excessive preoccupation with private projects such that individuals lose interest in how they are ruled, endangering both public and private freedoms. And, conversely, that large area of life lived apart from government, also attractive on its own terms, combats exaggerated claims on behalf of either authority or popular rule.[16]

I have been arguing that there is a liberal case *for* the experience of ruling. And, not surprisingly, democrats on the left frequently call attention to this side of Mill's liberalism, noting however, the ways in which his democratic theory overcomes rather than extends the liberal principle itself. What the critics properly detect is Mill's ambivalence about popular rule: his concern with "class legislation" and his willingness to trade off some measure of popular participation to enhance the quality or competency of democratic leadership. These characteristics of Mill's thought make it more apt, perhaps, to describe his democratic extension of the liberal principle as a "citizenship theory," rather than as a participatory theory of democracy.

Dennis Thompson has described as citizenship theories those types of democratic theory which presuppose the "autonomy and improvability of citizens."[17] Mill, for example, believes both that citizens should be treated as though they are the best judges of their own interest and, on the other hand, that, given opportunities for political participation, they are capable of exercising better judgment in the future. In short, Mill is a liberal whose theory of democracy attaches some considerable weight to popular participation. None of this is illicit within the terms of the liberal principle, and even seems to be part of its natural extension.

But the liberal principle and liberal theory more generally always require us to consider any sort of "developmental" (or community) claim on behalf of liberty or popular rule in comparison to the dangers of misrule and social tyranny. The liberal's belief that self-government is always something of a misnomer for the rule of each by all of the rest and, second, that the sort of community identity presupposed by "strong democracy" is unavailable (possibly, undesirable) to citizens living in a modern society marks the border separating it, not from belief in the good of popular participation in ruling, but from the belief that popular rule is an unqualified good. In this sense, liberalism is incomplete in putting together ruling and being ruled, committed instead to balancing the fear of misrule with the demand for popular rule. But so long as popular rule is always something of a base metal—an alloy of ruling and overruling—that ambivalence and incompleteness may be more faithful to our own circumstances.

Liberalism's critics can hardly be expected to endorse a tentative and halting argument on behalf of participatory democracy. The problem, they argue, is that the institutions and beliefs to which the liberal's principle commits him either prevent effective political participation or lead citizens to undervalue it or to value it for the wrong, i.e., instrumental, reasons. The liberal principle seemingly gives too much support to individuals doing what they are already inclined to do—pursue aims of their own choosing that are not widely shared. Liberal individualism, it has long been argued, cannot bear the weight of the idea of politics as a "public" domain that instantiates such values as community and fraternity. Preoccupied with protecting a private domain, civil society, from public interference, liberalism privatizes political life. In short, Mill's notion of individuality praises democratic rule, but the liberal principle cannot sustain the praise.

In the next section, I look at one particular expression of these more general attacks on the liberal principle: the argument that the liberal principle provides individuals with an identity that precludes a meaningful democratic politics.

Liberal Strangers and Democratic Citizens

Life in a society organized around the liberal principle is frequently characterized as though it were little more than a series of anonymous exchanges among strangers. Michael Walzer writes, "Liberalism, even at its most permissive, is a hard politics because it offers so few emotional rewards; the liberal state is not a home for its citizens; it lacks warmth and intimacy." That cold and homeless condition, Benjamin Barber might add, is not surprising, since the "stranger" is the best analogue for the liberal individual. The liberal conception of the individual and of individual interest, he writes, "undermines the democratic practices upon which both individuals and their interests depend." And, for Michael Sandel, liberal strangers are not even individuals; they are mere apparitions—"disembodied" and "dispossessed."[18] Of course, Walzer, Barber, and Sandel are not making exactly the same complaint. Yet, there is similarity here in the juxtaposition of the liberal individual and the democratic citizen. The former are strangers, autonomous but lacking a sense of mutuality, independent but suspicious of all public entanglements; the latter are "citizens," encumbered by their social relations, situated in a public, committed and self-governing.

This contrast between liberal individualism and democratic citizenship is very sharp and quite probably overdrawn. It is overdrawn, in part, because it understates the obvious sense, although not one intended by these authors, in which most citizens are strangers; they do not know one another. Not knowing each other, however, does not necessarily mean that they are isolated from one another. Arguably, the complexity of social exchanges and extensive division of labor in modern society increases rather than decreases our dependence on one another. The dependence, however, does not obviously bring us closer together, since the impersonality of the mechanisms that make possible the satisfying of our various needs do not require that we "meet" as individuals, only that we play our part in the exchange. While it is quite possible to establish that, as participants in some social system, each person's well-being is bound up with everyone else's activity, that does not lessen the distance that separates them on a more personal level. Close personal ties are just that: near and transparent. Where such bonds exist, there is no need to appeal to some other exogenous standard to discover how we should behave. The relationship itself—friendship, affection—provides its own reasons for action. But the more diverse the society and the quicker it changes, the less sense it makes to speak of a common identity that includes "all possible others." When roles replace persons as the main actors in all sorts of social interactions or when institutional "agents" displace individuals, it hardly seems credible to attribute the subsequent social "distance" to either the liberal principle or the liberal "image of the self."

Liberal individualism (and its image of the self) does constrain, however, how we might think about democratic citizens in various ways. First, since individuals have a self-orientation and it is a prima facie good for them to act on that orientation, the role of citizen cannot displace that self-orientation. Further, in a society composed of individuals whose tastes, occupations, values, and ambitions differ widely, any correspondence of self-interest and common interest must depend on something other than an emotional identification of each with all the rest. A socially diverse society "unencumbers" us, expands our range of choices, and increases the number of persons toward whom we are indifferent. In such circumstances, the juridical characteristics of the liberal democratic state acquire greater prominence because of their increased importance. Put differently, the liberal principle abbreviates or, perhaps, anticipates a large and diverse population living together, aware that their own activities and interests are bounded by the need to allow others freedom to pursue their interests, a need that gives rise to various standards—obligations, rules, rights, etc.—that express this mutual consideration. "The more," John Plamenatz writes, "we depend on the services of persons unknown or little known to us, the more we need standards governing our transactions with them which they and we respect and which enable us to rely on one another in spite of our remoteness from each other."[19]

At its most philosophical, liberalism deploys a view of the self, largely free of any partisan identification, to chart the ways in which this self-orientation and the "subjectivity of interests" can be brought under the control of more interpersonally generated judgments, e.g., those located in principles of justice or the practice of political and private rights. So whether "unencumbered" by being imagined in a state of nature or behind a "veil of ignorance," liberal citizens are asked to do the difficult but not the impossible. They are asked to pretend that who they are and what they might think of one another should not control how they treat one another. Whether or not that pretense is a form of "benevolent hypocrisy,"[20] liberalism wants citizens whose fair treatment of one another is not contingent upon their liking one another. Admittedly, liberal individualism can be carried in directions that portray society as merely an aggregation of "atomic units" and politics as simply the medium for carrying out their rivalry. But a more generous reading of the liberal principle can see in its defense of individualism and image of the self an attempt to add a more public life to the life of "strangers."

Critical to liberalism's strategy of both separating *and* integrating the public and private is the judgment that we are not confronted with simple either-or choices between liberalism and democracy, liberal individualism and more communal notions of political life. So, for example, Richard Flathman has usefully argued that rights do, in fact, "warrant and protect self-directed and even self-serving action." But they do more:

> Participation in the practice of rights enmeshes individuals in and makes their actions both logically and practically dependent upon an elaborate network of social rules and the shared beliefs, values, assumptions, and so on, that an accepted set of rules involves. Thus, there is a very important sense in which participation in the practice of rights enmeshes individuals in a network of social relationships and a social structure. The autonomy of action that rights warrant and protect is autonomy within that network.[21]

So even in a liberal society, members are never really strangers. While rights are part of liberalism's program to protect individuals from society and the state, they also provide them with some sense of "a *place,* an *identity,* a *role* in the social milieu." The practice of rights does not preclude a more public life; the practice itself is partially constitutive of that life. But in a rapidly changing and diverse society, the substance of that way of life will be hard to fix once and for all. Consequently, elsewhere in this volume Flathman has argued for a more political reading of liberal principles of justice in which the particulars of those principles are not immune to reconsideration. We must not, he warns, "deprive ourselves of the freedom that is arguably the most fundamental of all, the freedom to go on deliberating the scope of our freedom."

That concluding step in Flathman's essay recalls the ease with which Mill insisted on the close interplay between liberal freedoms and political freedom. Where citizens control the government under conditions of a universal franchise and "the utmost publicity and liberty of discussion," the "whole public are made to a certain extent, participants in the government."[22] And, Mill might have added, it is how liberal "strangers" become a democratic public considering and reconsidering the ways in which they might expand every person's opportunities, secure their rights, and rearrange institutions so that one person's project is not necessarily destructive of another's. Within a liberal democratic order, private projects, special attachments, and competition are not displaced or dreamily transcended, but "strangers" participate in a variety of practices in which each recognizes not only himself but his fellow citizens. Where that recognition encourages respect for distant "others" and provides a more attractive range of alternatives for individuals to pursue, popular rule now bolsters liberal individualism. The democratic consequences of liberalism affect, then, more than an institutional change in government;

they give moral force to the notion that, where all are implicated in the institutions that structure available alternatives, all have a claim to be involved.

This democratization of liberalism narrows the gap between ruling and being ruled, but it does not close it. Both practical and philosophical considerations intervene. Practically, even in a more egalitarian society where participation is widespread, there will still be the need for a state that issues authoritative commands that are binding on society's members. Nor does it seem possible to conceive of any modern industrial society carrying out its activities, making and enforcing various standards, without some for whom such activities are a full-time and specialized activity. Representation is one way to organize that activity. And that entails a complex of roles accompanied by differential authority. Since roles cannot be equalized, the liberal political strategy is to counter that inequality with an equality that gives to all the same standing as members of the community. And critical to that status are guarantees against misrule, guarantees that limit how much can be claimed for democracy itself.

The range of liberalism's democratic consequences and its account of the role of citizen are further circumscribed by what it sees as "two fundamental truths of the human condition: the diversity of human types and the inherent incapacity of the public sphere to encompass more than a portion of human activity or to fulfill more than a part of human aspiration."[23] Combined with liberalism's wariness about all rule, including popular rule, these practical judgments or "truths" mark the limits of liberalism's conception of the individual as citizen, as political agent. To claim more for the citizen's conception of himself (for example, that ruling is the site of an activity which unites each with all of the rest so that they "perceive in the common force the working of their own wills") is to move outside and beyond liberalism. Ruling is here conceived as something done by each person *along with all others* so that being ruled is only to be governed by decisions that *he* along with all others has made. So rule is, in fact, self-rule; misrule, an indication of civic corruption. This view of a more participatory democracy is underwritten by a notion of community that cannot be reconciled with the individualism of liberalism. That irreconcilability is worth pursuing, however, since it provides another way to talk about liberalism's democratic consequences (and their limits).

The Liberal Presuppositions of "Strong" Democracy

Benjamin Barber's *Strong Democracy* argues for a theory of democracy that makes the relationship between ruling and being ruled less problematic by dramatically reducing, although not eliminating, the occasions when the individual's interests and the society's claims diverge. In this he follows Rousseau, whose goal in the *Social Contract* was to describe a form of political association "in which the whole strength of the community will be enlisted for the protection of the person and property of each constituent member, in such a way that each, when united to his fellows, renders obedience to his own will, and remains as free as he was before."[24] Where the individual's identity is importantly constituted by membership in the community and where everyone has an equal say in making decisions, Rousseau argues that rule is properly thought of and experienced as self-rule. Any feeling that others were overruling your choices or interests would be outweighed by your identification with the decision as an expression of the community's interest and, correspondingly, your interest *qua* member of the community. The good of ruling need not be compared to the good of being ruled well; in each, one sees the silhouette of the other. Or as Barber, in one of many endorsements of Rousseau's project, writes,

> Reasonable choices are generally public choices. That is to say, they are choices informed by an extension of perspective and by the reformulation of private interests in the setting of potential public goals. To be reasonable is therefore not to deny Self, but to place Self in the context of Other and to inform it with a sense of its dependence on the civic polity.[25]

This interlacing of ruling and being ruled required, as Rousseau realized, intense levels of political participation within a small community. What distinguishes Barber's *Strong Democracy* is the thesis that participatory democracy and the artifice of citizenship can recreate that identification of self and community within modern society.

Much of strong democracy is defined by contrasting it with the "thinness" of liberal democracy. Barber indicts liberalism in all its various manifestations—as a mode of reasoning, as a political doctrine, as a view of human nature—for undervaluing the public domain in general and hollowing out democracy in particular. Presented with unusual verve, the list of liberalism's offenses is, however, familiar. Liberal individualism is a politics for "atomic individuals defined by their solitude"; the chief point of liberal democracy is to "leave men alone" to pursue private interests; liberal citizens are tolerant but anemic, incapable of recognizing "public interests," without the convictions necessary to "concerted action." Cautious, instrumental, and representative, liberal democracy is "thin" in the sense that politics and public life are always seen as a threat to the "independence" of a life lived apart from the community: "every foray into the world of Others, cries out for an apology, a legitimation, a justification."[26]

The positive agenda of "strong democracy" is equally exhaustive, but at its core is the transformation of conflict and individuals to bring about a condition of social harmony. Both Barber's complaints about liberalism and his hopes for strong democracy turn, in part, on his judgment that the artifice of citizenship can reproduce in modern society precisely those community-oriented dispositions that Rousseau claimed for much smaller and more homogeneous societies. Strong democracy is, finally, a veritable collage of "commonality": common talk, deliberation, action, vision, consciousness, force, and so forth. And politics—the public domain—is the only possible site in which such community experiences can become manifest; the role of citizen, the only form of action appropriate for expressing such an associated way of life.

All of this Barber presents with an enthusiasm that seemingly exposes the liberal principle and liberal caution as little more than a failure of nerve. It comes, therefore, as something of a surprise to learn later that communal politics or strong democracy always verges on the profane, that community can become a euphemism for social tyranny, and political activity, an excuse for "totalism." More intriguing are the guarantees that prevent the corruption of participatory or strong democracy:

> When safeguards are ignored, when impatience for utopia overwhelms the need for a proximate resolution of transient conflicts, when the ideals of duty, fraternity, and community and the sovereignty of politics over society and of public over private are deployed without their indispensable strong democratic concomitants—equality, autonomy, pluralism, tolerance, and the separation of private and public—then to be sure democracy can become unitary and collectivistic.[27]

The "stronger" the democracy about which we are talking, the greater the authority of the community over its members, the more important are those "democratic concomitants" typically associated with the liberal tradition. "The objective," Barber adds, "is to reorient liberal democracy toward civic engagement and political community, not to raze it—destroying its virtues along with its defects."[28]

These comments by Barber suggest that the quarrel between "strong democracy" and that more complex democracy labeled as "thin" by Barber turns less, or at least not simply, upon how liberal each is, and more upon an estimation of how best to express and define the democratic ideal. So, for example, Barber concludes his book by noting:

> The case for democracy has two advocates: one speaks from human weakness and, pointing to the sand on which every claim to knowledge finally must rest, says with regret, "We must govern ourselves together;

> there is no one else who can govern for us." It is that voice to which the call for limits responds.
>
> But there is another, more affirmative advocate—one who perceives in speech itself, in the Greek faculty of reason called *logos,* the distinctive feature that sets humankind off from the animal kingdom and bestows the twin gifts of self-consciousness and other-consciousness. To this advocate the right of every individual to speak to others, to assert his being through the act of communication, is identified with the precious wellspring of human autonomy and dignity.[29]

The choice that Barber poses here between liberal resignation and "strong talk," granting that the choice is properly posed, sets aside as many issues as it settles. There is, for example, the questionable assumption, a sort of recycling of Aristotle, that only through political activity can an individual function as a morally conscientious person. But, finally, what makes strong democracy a solution to ruling and being ruled is the equation of political life with the life of the community, self-rule with social harmony.

What distinguishes this agenda from liberalism is not its celebration of a more public life, but its denigration of any more private life. While Mill and other liberals are sensitive to the ways in which political participation can uncover new ends around which individuals might cooperate, tolerance of a variety of ends that will vary from person to person, group to group, is equally critical to the liberal understanding of a more democratic way of life. It is part of the task of political thinking, then, to distinguish between those matters about which persons must agree or that are constitutive of their public identity and those private projects that are equally critical to a free and full life. Strong democracy, in contrast, outfits each individual with one garment, the mantle of citizenship so that all appear alike. Citizenship is not simply a way to acknowledge or publicly recognize all members of the community; it creates resemblance and mutuality: " 'I am like others,' and 'I like others,' " There is, however, something false-sounding about an empathic feeling that is a "contrivance of politics," the producer of an "*artificial* friend."[30] Throughout, Barber's account of strong democracy appropriates a vocabulary more commonly used to describe face-to-face relationships to characterize political activity, in general, and the role of citizen, in particular. That interpretative maneuver is his solution to Rousseau's problem of scale, i.e., how to nurture those sentiments necessary to fraternity in a large and socially diverse society.

But Barber's (metaphorical) community, unlike Rousseau's, is amorphous. That is, it is easier to see how through "talk" and "concerted action" the community is always in the process of being discovered; it is less easy to say when the community has, in fact, acted. From the strictly conceptual and communitarian point that the citizen is a "*we*-thinker," Barber too easily slides over to the equally formal and conceptual observation that all conflicts of interest are an occasion for "mutualism." But that sort of conceptual linkage does not respond to the fact that in modern society, each person has interests, experiences, and beliefs that add up to a life that cannot be summarized as a shared or communal existence. In societies that provide individuals with a large number of possibilities and the freedom to choose among them, the virtues constitutive of satisfying personal relationships, e.g., love and friendship, do little, if any, political work. The appeal to them is callow and evasive.

Given what I have termed social "distance" and social diversity, the liberal principle is ready to settle for less: asking that each recognize their equality *as* citizens, that there be guarantees against misrule, and that all be assured the equal opportunity to participate in politics. The liberal's fear of misrule and affirmation of popular rule interact in ways that complement and qualify each other. But the democratic consequences of liberalism are not so powerful (nor so implausible) as to reconcile perfectly ruling and being ruled. The subsequent liberal balancing act in which the very definite claims for political activity are often expressed as the reverse side of its very definite limits is not easy. To find that "balance" is not an end achieved, but is a fairly continuous activity for which liberalism provides some guidance. Occupying a position somewhere between a hyperperfectionist view of politics and a misanthropic outlook on society, this more democratic and prudent liberalism[31] reminds us, finally, not to ask too little of democratic citizens *(vide* Sartori) by expecting too much of them *(vide* Barber).

Notes

1. Judith N. Shklar, *Ordinary Vices* (Cambridge: Harvard University Press, 1984), p. 238.

2. Giovanni Sartori, *Democratic Theory* (Westport, Conn.: Greenwood Press, 1973), pp. 369, 372. Also, see his essay on "The Relevance of Liberalism in Retrospect," in *The Relevance of Liberalism,* ed. the Research Institute on International Change (Boulder: Westview Press, 1978), pp. 1-16.

3. Benjamin Barber, *Strong Democracy* (Berkeley: University of California Press, 1984), p. xi.

4. Ibid., p. 133.

5. Rousseau, *Social Contract,* I, vi and II, iv, passim.

6. Mill, *On Liberty* (New York: E. P. Dutton, 1951), p. 88.

7. Stephen Holmes, *Benjamin Constant and the Making of Modern Liberalism* (New Haven: Yale University Press, 1984), p. 20. Throughout, Holmes's thesis is that Constant rejected all simple divisions between liberalism and

democracy. Rather, Constant "urged his fellow citizens to integrate public action and private independence in a new pattern. Ancient and modern liberty should not be merely balanced but *combined*" (p. 78).

8. Richard Flathman, *The Practice of Rights* (Cambridge: Cambridge University Press, 1976), p. 7.

9. *Collected Works of John Stuart Mill,* vol. 3 (Toronto and London: University of Toronto Press, 1965), p. 938. Cited in C. L. Ten, *Mill On Liberty* (Oxford: Clarendon Press, 1980), p. 115.

10. Mill, *Representative Government* (New York: E. P. Dutton, 1951), p. 280.

11. Ibid., p. 289. For a fuller discussion of "freedom from interference" and "individuality" in Mill's thought, see Ten, *Mill on Liberty,* chap. 5.

12. Michael Walzer, *Spheres of Justice* (New York: Basic Books, 1983), p. 277.

13. *Principles of Political Economy,* v, vii, 6, p. 944. Cited by Graeme Duncan, *Marx and Mill* (Cambridge: Cambridge University Press, 1973), p. 249. The phrase "art of separation" is Michael Walzer's; see his "Liberalism and the Art of Separation," *Political Theory* 12 (August 1984): 315-30.

14. Robert N. Bellah, Richard Madsen, William M. Sullivan, Ann Swidler, and Steven M. Tipton, *Habits of the Heart* (Berkeley: University of California Press, 1985). While generally critical of American "individualism," the authors do find in their study of American commitments that "A rewarding private life is one of the preconditions for a healthy public life" (p. 163).

15. *On Liberty,* p. 156.

16. On the importance of "chastening authority" and avoiding excessive conceptions of the good citizen, see, respectively, George Kateb, "The Moral Distinctiveness of Representative Democracy," *Ethics* 91 (April 1981): 357-74; Richard Flathman, "Citizenship and Authority: A Chastened View of Citizenship," *News for Teachers of Political Science* (Summer 1981), pp. 9-20.

17. Dennis F. Thompson, *The Democratic Citizen* (Cambridge: Cambridge University Press, 1970), p. 10

18. See, respectively, Michael Walzer, *Radical Principles* (New York: Basic Books, 1980), p. 68; Barber, *Strong Democracy,* p. 71; Michael J. Sandel, *Liberalism and the Limits of Justice* (Cambridge: Cambridge University Press, 1982), passim.

19. For this and much else on this point, I am indebted to the discussion of community and fraternity by John Plamenatz in *Karl Marx's Philosophy of Man* (Oxford: Clarendon Press, 1975), chap. 14.

20. Cf. Shklar, pp. 76-77. In a useful commentary on an earlier (convention) draft of this paper, Joan Tronto properly worried, among other things, that I had finessed the issue of the sort of human knowledge that is critical to the liberal's democratic ideals. In claiming that liberal practices teach citizens a great deal about one another, I had, she noted, ignored the obvious possibility that citizens might not even see others as part of, say, the practice of rights. So they remain "strangers." Any satisfactory response would, I think, have to start with the distinction between personal relationships and those more public exchanges in which our interactions with others are often highly formal and episodic. The type of knowledge relevant to the latter exchanges does not require that we "know one another"; rather, we need to know how to act when placed in different settings. The strategy of a more democratic liberalism is to structure political life so that justice can operate

independent of such motives as benevolence or affection by encouraging behaviors and dispositions necessary to the success of the practices themselves. It is some sense of this strategy that I have tried to telegraph in substituting the phrase "mutual consideration" for "mutual respect." To ask that citizens accord each other "equal respect" would, in fact, require a sort of knowledge unavailable to citizens *qua* citizens.

21. Flathman, *The Practice of Rights,* pp. 185-86.

22. Mill, *Representative Government,* p. 326.

23. William Galston, "Defending Liberalism," *The American Political Science Review* 76 (September 1982): 628. This is a point that more sociological democratic liberals have long noted: "Is there one kind of social unity," Robert MacIver asked, "to which man owes his entire allegiance, one kind that fulfills all his needs? If we are content to take human society as it is the answer is clear: there is no one group, no single form of organization, that incorporates all the rest and wholly circumscribes the social life of man. Diverse groupings exist because man needs them, because no one suffices." *The Web of Government* (New York: Free Press, 1965), p. 309.

24. Rousseau, *Social Contract,* I, vi.

25. Barber, *Strong Democracy,* p. 112.

26. Ibid., pp. 20, 91, 106.

27. Ibid. p. 159.

28. Ibid., p. 308.

29. Ibid., p. 311.

30. Barber, "Political Talk and Strong Democracy," *Dissent* (Spring 1984): 220. Contrast Glenn Tinder's powerful defense of liberal tolerance as the foundation of community in *Tolerance* (Amherst: University of Massachusetts Press, 1976), pp. 54-86.

31. On the role of prudence in political thought in general and liberalism in particular, see John Dunn, "The Future of Liberalism," in *Rethinking Modern Political Theory* (Cambridge: Cambridge University Press, 1985), pp. 167-70.

– 10 –

Citizenship and Liberal Institutions

ELAINE SPITZ

This essay aims to rescue, from the depredations of liberalism's critics, that much maligned figure, the citizen of a modern democracy. Citizens appear in the critical literature in one of two guises: either we find them serving as shareholders in a Lockean joint–stock company,[1] furthering the welfare of the corporation only insofar as that does or does not increase their holdings or, alternately, they show up as pusillanimous persons, spectators passively watching the game of politics played by elites elected when a portion of the hopelessly manipulated electorate gets itself to the polls.[2] Both of these unflattering portraits gain plausibility as accurate renditions of a citizen by their contrast with the civic-minded republican depicted in direct democracies. Whether the scene takes place under an oak tree in Switzerland, in the agora at Athens, or at a town meeting in New England, citizens get together face to face, talk earnestly, listen intently, and vote openly. Deviations from this ideal apparent all around us—our use of intermediaries, secret ballots, and so on—reflect the fallen nature of man, the exigencies of efficiency, or the pernicious results of capitalism and its political offspring, liberalism—all regrettable matters.

Disrespect for the modern citizen leads to attacks on liberal democracy as a mere formal system, a woefully inadequate dilution of the democratic ideal experienced in some previous golden age, a polity drained of fraternity and equality and, therefore, too weak a version of self-government to merit strong support.

Now the citizenry of a modern state clearly is not composed of neighbors bonded by the intimacy of friendship, or comrades brought together by a common cause, or eschatological communities of believers building a New Jerusalem. Modern citizens may pursue a species of justice and recognize that equality of a specifiable kind obtains among them, but there the resemblance to "pure" democracy ends, and relationships less stringent and more precarious cry out for recognition. The model of direct democracy, however, turns a deaf ear, insists on standards that correspond to no significant operative institutions in the West, and by implication, denigrates those forms and procedures that are in active use, namely representation, Parliaments, and majority rule. These standard features of Western regimes, I want to contend, are not sickly substitutes for the superior, albeit impractical, forms of direct democracy. As communicative processes reflecting the structure of relations among modern citizens, they make moral claims of their own, claims that town meeting models of democracy cannot match. If we can develop a persuasive case for the importance of these characteristic institutions from a moral point of view, perhaps we can refurbish these portraits of the ugly citizen and paint the more complex creature who animates political life in contemporary democracies.

I

It would be a mistake to dismiss direct democracy as simply utopian. Nonfeasible modes can serve as inspiring ideals, and a model that provides for public life in a public sphere, with secure access for all, possesses formidable credentials.

One source of the model's strength derives from its recognition of a life in common and its appeal to a common sense. Questions faced by citizens revolve around what the group as a unit should do, not around what individuals want. Their united concern to solve a common problem contrasts with the tendency of representative democracies to encourage disparate subgroups in the polity. Separable interests elect representatives; a whole person votes directly. Special interests back candidates and policies in pluralist systems; in direct forums a public interest is sought. Trouping to the meeting itself expresses a commonality that retreat to private associations negates. Unlike the isolated hermit, familiar in the literature of behavioral political science, who emerges periodically to pull a lever in a voting booth, citizens in a direct democracy are social creatures and form opinions that reflect their estimate of what others think and their assessment of strategic possibilities of enactment. Their votes indicate, in addition to their sentiments for or against this or that policy, their willingness to throw in their lot with a particular community and to sustain its existence.

Second, direct democracies exclude no one and extend a welcome without regard to birth, wealth, knowledge, or talent. Each person has a right to speak. No one gets more than one vote. In representative assemblies, on the other hand, only those elected attend, rules of debate limit speakers, and committee structures fragment each one's vote.

In their strongest form, direct assemblies part company with debating societies, and their discussions—rather than being aimless, or exploratory, or speculative—lead to conclusive decisions. They result in the purchase of a new fire engine, a change in the tax rate, or some other direct contributions to the quality of life in a community. (Proportional representation theories that focus exclusively on reproducing a mirror image of the electorate ignore this orientation to action that characterizes self–government.)

Two common criticisms of direct democracy turn on arguments whose merits will not be addressed, and from which the position I want to develop should be disassociated. Standard-bearers in one political camp agree that "direct democracy is a more genuine democracy" but worry that it may be "too fragile."[3] Instability results, Giovanni Sartori claims, when societies divided along class lines meet face to face and try to settle their differences politically, while indirect democratic mechanisms promote the diffusion of confrontational sentiments into plural, usually commercial activities. The fit here between disapproval of direct democracy and stability seems problematic. No one has spelled out just why representation should mute irreconcilable conflict and face to face encounters provoke it. Aristotle's strictures about the importance of middle classes may apply in some unspecified way, or critics may have in mind the empirical evidence of rapid oscillations in ancient Greece between tyranny and democracy, or behind Sartori's observations may lurk an image of intelligent elites interposing standards of justice between hot-headed rivals. Volatile emotions, especially in large crowds, concern anyone hoping for rationality in political affairs, but surely some features of direct democracy encourage as much deliberation or reflection as elections of representatives; more strongly, partisans of participatory modes have argued that standing up before one's neighbors inculcates responsibility and squelches prejudices with a success that secret ballots cannot match.[4]

I do not pretend to know what produces stability in governments, but I suspect that stability itself is a weak value, desirable only in proportion to the merits of the status quo. From a moral point of view, the substance of change matters more than its size or mere existence. Few want peace at any price. For these reasons we can afford to bracket arguments of the instability stripe.

In the other quarter, trumpeting a challenge to direct democracy are those who recognize self-government as a good political strategy but not a good in itself. According to Leo Strauss and his followers, because universal suffrage and widespread popular participation create consent otherwise unobtainable in the modern world, prudence demands acceptance of liberal democracy. Still, this should not lead to confusion about egalitarianism. Excellence, on this view,[5] remains the proper standard for societies, even if they fail to recognize the uneven distribution of good character and understanding and fail to institutionalize an appropriate hierarchic order. Representative democracy wins support over direct variations, for those who share this perspective, because by providing some filtration of gold from dross, leaders may attain their rightful place and find scope for their talents.[6] Face-to-face assemblies lack bulwarks against pernicious leveling, and therefore, where tradition obviates aristocracy, regimes that train a responsible elite and inculcate respect for the liberally educated among the masses remain the best strategic alternative.

Direct democracy, this school concludes, does not facilitate the reign of virtue or its guardians, while representative democracy, with the protection offered by its system of rights and with the opportunities for leadership presented by its multi-layered election system, looks more attractive. Since Socrates, face to face with the Athenian assembly, was convicted, these critics of direct democracy may have a point. (Although, as Strauss concedes, a democracy tolerated Socrates for seventy years, and that may be the best we can hope for in an imperfect world.)[7] Liberals, nevertheless, might agree with their own "saint of rationalism" John Stuart Mill, who wrote that "from the general weakness of the people or of the state of civilization, the one and his counsellors, or the few, are not likely to be habitually exempt . . . ," and therefore "it would be absurd to construct institutions for the mere purpose of taking advantage of such possibilities."[8] Liberals might insist on the primacy of experience in political intelligence, and the consequent inappropriateness of hierarchy. Comparable infirmities, as Mill argued, have afflicted governments not directly dependent upon mass opinion, and democracies that afford people alternatives and provide forums for discussion that can improve the quality of public opinion are as far along the road to human betterment as any political system can take a people. Although concern for the kind of equality relevant to communication among citizens will form part of the core argument launched below, that argument will not turn on the case for wise and virtuous rulers or on the natural rights of natural leaders. Those doctrines are simply rejected as inappropriate for democracies.

II

We can begin to face the issues that do concern us by asking, who comprises the public expected to display public spiritedness in a democracy? What connects those thrown together by fate on the same piece of real estate in the twentieth century? A diverse group of semi-strangers, they share only a superficial culture, a thin thread of history, or common language, or institutions that cannot bear much weight. Geographic mobility encourages migration and discourages attachment to a particular landscape. Christendom has splintered into multiple denominations, numerous sects impress themselves on religious consciousness, and the absence of shared attitudes toward basic questions about life and death has begun to strain mutual vocabularies, as the debate about abortion attests. Burke's "little platoons," in which people once gained their sense of self and out of which they once spun their relationships, now have international dimensions: athletes compete across national boundaries, professionals hold worldwide conferences, vacationers sample all the mountains and beaches of the globe, lovers crisscross continents, and movie fans watch the same films in any of the world's capitals.

Mass migrations have supplemented individual cosmopolitans, moving French Algerians north for political reasons, Greeks and Turks west for economic purposes, Asians east in response to demographic pressures. All the world is America now in a sense Locke never imagined, with shifting populations mixing traditions and minimizing relatedness. Appeals to mutuality in this setting strike one as odd, sugarcoating for the difficulties of operating a territory with those of diffuse loyalties and tenuous local political attachments. No one who has lived through the twentieth century can pretend that nationalism lacks potency. Nevertheless, the tenacity of the nation-state should not blind us to those eroding forces also at work.

Mass society compounds the problem of civil association by broadening the range of those included in political affairs so that any general meeting is likely to embrace a motley crew. Hannah Arendt romanticizes about self-selected leaders detached from personal interest and motivated by concern for the general welfare,[9] while anyone who has ever attended an open community meeting has found an assortment of egoists, single-interest fanatics, well-intentioned bumblers, neurotics "acting out," and other tedious types. "Empathy," "affective ties," "learning to value one another," and other jolly phrases that pepper the commendatory descriptions of communitarians hardly seem warranted by the tiresome efforts necessary to maneuver at a meeting of a random sample of one's modern neighbors.[10]

Psychological patterns of domination and subordination that run just beneath the surface of public meetings explain a goodly part of their limited utility as forums where genuine exchange of views can take place. The timid sit alongside the domineering, eloquent voices confound the articulate, and particular relationships—husband and mother-in-law, student and teacher, doctor and patient—complicate communication. Public discussions, therefore, may reflect the strength and weakness of various personalities rather than the actual political sentiments coursing through a community.

Economic relationships augment the lack of authenticity imposed by psychological and cultural configurations and increase the pressures for conformity. Will the small businessman at a town meeting contradict the loan officer of his bank? the grocery clerk oppose his boss, the store owner? Karl Marx could have written a chapter on the fetishism of participation! Participation talked about apart from structural constraints obscures the way individuals enact different aspects of their being in different settings. Masks put on to play parts in the human drama do not fall off at public meetings to reveal abstract creatures unembedded in social roles. Habermas's ideal speech situations appear unpersuasive in part because they ignore the social construction of being and posit abstract people without concrete jobs or personalities or social standing. We do not know what would remain if we peeled off all identifying layers of a person, but some have suspected that what would stand revealed is not the pure essence of personhood, but emptiness or a creature not recognizably human.

Small face-to-face groups tend to exacerbate the brute force of inequalities because they deprive individuals of the resource that can modify economic and social pressure, namely factional friends. Families interpose love and loyalty between dominations within the unit and support members when they venture beyond its confines. Labor unions substitute group solidarity for the weakness of individuals on their own in the marketplace. Churches provide networks of parishioners committed to helping each other. Free people, as anyone can observe, usually function through organized associations that mediate their civic relationships. Stripped of allies, naked among unequals, individuals cannot hope to fare well.

A radically individualist scenario undoubtedly has a certain appeal to Calvinists, exemplified by Rousseau's warning against subsidiary corporate allegiances: "It is important, then, in order to have a clear declaration of the general will, that there should be no partial associations in the state, and that every citizen should express only his own opinion."[11] But when only a unitary, society-wide group exists, there, liberals suspect, politics becomes superfluous, and tyranny of the one, the few, or the many takes over.[12] The absence of pluralism detracts from the persuasiveness of direct democracy as an appropriate inspiration for politics, and suggests that we ought to look more closely at the alleged moral attributes of direct participation.

Given the attenuated relations between citizens in mass societies, what recommends face-to-face politics as a contribution to the good life? Supporters of "pure democracy" claim that public life is a good in itself[13] and that a taste for it, like a taste for the fine arts, broadens and ennobles the individual. Moreover, democratic egalitarianism, they say, requires equal participation. Let us consider these claims.

A good citizen, most would agree, cares for matters beyond the personal: giving a marvelous birthday party for one's child does not count; collecting for the heart fund does. But two problems immediately beg for attention: one concerning the distinction between public and private action, and the other, the criteria for a priority ordering of activities. In Europe, governmental subsidies provide for an array of local and national operas, ballets, and symphonies. In the United States, private groups make provision for the fine arts, raising money for productions, arranging tours, hiring artistic directors, and so on. It seems arbitrary to label the very same activities public in one country and private in another. Welfare provides another example of an arena alternately labeled public or private, depending upon whether activities are conducted by male ministers or an established church collecting and distributing taxes, or female members of voluntary associations raising and dispensing contributions. Selective perceptions operate here as much as palpable differences in power.

Nor does there seem to be a hierarchy of publics so that one can claim that working for the American Association for the United Nations constitutes a higher-order activity than promoting the welfare of New York City. Aristotle's self-sufficing criteria no longer apply to any units, and no logic produces a hierarchy of public functions among cities, states, international organizations, professional associations, scientific teams, churches, or charities. The question of whether or not to purchase a new fire engine for the local hook and ladder company, a decision made by a governmental unit, does not have higher (or lower) status than the question of what percent of the local Episcopal Church's revenues will go to shelter the homeless, a decision up to a private association of coreligionists. Does power exercised in one sort of public activity take moral precedence over other sorts? Accounts that try to establish a meaningful hierarchy tend to reduce politics to questions of war or peace (e.g., C. Wright Mills, *The Power Elite*) a move no longer adequate for discussions of international affairs, much less for domestic policy.

We have developed multiple forums to handle our multiplicity of interests and the diversity of people with whom we are involved. It is not obvious that a single forum attended by all would serve a better, more glamorous cause. Worse, a single unit with one overarching purpose may take a pernicious path, and then increased participation may frustrate the good more than promote it. In South Africa, some have argued, the more one participates, the more one legitimizes the regime one hopes to defeat.[14]

Undoubtedly, participation in life beyond the confines of narrow self-interest has character-building propensities, perhaps of heroic dimensions. Its advantages, however, adhere to the making of *some* choices, those most important to the individual, as well, if not better, than making *all* possible choices.[15] John Stuart Mill's argument, in which he firmly ties self-development to utility, necessitates widespread participation in order to insure self-protection. One gets in the habit of functioning politically, and studies of town meetings confirm that those most practiced in the art fare better than novices.[16] Even so, effective experience can be less than universal in scope.

The problem of equality still remains, for differential amounts of participation on different stages may not leave intact the equalities essential to democratic citizenship. Robert Dahl taught a generation of American political scientists that elites, with the acquiescence of their constituencies, do control, albeit each elite only within its own bailiwick. We have no reason to suppose that X amounts of power over education equals Y amounts of power over housing. Does this situation negate the sort of equality necessary to democracies? Only, I think, if we ignore those allegedly passive constituencies. Everyone, Dahl would agree, retains the right to withhold his or her consent, and that means we must consider each as the person who might cast the decisive vote. Equality of concern functions, therefore, to maintain everyone's equal standing in that sense of "equal" most important in political life. Sameness of activity seems unnecessary; equality of condition, irrelevant.

But some inequalities (which ones may vary with time and circumstance) do matter. Power differentials that interfere with the articulation of an independent viewpoint, for example, do undermine equality in an important sense, and thus lead to consideration of one major weapon against such disparities of power: representation.

Forging connections between "pure" democracy and numerous virtues has become commonplace, while the moral status of representation has been either neglected or bemoaned for its dilution of an individual's ability to impress his sense of justice on politics, its debasement of the self-development potential of political participation, and its alleged inducement of citizen passivity and production of radical inequalities between representatives and constituents. While some filtration of opinion undoubtedly occurs when we resort to representation, this assessment is less then fair.

People join groups in order to augment their influence over aspects of their lives. Tocqueville, recognizing the importance of those "partial associations" Rousseau disparaged, put it this way:

> As soon as several inhabitants of the United States have taken up an opinion or a feeling which they wish to promote in the world, they look out for mutual assistance; and as soon as they have found one another out, they combine. From that moment they are no longer isolated men, but a power seen from afar, whose actions serve for an example and whose language is listened to.[17]

Groups and their representatives maneuver in the political realm more effectively than individuals. We join groups or commission others to do what we find difficult or distasteful, and thereby acquire the resources of expertise and the strength of allies. The range of interests we can pursue increases dramatically.

Does this use of representatives turn citizens into Casper Milquetoasts who watch others do what Cincinnatus did for himself? The question is but another way of stating the familiar charge that freedom in democracies prevails only on election day, and after that, elites take over. If we think of representatives as those who make present the will of their constituents, the charge has plausibility. Wills, however, do not exist out there as part of the landscape like trees and mountains. Wills have to be created. They form in the process of political give and take. Constituents do not have wills about political particulars and cannot know in advance, on election day, just what the important, practical political questions will turn out to be. Constituents do possess, however, an idea of justice, an orientation toward moral rules both substantive and procedural that ought to apply in practical life, and they can expect their representatives to inject into the resolution of political problems the sense of the right with which they feel sympathy.[18]

What determines a person's orientation toward justice is his political judgment, his general assessment of the political scene. Citizens do not watch passively the plays called by others. Rather, they actively judge those plays and, like Monday-morning quarterbacks, approve or disapprove every move, often making clear that the coach's tenure in office depends on their opinion about how the game might have been won, and how the next game should be handled. A barrage of material informs the generation of political judgments, flooding mailboxes with exhortations to join, support, or contribute. Information comes from a newsletter from the archdiocese, a report from an elected official, a notice from the PTA, or a flyer from a local civic association, and exchanges of opinion occur in bars, on park benches, or over dinner. Not one day a year, but every day people observe and react, i.e., they judge the play of politics and develop opinions about how the game should go forward. They resign from group A in disgust and welcome group B as a superior replacement. They judge their representatives and decide whether their personal views have had a proper hearing and whether their interests, broadly conceived, have been adequately looked after. In democracies, where any disparity between public opinion and power tends to delegitimate the state, citizens exercising political judgment have considerable impact.

"Pure" democracy depicts radical individualists in friendly conversation with equals, instead of semi-strangers among whom unequal power relations obtain. Representatives in antiliberal attacks always diminish a person's ability to make operative his own sense of justice, while in the alternative view put forward here, representation enhances one's ability to function politically and authentically over a wide range of activities and, through exercise of the faculty of judgment, to maintain an active part in political life. Representative government, of course, has weaknesses of its own unrehearsed here. That should not detract, however, from the importance of recognizing its moral strengths.

III

Just as friends converse *tête-à-tête* but citizens prefer intermediaries, so lovers arrange a rendezvous but citizens elect Parliaments. Why is it less than satisfactory, when a public matter needs attention, to follow the advice of the American folksinger to "pass out a leaflet, call you a meetin', get together, talk it over, speak yer mind, decide to do somethin' about it?"[19] Perhaps we have lost something we ought to retrieve in the simplicity of the general open assembly. By contrast with a town meeting, Parliaments appear formal and arcane. Only representatives can attend, not the public at large; they splinter into myriad committees; they depend on organization by political parties; and notoriously, they institutionalize opposition, not harmony.

The power of the town meeting model may reflect its success in capturing the democratic sense of sovereignty. To the extent that the logic of a legal system or the legitimacy of a nation requires the presence of a court of last appeal, a sovereign person or institution believed to have final say in a democracy, the repository of that power must be the people themselves in their corporate capacity. It is they who can change the constitution, elect and depose executives, and otherwise make policy. What better exemplifies the whole people in action than decisions taken face to face in a meeting open to all citizens? Revolutionary situations apparently confirm the validity of such meetings as expressions of the general will, for spontaneous grassroots councils arise in volatile times and take into their own hands the tasks at hand. Hannah Arendt cites approvingly the Soviets in Russia, the Paris Commune, the Rate in Germany, and the councils of the Hungarian revolt.[20]

The very strength of general meetings as repositories of a general will, as forums for the expression of unity of purpose and commitment, suggests the source of their weakness. If politics is not simply the imposition of a unified will giving direction to a whole, but the adjustment to each other's diverse wills of competing, cooperating, and compromising semiautonomous associations, then general meetings may lack the facilities for political management that Parliaments possess. For many of the things we ordinarily mean by "ruling," sovereignty proves an insufficient concept. Passing laws remains an ineffectual process, for example, until supplemented by administration and enforcement, the spirit and substance of which can undermine or enhance the intent of lawmakers. But a citizen assembly does not have a full-time General Accounting Office or permanent investigating committees to oversee administration. A similar lacuna in general meetings afflicts initiatory legislative processes. Parliaments, organized by political parties, select issues from among competing concerns, piece them together as one particular set of problems rather than another, negotiate a priority order, and only, at the end, frame a specific question that narrows choice to a manageable number of alternatives. At town meetings, the final form of a question depends arbitrarily on the last speaker. Weighing and winnowing is left to the mercy of chance. Constitutional and institutional rules designed to process the claims of organized forces and keep them in competitive equilibrium have no counterparts in direct democracy models. Citizen assemblies, consequently, must depend on executive committees with significant powers to set agendas and monitor administrations that are hidden from view. In classical Greece, one scholar has claimed, "the advance of democracy found its main enemy as a rule in the competence and power of the Council," an executive committee with deep roots in the clans and the priesthood.[21] The more town meetings attempt to overcome their deficient ability to handle pre- and postlegislative functions, the more they come to resemble representative Parliaments where formal hearings, loyal oppositions, and other institutions routinely provide legislative leadership for a wide range of governmental activities.

Adversary styles and majoritarianism suit liberal societies struggling to articulate multiple ends and to foreclose as few choices as possible, while direct democracies have an affinity for consensus politics and unanimity. "The basic principle of democracy," Ralph Barton Perry wrote, "is not majority but unanimity."[22] People's inability to get hold of the truth, from this point of view, necessitates majority rule, a procedure always stigmatized by its failure to achieve harmony and its resort to coercion of those who disagree. In one New England town studied by a political scientist, the townspeople denied their fundamental disagreements and explained political contention in terms of "conflicting estimates of who can best pursue the common good" or a technical matter of finding the correct solution.[23] For those moved by a classical vision of unity, the "sense of the wholeness of things" which was the "most typical feature of the Greek mind,"[24] the language of contracts and bargains and coalitions strikes harsh chords.

Rousseau sounds better. "The sovereign," he said, "needs only to exist in order to be what it ought to be."[25] Since society is morally preferable to the state of nature, the moral good must consist of what is good for the community, those policies that, in Rousseau, constitute the sector where individual interests overlap. Each realizes his highest ends in submission to the will for the common interest, and the state's sovereignty coincides with its moral preeminence over all other forms of human association. No one can object to state power in the name of justice, because ultimate authority itself defines political right. To join a community is to promise oneself to its good, and the concept of the general will for that good thus circumvents the question of individual freedom. The moral sovereignty of the community leads to its expression in a civil religion or other symbols of public solidarity.

An alternate liberal vision of politics depends less on moral absolutes and more on the unexalted constant adjustment of reactions to circumstances. In the tradition of republicanism to which John Pocock has called our attention, for example, a shifting balance of forces motivates political life, and the common good refers only to equilibrium.[26] In the same spirit, modern liberalism does not flee "the babble of raucous interests and insistent rights," as one communitarian has disdainfully put it,[27] but embarks instead upon the adventure of fashioning a world from agreements endless in their number and variety, and building institutions to process fairly those raucous interests and insistent rights.

Direct assemblies do not work well as arenas in which to balance forces. Face to face, we tend to observe the norms of conversation and drawing room decorum. The noisier business of a heterogenous people, only tenuously related to each other, demands the skill of lawyers and other intermediaries capable of serving as advocates of contending parties, inventors of bargains and agreements, leaders of coalitions, or judges pinning down interpretations of extant rules. Admittedly useless or nuisances when a moral vision of what is good for the community needs to be discovered, politicians and lawyers flourish in procedural states that dare to operate with no more orthodoxy about the substance of the public weal than that produced by fair rules under which shifting alignments of citizens solve problems in piecemeal fashion.

Parliaments, then, like representatives, can be understood to augment, not diminish, the political efficacy of citizens. Sovereignty commands consent to the maintenance of the unit without encompassing the wider range of governmental activities crucial to a politics centered on the mutual adjustment of groups under agreed-upon rules. Geared to balancing forces and creating coalition majorities rather than expressing a sovereign will, current Parliaments presume little cohesion among the disparate purposes of citizens and their organizations. What citizens have in common is primarily their common attention to the same political performances. As makers and shapers of political judgment they lend legitimacy to democratic republics and impart a style to their political life.

IV

Political arguments about the positive features of liberal democracies do not address directly the philosophic question of what constitutes desirable political agency. Just what sort of institutionalization and distribution of the power of political agency would conform to liberal canons of justice?

Liberalism has generated a variety of answers. Lockean liberals would look to agreement and count as acceptable whatever social contract citizens sign, tacitly or explicitly; others, following Kant (perhaps in a modern Rawlsian restatement), would wait to invest their answer with more substantive content; while in the John Stuart Mill tradition, some version of utility would be found persuasive. Disparate philosophic grounds among liberals, however, have often led to similar priorities and practices: open societies, with ingenious procedural mechanisms to process diverse claims.

More important, many liberals would resist the very question about justice because it involves a deontological conception of politics they reject. Societies do not begin with a programmatic notion of right and devise policies derived from it; policies arise from mutual adjustment and not from a preconceived vision of the public weal, or so some liberals would contend.

Nevertheless, liberals might wish to stipulate qualities that any system of political agency ought to include. They might agree that there are good forms of agency and bad, and that some distributions appear more desirable than others.

A half-dozen appropriate criteria come quickly to mind. Whatever system of agency is employed, for example, it must be reversible and modifiable in deference to liberal notions about the importance of always maintaining a prudential allowance for error. Second, agency goes hand in hand wtih accountability, which means set periods of office-holding, recall and impeachment mechanisms not too corroded by disuse, and alternation of those in office through popular elections. The number of interests, classes, and groups should be inclusive, with encouragement offered unorganized voices that might be struggling for articulation. Buttressed by sunshine laws, information must circulate freely through mass media and parochial presses. And, many would insist, the quality of discussion matters. A citizenry beguiled by style, not substance, is likely to form political judgments of an inferior variety. Although political rhetoric will always have a place in politics, elements of taste will inform the level of judgment and affect outcomes. Finally, disparities of power loom important insofar as they affect the ability of individuals and sets of individuals to make their authentic views part of the political process.

Behind these criteria lurks the concept of political judgment, the activity of citizens that involves them in appraisals of the political scene and injects their reactions into the political arena. More than a practical activity because it conforms more or less to standards, less than an activity of pure justice because it depends thoroughly on circumstances, political judgment is the preeminent task of citizenship. A people forms and becomes a public unit through the discussions and exchanges of information that go into the development of political judgment.[28] Everyone has opinions (not, *note bene,* reducible to interests) that enter political life through representatives and representative institutions.

Here is a daring conception of politics separated from truth and orthodoxy and distinct from direct democracy, which is not obviously superior or deficient only in scale. The strengths offered by communitarian models, liberal democracy can duplicate or better: public spaces replace a single agora, the welcome mat for everyone includes organizations not just individuals, and the range of power stretches beyond sovereignty to aspects of ruling more important than pronunciamentos by an ultimate source of legitimacy.

Because the critics of liberalism have failed to come to grips with many features of liberal democracy, their portraits of modern citizens lack verisimilitude. In the United States people devote astonishing amounts of time and energy to public service—coaching sandlot ball clubs, serving as docents in museums, planting bulbs in public parks, raising money for community projects. A society that starts its children out selling Girl Scout cookies and graduates them to *pro bono* work as lawyers may be the most participatory the world has ever known. In these activities, as well as at school and work, interacting with others in the community, the citizen develops judgments about those among whom he lives, about their needs and wants and opinions. When issues arise he or she has a sense of what can or ought to be done. But as active moral reasoners, citizens need not venture alone into the uncertain world of face-to-face encounters. Liberal representational institutions, providing experts and cohorts, present more pleasant and effective alternatives.

Notes

1. C. B. Macpherson, *The Political Theory of Possessive Individualism* (Oxford: Clarendon Press, 1962).
2. Benjamin Barber, "Political Talk, Strong Democracy," *Dissent* (Spring 1984): pp. 215-22.
3. Giovanni Sartori, *Democratic Theory* (New York: Praeger, 1965).
4. Barber, "Political Talk," p. 220.
5. Leo Strauss, *On Tyranny* (Ithaca: Cornell University Press, 1963), p. 207.
6. Martin Diamond, Winston Mills Fisk, and Herbert Garfinkle, *The Democratic Republic* (Chicago: Rand McNally, 1966), p. 82.
7. Leo Strauss, *What Is Political Philosophy?* (Glencoe, Ill.: Free Press, 1959), p. 363.
8. John Stuart Mill, *Representative Government* (London: Oxford University Press, 1912), pp. 224-25.
9. Hannah Arendt, *On Revolution* (New York: Viking Press, 1965), p. 282.
10. Barber, "Political Talk."
11. Jean Jacques Rousseau, *The Social Contract,* trans. Willmoore Kendall (Chicago: Regnery, 1954), p. 29.
12. Bernard Crick, *In Defense of Politics* (London: Weidenfeld and Nicolson, 1962).
13. Hannah Arendt, "The Crisis in Culture," in *Between Past and Future* (New York: Viking Press, 1961), chap. 6.
14. William Nelson, *On Justifying Democracy* (London: Routledge and Kegan Paul, 1980), p. 45.
15. Ibid., p. 47.
16. Jane Mansbridge, *Beyond Adversary Democracy* (New York: Basic Books, 1980).
17. Alexis de Tocqueville, *Democracy in America,* Reeve Text as revised by Francis Bowen (New York: Vintage Books, 1959), vol. 2, pp. 117-18.
18. A. Phillips Griffiths, "How Can One Person Represent Another?" in *Representation,* ed. Hanna Pitkin (New York: Atherton, 1969), pp. 133-56.
19. Peter Seeger, M. Lampbell, and L. Hays, "Talking Union" (Columbia Records, 1940).
20. Arendt, *On Revolution,* p. 975.
21. Victor Ehrenberg, *The Greek State* (New York: W. W. Norton, 1964), p. 61.
22. Ralph Barton Perry, *Puritanism and Democracy* (New York: Vanguard Press, 1944), p. 490.
23. Mansbridge, *Beyond Adversary Democracy,* p. 77.

24. H. D. F. Kitto, *The Greeks* (Baltimore: Penguin, 1951), p. 169.

25. Rousseau, *Social Contract,* p. 18.

26. J. G. A. Pocock, *The Machiavellian Moment* (Princeton: Princeton University Press, 1975), pp. 3-48.

27. Barber, "Political Talk," p. 216.

28. Ernst Wollrath, "Reflective Judgment and the Concept of the Political," IPSA, Paris, July 1985.

– 11 –

Pragmatic Liberalism: Uniting Theory and Practice

CHARLES W. ANDERSON

Liberal political theory is conventionally concerned with the most fundamental questions of political order, with first principles and basic constitutional arrangements. It teaches us to regard the great issues of legitimacy and obligation, of the relation of the powers of government, of democratic process and individual right, of the relative priority of liberty and equality, as the essential questions of political thought. Liberal theory makes it seem that the first task of citizens, and the basic object of political deliberation, is to engage in a persistent reconsideration of the constitutive principles of the regime. It is as though the body political were to be understood as a constitutional convention perennially in session that could, if it would, wipe the slate clean at any time and begin anew on fresh foundations.

Formal liberal theory is written from the point of view of the lawgiver and the constitution-maker. And it is this quality of formal liberal theory that makes it seem remote, academic, and an imperfect guide to practical political reason. For despite our memory of the extraordinary venture in political architectonics that accompanied America's beginnings, we recognize that the deliberate reconstruction of a regime is a most unusual form of political action. We better understand ourselves as parties to an ongoing political project, one which it would be imprudent, if not impossible, to unravel and recast along fundamentally different lines. Our public problems arise within a complex legacy of ideas and institutions, and the issues that call for deliberative action concern the fitting of that legacy to new contingencies and opportunities.

Furthermore, questions of the regime are remote from practical experience. Deliberation on the fundamental issues is largely a matter of speculative musings, topical conversation, an affair of off-hours. The significant problems of political judgment for the citizen are immediate and local. They arise as much from the contexts of work and social function as from formal political responsibility. Even when the citizen functions as public official, as legislator, administrator, or judge, the focus of deliberation is not apt to be on fundamental principles in themselves, but these only in relation to a set of concrete projects, programs and functions.

Thus, we enter public life always in mid-stream, never at the beginning. We are seized with a particular project: the construction of a road, the location of a factory, the adoption of a land use plan, a question of curriculum or research priorities in the university, a decision on doctrine or standard operating procedures for an enterprise. We confront the dilemmas of public life from the vantage point of a specific role or position of responsibility. We are mindful of the expectations of those who will be affected by our actions. Our deliberations reflect conceptions of purpose, tradition, and normal practice of a particular going concern. And out of such partial, piecemeal decisions, the larger constitutive order of the liberal polity gradually emerges and takes on settled form.

The problem then is to connect this immediate, contextual quality of political action in the pluralist polity to the larger theory of the liberal regime. In what is to come, I shall sketch a conception of such a relation of theory to practice. To do so is to restate and reinterpret a particular variant of liberal theory, that which has its roots in the tradition of philosophic pragmatism. In this version of liberalism, the emphasis is not on constitutive principles or the elemental relations of the individual to the political order. Rather, pragmatic liberalism focuses on the adaptive relations of individuals acting as participants in a wide variety of associations and undertakings. These enterprises, for pragmatic liberalism, partake of the public functions of the liberal regime. The regulation and husbandry of the regime of pluralist associations become a primary political concern. Furthermore, insofar as these associations are presumed to play a public role, their governance is a form of political responsibility.

Such a theory, then, must address the problem of political judgment from two distinct points of view. The first is that of the citizen of the polity, concerned with the government of the pluralist order. The second is that of the citizen of a specific enterprise, concerned with its performance.

Similarly, there are two basic problems to be considered. The first concerns the way in which the social function of the enterprise is performed. The second involves an appraisal of the internal political order of the organization, its character as a private government. Both perspectives, and both problems, entail the application of liberal principles to "practice," practice here understood as the systematically organized "ways of doing things" that arise within liberal society and give it form and substance.

I shall first discuss the theory of public decision and political judgment, the ideal of method for relating principles to practice, that might be associated with pragmatic liberalism. I shall note particularly how this conception of method is related to formal, rationalist liberalism and how it differs from classic doctrine. I shall go on to consider some of the larger questions of politics and the regime that seem to follow from this idea of practical political reason.

Pragmatic Liberalism and Political Judgment

We do not tend to make up public problems. Rather, we are confronted by them, or charged with them, in a specific context and role of responsibility. Our deliberations tend to focus on "my station and its duties" and on the immediate ends in view.

Of course, it is precisely the intent of liberal theory to detach us from the exigencies of the situation, to place us, in imagination, in the position of the dispassionate observer, stripped of preconception and interest, who can judge from a stance of impartiality and neutrality. The purpose of the great artifacts of liberal thought, of such devices as the state of nature and the individual contractor, is to create a situation in which we would be called upon to reflect on those fundamental principles of public life to which all rational persons might consent. Thus liberalism seems to suggest that we must return to the foundation questions as a necessary prologue to action.

The practical intent of liberal theory, however, is also to fashion a decision rule, a maxim, that would yield beneficial public results if applied consistently to any situation of choice. In any contested issue there must be a point on which the decision turns, and the utilitarian argues that this should be a calculation of aggregate social utility; the classical liberal, a preference for the option that best maximizes individual choice; the Rawlsian, a concern for equality at the margin, once considerations of rights are duly accounted for. Each of these may be understood as a rule of marginal choice, a counsel of what to do when the situation itself yields no evident resolution. And applied routinely in local, immediate contexts, the result of relying on any of these maxims would be to move society, gradually and incrementally, toward the realization of some conception of the larger liberal ideal.

Liberal theory requires that public decisions rest on known and universal principles. Liberalism, historically, is a long endeavor to reduce the degree of arbitrariness in public affairs.[1] For this reason policy making cannot be understood merely as a matter of art or style. The public official has no right to base decisions on hunch, instinct, or even an experienced "feel" for the requirements of the situation.

Liberalism is a language of justification, and it is not good enough to say simply that one "knew" the right thing to do or "had a sense" that one should proceed in a certain way. Liberalism becomes a discipline of practical reason as one searches for a rule, a principled ground of choice. The search for principled justification becomes a corrective to initial impulse. The solution that "seemed right" may not stand up under scrutiny. One perfects a design for public action in contemplation of the reasons one must eventually give for it.

Nonetheless, the requirements of liberal justification are exceedingly demanding, and from these the dilemmas of liberal political theory arise. Classical liberalism shares with classic science a commitment to the ideal of rational proof, rooted in the conviction that a free person need accept no conception of truth or social good unless, in the full light of reason and evidence, they find that they can "do no other." And this implies that the foundation principles of the liberal polity must be demonstrated formally, beyond disinterested criticism or reasonable doubt.[2] And this test liberal political theory could not meet. It is possible to create systems of liberalism, but liberalism has never been reduced to a system.

In the end, the requirement that practical decisions be grounded in universal principles becomes an act of conviction on the part of the policy maker. In acting on principle, one commits oneself to pursue an image of liberal society, consistently and incrementally, as a rule of choice for each relevantly similar case that arises within the purview of one's authority. Nonarbitrariness becomes ideological integrity. Decisions are not whimsical, random, or interested so long as they can be shown to be related to *some* coherent system of liberal values. So long as officials make the value bases of their decisions clear and act consistently from them, the citizenry can appraise their conduct and decide, electorally, whether to pursue this version of liberalism in the next period or change it.[3] Liberal theory becomes democratic theory as the system of liberal principles to be pursued comes to rest, in the end, on the preferences of citizens.

In such an image of practical liberalism, it is presumed that we hold our principles *a priori,* that we *enter* the political arena as committed advocates of free markets, utilitarianism, Rawlsian justice, or whatever. To act consistently from principle, to achieve detachment from the contingencies of role and situation, we must know in advance the ultimate maxim under which particular cases will be subsumed and decided. Comprehensive philosophic reflection, culminating in coherent system, is a necessary prologue to action. One is not fit for political participation until one has arrived at a definitive ideological position, and politics is played out among the adherents of fixed positions. There is no room in the political arena for those who entertain doubts or ambiguities about matters of ultimate conviction.

There are many for whom such an image of liberal politics would be congenial, of course. But for many others, this is caricature, a *reductio ad absurdum* of the liberal political style.

It is true that liberalism implies acting on principle. But liberalism, ideally, is a deliberative process, and this begins in a mood of uncertainty and openness to the ambiguities that attend the act of judgment. The situation of choice is initially amorphous; it could be characterized in different ways. This could be an issue of rights or of social efficiency. How we define the governing rule depends on our construction of the situation. We attend to the arguments, contentions, and claims of others, considering each as a potential basis of choice. In the end, we must construct our own interpretation of the situation and articulate our own principle of action.

In this version of liberalism as a method of practical reason, we do not know our principles in advance of action. Rather, we *discover* them through a process of inquiry. They emerge from a consideration of the particulars of a situation in which we are involved and for which we are responsible, and they arise in relation to the point and purpose of a specific undertaking.

The process of justification, the effort to give good reasons for a decision is then an heuristic for thought and an exploration of the mind. Our initial assertion of a ground of decision is hypothetical and provisional. We examine the implications of the rule we have enunciated, asking whether we could endorse it consistently in further cases. We consider the consequences of following such a rule. We revise, qualify, delimit, or reject the intuitive first ground of decision depending on the outcome of a process of deliberative, critical inquiry.

This, of course, is the method of the common law. It also seems consistent with Rawls's notion of reflective equilibrium,[4] a working back and forth between a series of moral intuitions and the principles that seem to govern them, modifying either principles to fit the intuitions or the intuitions to fit the principles. The method seems compatible with modern notions of rational inquiry and scientific procedure and, in this respect as well, with the tradition of philosophic pragmatism.

The conception of method that we now begin to associate with pragmatic liberalism may have a bearing on a current controversy about the foundations of liberal theory. For writers such as Roberto Unger, Alasdair MacIntyre, Michael Walzer, and Michael Sandel, a prime objection to the rigorous formalism of much liberal theory is that the individual is perceived as standing outside culture and tradition, prior to and independent of purposes and ends.[5]

It makes more sense, such writers insist, to see the individual as situated in a context and tradition, as a party to particularistic communities of ends within which specific conceptions of justice and virtue arise. For MacIntyre, ideals of virtue and excellence function within the context of a practice, "a complex, cooperative human activity engagement with which allows the realization of goods internal to that activity and also the achievement of standards of excellence that partially define the activity but also define excellence in general."[6]

This is an argument in which the pragmatic liberal need not take sides. Pragmatic liberalism sees the individual as a member of a realm of purposive communities but also as a party to a larger public realm, defined by the liberal tradition, its principles and precepts. The problem of liberal political reason is to define the relationship between principles and practices, to scrutinize the bearing that claims based on liberal principles have for the conduct of a practice within the liberal polity and, at the same time, to consider how liberal principles shall be construed in relation to the specific communities of practice that emerge and evolve within the particular polity and give it a distinctive character and culture.

Theory and Practice

When theory is contrasted to practice, "being practical" often suggests expediency. But practicality more appropriately means acting in a disciplined, systematic, or customary manner, guided by theory, as when we speak of the practice of medicine or standard building practice. Thus, the tension between theory and practice is often a tension between different forms of theory or different forms of practice. Herein we are concerned with the relation of liberal theory to the diverse modes of consciously organized, practical activity that arise within the liberal polity.

The forms of practice include the production techniques and operating rules of various industries, the standards of performance of the professions and crafts, the doctrines of churches, the programs of the scholarly disciplines, dominant styles of artistic endeavor—any activity that has been consciously systematized on the basis of canons of correct or outstanding performance.

To follow a practice, then, means to be guided in deliberation and action by a collectively understood framework of technique and method. Our conceptions of what is and is not a problem, what will and what will not count as a solution, derive from the critical standards, the legacy of skill and craft, the logic of inquiry, of a "community of good practice" or, to use Stephen Toulmin's term, a "rational enterprise."[7]

To speak this way is to apply the language of scientific paradigms and research programs to all the diverse forms of collective, purposive endeavor that arise in pluralist society. This suggests another link to the pragmatic tradition, for Dewey regarded the polity as analogous to an ideal scientific society, a community of inquiry, engaged in an experimental, ongoing search for coherent solutions to public problems. As we shall see, to regard pluralist enterprises as similar to communities of inquiry has significant implications when we come to appraise them politically.

The community of practice may be a more useful level of analysis for reflection on pluralist politics than the organization or the association, the interest or the class. One can speak of the theory of the firm, but GM, Ford, and Chrysler are more alike than different; they share a common heritage of institutions and techniques, of assumptions and discourse that is distinctive to the auto industry, and the paradigmatic structure of the auto industry is probably as different from that of petroleum, insurance, or meatpacking as that of physics is from anthropology, literary criticism or philosophy. These invisible colleges create subcultures within the society perhaps more differentiated than those of ethnicity, class, and region, and certainly of greater normative import, for each is identified by a conception of how an important social function is properly performed.

As I suggested earlier, in modern, complex society we normally enter the public realm as parties to a rational enterprise or in contemplation of the performance of a rational enterprise. Our more significant acts as citizens arise from our occupational roles rather than from those residual acts, such as voting, which we identify formally with citizenship. At the same time, some of the most contentious issues of legislation and adjudication arise in connection with the operating rules of some purposive community or set of communities.

The conceptions of practice that arise within pluralist society are diverse, specialized, and differentiated. The practitioners inhabit different worlds and often find the ways of other crafts strange and suspect. The individual finds the ordinary processes of life increasingly remote and alien, that to deal competently with everyday transactions requires one to penetrate the mysteries of specialized languages. (Consider the arcane conventions of mortgage finance, or banking, or income tax preparation.) Yet it is precisely the elaborate, painstaking, critical process of rationalization of even the most mundane forms of practical activity that yields the sense of mastery of modern civilization, its distinctive virtues and capabilities.

Nonetheless, it is not as though we did not have a common ground for deliberation of the political and practical implications of the universe of specialized activity. On reflection, it becomes apparent that any question of policy that arises in the course of practical activity will turn, in the end, on some element in the liberal lexicon of values.

The appraisal of a performance will be grounded in considerations of efficiency or economy; or concerns for fairness in the provision of the product or the relations among practitioners; or regard for continuities of expectations, expressible also as a matter of rights; or questions of the ability of a community of practice to reflect the autonomous choices of individuals, equally considered.

The communities of practice exist, after all, within the larger context of the liberal polity. They take their bearings and their justification from it. There is a strain toward consistency in the liberal regime. It is the anomalies, the instances where the operating rules of the practical enterprise are incongruent with the principles of liberal order, that create the occasion for political inquiry and policy making, whether in the governance of the enterprise or of the liberal regime.

Liberal theory, of course, is presumptively neutral with regard to the aims of collective undertakings. It does not prescribe the character or quality of the economic product, the legitimate forms of worship, the programs of the scientific disciplines, or the proper modes of artistic performance. Liberal principles pertain instead to certain *qualities* that would, ideally, be realized in any practical endeavor.

The problem, then, is to fit principle to practice in such a way as to preserve the integrity of the undertaking. The issue is how to render a service more economically without destroying quality, how to make a profession more responsive to those it serves without compromising its autonomy. Such problems of adaptive fitting are familiar: they have often been the essence of the craft of politics in advanced industrial nations in this century. Such questions are never appropriately addressed by simply applying a general rule, indiscriminately, to all human undertakings, by appraising each only in its economic aspect and asking merely how its productivity could be enhanced, or by considering how each could be restructured along market-like lines so as to enhance individual freedom of choice, or by seeking to democratize all such institutions as a means of enhancing civic virtue. What is required is an appreciation both of the distinctiveness of the particular community of practice, its objectives, traditions, and normative structure, and a critical sense for the ways in which liberal precepts and ideals may suggest improvements in its performance, improvements that serve to bring the particular enterprise into greater conformity with the underlying ideals of the liberal regime.

This conception of the problem of practical reason is almost totally neglected in contemporary liberal theory. Nevertheless, it was central to the heritage of pragmatic liberalism (as it was in various forms of pluralist, corporatist, and social Christian thought). It is important to outline, however briefly, the essential logic of this position.

Pragmatic Liberalism and the Nature of the Regime

It is a first premise of liberalism that the state should not be the architect of social order. That would arise spontaneously, from the engagements voluntarily entered into by individuals in pursuit of their distinctive interests and life plans.

For classic liberalism, all human enterprises, all forms of collective purposiveness, were to be understood as forms of contract. They arose in response to individual will and interest and they were legitimate insofar as they could be shown to rest on the autonomous consent of equal individuals, deciding on a satisfying pattern of life engagements in the presence of alternatives. The law of contract, once understood as pertaining primarily to business transactions, expanded in the formative years of the liberal regimes to become the basic metaphor for all social organization.[8] The family, the church, the club, and the business enterprise were all to be understood as forms of voluntary contract, as was the state itself, which, at least mythically, was presumed to arise out of an initial deliberate bargain, a social contract, among free, consenting individuals.

The close corollary of contract in classic liberal thought is the idea of the market. If contract provides an image of the statics of liberal society, the market describes its dynamics. If a perfectly competitive market could allocate goods and services so as, ideally, to fit the expressed preferences of individuals, then analogously a free market in intellectual programs, artistic and cultural endeavors, religious practices and the like would reach "equilibrium" in a pattern of social order better expressive of the deliberate wills of the individuals concerned than any conscious plan could contrive.

Pragmatic liberalism accepted the principles of contract and the market as an ideal of associational legitimacy and a standard of social criticism, but it did not endorse this as a description of the development of liberal social order. The ideal conditions of contract, if they existed at all, were exceptional and transitory. The human enterprise might arise as a project of autonomous individual will, but if it survived and succeeded, it took on institutionalized form; it became a going concern. It took on organizational structure, developed an internal normative culture, and became a systematized, rationalized way of "doing things." Individuals no longer bargained for goods or patterns of social engagement that fit their particular needs or interests. Rather, choice was between established, institutionalized concerns. Simple contract became, in the language of law, a contract of adhesion. One did not design one's own insurance coverage; one bought a standard plan. One did not express one's personal religious commitments; one became a Lutheran. One did not develop a program of inquiry; one practiced the profession of physics. Practical action was not the calculated expression of will; it was the adoption of a discipline. Pluralist society did rest on freedom of choice; but it was, in many realms, a choice between institutionalized alternatives. And with such choice, particularly in the realm of work and practical endeavor, came enculturation, responsibility for and affiliation with purposive communities that more defined one's interests and life plans than they were defined by them.

Pragmatic liberalism saw this evolution from contract to institutionalized going concern as a natural process. The collective undertakings that emerged within the liberal polity regularized and routinized the performance of social functions. They represented not only socially significant ways of doing things, but valued ways of life as well. They emerged from a complex, evolutionary process of inquiry and adaptation. At the same time, however, all such enterprises were to be understood as experimental and contingent. They were subject to conscious, continuing reappraisal, not only in terms of their inherent "fittedness of purpose" but in relation to the larger, normative expectations of the liberal regime as well. Nor did pragmatic liberalism rely simply on the autonomous forces of the market to generate the necessary adaptive responses to change. Adaptation was also a matter of organized intelligence, a process of critical argument and systematic action that was political in nature and had much in common with the nature of scientific inquiry.

Pragmatic Liberalism and Rational Order

Pragmatism rejected the classic ideal of rationalism as appeal to abstract metaphysical system and a priori truths. But there is another sense of rationalism that is congenial to the pragmatic idea of method and has similar implications in the realms of scientific inquiry, the organization of purposive enterprises and in politics.

In each of these realms the object is to reduce the personal, idiosyncratic, whimsical, capricious, and arbitrary to orderly system. The purpose of science is the generation of reliable knowledge.[9] The object is to determine the extent to which theoretical propositions actually yield repeatable, consistent statements about the world. The function of science is to render nature comprehensible, which is to say, predictable and routine. By the same token, in the various realms of social endeavor and in politics, the object is to design institutions that will render human performance knowable, orderly, consistent, and in that sense, predictable and routine. As the discipline of the scientist is to subsume personal observations under lawlike statements that can be sustained, in experience over time, so the discipline of the policy maker is to subsume decisions under general principles of rightful authority that can be applied consistently in like cases, over time.

The justification for this search for order and system in all realms of human inquiry would seem to rest ultimately on a certain conception of freedom. As Hayek expressed it, the purpose of law (and here we may think analogously of physical law as well, and of "system" in organized social endeavor) is to create a stable, comprehensible framework within which people may design life plans with some assurance as to their outcome.[10]

The virtue of rationally designed laws, airline networks, telephone systems, motel chains, and physical principles is that they will work as they are expected to when one calls on them. Rationality implies efficiency, which is not the same as economy. Economy, that a function should be performed without social waste, is but one attribute of efficiency. Efficiency, in the broader sense, implies not only fittedness to purpose but also that a performance should be consistently repeatable—in a word, reliability. Fittedness to purpose, reliability, and economy are all grounds for evaluating a technology, a social practice, a scientific program, or a construct of law or policy.

Rational enterprises, then, represent reliable ways of knowing and acting within the larger society. They provide a background of relative stability, an infrastructure of settled meaning, within the general atmosphere of transitoriness and flux that characterizes liberal society. The order that is so essential to freedom arises not so much from the marketlike arrangements that classic liberalism took to be the essential instrument of free commitment, but from the communities of good practice, the guildlike arrangements, that are embedded within and derivative from the skeletal ordering precepts of contract and market.

The justification of a rational enterprise lies not in predictable routine itself but in the claim that standard practice is as well "best practice," that it arises from a practical codification of the results of a self-conscious and collective process of trial and error, internal analysis and criticism, a sustained scrutiny of how a particular function is properly performed. The goal of rational system is not to standardize custom or common practice but to make the exemplary case general and routine.

In liberal society, the public justification for rational enterprise is that it arises from such a systematic process of inquiry. Liberalism properly regards as equally arbitrary those actions of public effect that arise only from personal caprice and inclination and those that rest on unexamined custom, dogma, or orthodoxy.

The rational enterprise then is to be understood both as a delivery system and as a community of inquiry. The professional is, on the one hand, charged with carrying out a function according to the norms of a collective order. On the other hand, the professional is also understood to be a contributor, potential or actual, to the community of discourse engaged in a continuing reappraisal of practice.

It is in contemplation of its rational performance that the political order, the system of governance, of the enterprise properly becomes a matter of public concern. Only to the extent that the enterprise is structured both as a community of inquiry and a community of good practice is it fully legitimate in this conception of rational, liberal order.

Within the rational enterprise, the demands of systematic, disciplined practice and internal criticism, experiment and innovation are always in tension. The balance between them is a perennial issue in the design of the going concern. Neither hierarchy (which puts a premium on orderly routine) nor methodological anarchism (the free-spirited conviction that "anything goes,"[11] maximizing exploration but imperiling responsibility for reliable performance) meet the necessary conditions. The more appropriate model seems the discursive community of inquiry, as described by Peirce, Dewey, Toulmin and others, grounded in a sense of purposiveness and appropriate procedure but always open to the self-conscious scrutiny of method, technique, and even paradigmatic commitments.

But what is the relevant community of discourse? Liberal pluralism strongly supports the autonomy of the communities of practice that arise within the polity. Thus we speak of the separation of church and state, of academic freedom, of an economy organized on market principles.

Part of our reluctance to make the performance of the rational enterprises a centerpiece of public discussion is our assumption that the ultimate object of political debate is state regulation and control. Yet political discourse need not culminate in law or policy. Its audience can be the community of practice itself. In Albert Hirschman's terms, we exercise "voice" rather than "exit" in attempting to perfect the performance of an enterprise.[12] We become parties to the ongoing review of doctrine, procedure, and technique rather than simply taking our business elsewhere.

Nonetheless, there is a strong case that the performance of any rational enterprise is subject to review within the liberal polity. Only in the formative period is it properly regarded as a simple matter of contract and individual affiliation. But as it comes to perform a public function, as people come to depend and rely on it, as it becomes, in effect, a source of rights for those who are parties to it, its disciplines of practice and its institutions of governance are properly a subject of appraisal in the light of liberal norms and precepts.

The rational enterprise is properly regarded as an ongoing experiment in social purposiveness within the liberal order. The openness of the pluralist regime is a commitment that the legitimate forms of human undertaking will not be judged a priori. But this does not mean that such enterprises cannot be evaluated after the fact, after their implications are known, after they have reached something like fully developed form.

The Public Interest in an Enterprise

The most fundamental problems of applying liberal theory to practice arise when we ask whether there is a public interest in an enterprise, whether it is appropriately subject to state regulation and control. Classic liberalism sets stringent limits on the role of the state. But pragmatic liberalism belongs to a tradition that understood that the creation and maintenance of the conditions of liberalism required the active assertion of governmental authority. The strictures of liberalism applied equally to the uses of public and private power. The result is an ambiguous doctrine. Pragmatic liberalism is neither "for" the state nor private interest. A strong presumption in favor of voluntary associations and undertakings must be weighed against general norms of individual right and collective interest. The resolution of this tension can never take place in the abstract, but only in contemplation of the particular practices that emerge and develop within the liberal polity.

The Prototypes of Contract and the Market. In appraising the propriety of state interventions in the realm of practice, pragmatic liberalism starts from an orthodox basing point. Despite the best efforts of the pluralist theorists, liberalism never found a secure place for collective solidarities in its conception of political order. Thus, liberals constantly return to fundamental constructs in taking the measure of the evolving regime of rational enterprises.

In principle, all forms of purposive undertaking are to be regarded as voluntary associations, resting on willful consent and contract. Yet this paradigm of rightful order sets strenuous tests for the legitimacy of any organized undertaking. In ideal liberal theory, the parties to a contract must be shown to be equals in all significant respects. Any disparities of power or opportunity, information or access, raise questions about the propriety of the undertaking. Furthermore, if the costs or benefits of a practice accrue to others than the contracting parties, these "externalities" become, potentially, a matter of concern. Still, intimations of dominance are always present in any organized activity, and few communities of practice are so self-contained that their effects do not spill over into public space.

It is not good enough, then, to show that a practical enterprise predictably yields good results. Social efficiency alone does not legitimate a community of practice. It must also be shown that the enterprise results from, and is constantly reaffirmed by, the revealed preferences of consumers and practitioners. Such choices must be fully informed, and they must be made in the presence of alternatives.

The ideal of contract, then, provides a ground for radical criticism of the evolving orders of complex organization and systematic practice. In each generation, programs of radical reconstruction are advanced. There is always a standing case for the restoration of rigorous market conditions at one end of the spectrum and for a general reconstitution of the regime along the lines of social democracy at the other.

For pragmatic liberalism, such agendas for total reform may be infinitely deferrable, but they are nonetheless suggestive. The rational enterprise is a provocative anomaly in liberal theory. And from time to time, opportunities arise for the experimental reconstruction of practices along the lines suggested by such fundamental critiques. Pragmatic liberalism maintains no ideological case whether for the market or for planning; either may be an appropriate instrument of public action, a mechanism for the progressive reform of practice, depending on context and circumstances.[13]

The patterns of regulatory law and policy associated with pragmatic liberal politics are usually justified by appeal to the various forms of market failure and presumed flaws in the contractual nexus. The need to sustain competitiveness within a practice becomes the warrant for antitrust. The law of industrial relations is grounded in a perceived imbalance in contractual power between the individual and the corporation. The ability of a firm to impose costs on parties outside the contractual relation becomes the basis for environmental protection legislation. In all such cases, fundamental liberal norms are applied in assessing the public interest in the evolving regime of rational enterprise. Yet, normally, such measures are corrective and not anticipatory. They arise not from a coherent program of liberal principles but as part of an ongoing, contextual reappraisal of forms of action undertaken by the developing collective concerns.

The Promotion, Diffusion, and Universalization of Practices. In theory, the liberal state is neutral among the various forms of human undertaking that arise within the society. In experience it is not. Every new technology, every innovation in organized social activity may be suggestive of a related public project. There may be thought to be a public interest in the promotion of a new mode of transport, in the creation of a banker's bank to add flexibility to the monetary system, in special and privileged structural arrangements for cooperative societies or savings and loan associations. The finding of such a public interest in an enterprise may arise from a general interest in improvement, from a Mercantilist concern to develop at home an institution that has flourished abroad, or from considerations of equality or equity, to make available a product or service more comprehensively than would be the natural result of market distributions.

The modern liberal state has largely developed through a selective process of favoring certain emergent forms of human enterprise, and assimilating them to the public domain. The process seems to follow no categoric principle of classic political thought. It is not governed either by the formal theory of public goods or Adam Smith's somewhat looser principle of public works. Rather, the pattern seems to arise from the opportunities suggested by the specifics of practice, and the justification for public involvement vary, depending on the technical characteristics of the enterprise.

Thus schooling, once a discretionary activity, becomes a universal and prescribed practice, part not just of rational order but political order as well. The practice of insurance becomes the foundation of the welfare state. The trade union, once a form of collective purposiveness of dubious propriety, is legitimated and incorporated into an official scheme of industrial governance. The state subsidizes and promotes the communities of inquiry of the dominant sciences and schools of creative and performing art, and to some extent it ratifies their prescriptive methodologies by establishing them as constitutive of the public university and by incorporating their doctrines into the curricula of the public schools.

The state may also underwrite the standards of good practices inherent in an enterprise through occupational licensing, a law of health, safety and consumer protection, and strict liability. A public interest is found in rational performance itself, and the state becomes a party to the community of inquiry that defines and standardizes the norms of practice. The state sanctions a specific conception of practice and thus, skeptics insist, diminishes the flexibility and adaptability, the critical and experimental qualities of the community of practice.

The Public Interest in the Governance of an Enterprise. As the enterprise evolves beyond the simple forms of contract, pragmatic liberalism holds, it takes on many of the characteristics of a government. Structures of authority develop; legislative, executive, and judicial institutions may be recognized. The enterprise becomes a source of law, creating a system of rights and duties backed by coercive sanctions, that often governs the lives of individuals far more intimately than does the state itself.[14]

Here again, applying liberal theory to practice yields radical critique. The norms of the liberal polity are democratic; those of the rational enterprise are, in general, hierarchic. If liberal political theory is understood fundamentally as an historic effort to curb arbitrary authority, its requirements would seem to apply to the realm of structured, purposive institutions as well as to the state.

Pragmatic liberalism promoted the idea that rational enterprises were to be understood as forms of private government. Given its dominant metaphor of collective activity as organized inquiry, it has pressed for democratization within the enterprise, as within the state itself. Borrowing from corporatist thought, it perceives the state, in prescribing the legal form of associations, as acting to define the constitutional principles of the pluralist order. Yet the pragmatic view that the mature rational enterprise, the going concern, is to be understood more as a political order than as a simple form of contract has never become conventional in liberal thought. In this area pragmatic liberalism retains a clear ideological distinctiveness and an unfulfilled agenda.

Aggregate versus Particular Liberalism

For abstract, formal liberalism, the state is to govern through general, impersonal laws that are impartial among the diverse interests and activities of its citizens. From this point of view, the incidence, character or performance of any specific undertaking is not a matter of public concern. The state is expected to be indifferent to the particular mix of goods and services generated by the economy, to the specific array of institutions and systematic practices that may emerge, so long as this pattern can be assumed to arise from the revealed preferences of individuals, acting through marketlike arrangements.

The state should be concerned only with the aggregate performance of economy and society, with the sum of satisfaction available to the citizenry. While the state may legislate in relation to matters of health, safety, and contractual probity, it ought not regulate the substance of the economic product, of art and culture, science, religion, or the practice of the professions.

Orthodox liberalism regards any structured relationship between the state and the pluralist enterprises as inherently corrupt. In recent years, particularly, the public decision to promote, universalize, or regulate a specific practice is interpreted as a matter of interest-group politics, a tawdry exchange of privilege for political support.[15] The original rationale for such relationships has almost been lost to liberal political discourse as Marxist and liberal analysts concentrate, with never diminishing fascination, on "revealing" the deeper structural foundations of such arrangements. Thus, liberal political theory becomes rarified and abstract as the protagonists deliberate only the constitutive principles of a contentless, impersonal order.

For classical liberals, the conditions are satisfied if a minimal state provides security for person, property and contract, and leaves the rest to the market.

For Keynesians, the state's role should be limited to securing the optimum aggregate performance of the economy. If the public finances can be so arranged as to generate steady economic growth, full employment, relative price stability and balanced trade, the collective social product can be assumed to arise from individual preferences. Any "industrial policy," or its equivalent in other realms, will lead only to "distortions" in the fabric of the political economy.

For a certain kind of reformist liberal, the aggregate performance of society is justified if it arises from manifest individual choice, but this can be certified only under conditions of relatively pure meritocratic competition. This requires that equality of opportunity be assured, that the conditions of the race be fair, and this warrants public efforts against discrimination and special assistance for the most conspicuously disadvantaged. Egalitarian liberals differ only in insisting that the aggregate outcome of liberal society can be justified only if relative equality of income and political participation are guaranteed.

The tradition of pragmatic liberalism is distinctive. It shares with formal liberalism a concern for the integrity and legitimacy of the liberal community, that the aggregate product must somehow reflect the deliberate wills of individuals, equally considered. It goes beyond this, however, to presume that liberal politics is a process of sustained inquiry into the substantive character of the order that emerges within the framework of liberal norms, and that the liberal community is appropriately concerned with the particulars of the performance of important public functions.

Thus, the nature of a nation's transportation system, energy system, or health care system, its practices of architecture, or journalism, or scientific inquiry are all appropriate subjects of political theory and political deliberation. Such activities are public in an essential sense, and their performance is appropriately appraised and persistently reevaluated in relation to the realization of the foundation values of the liberal regime, which include their own inherent "fittedness to purpose."

Pragmatism, then, is radical in its willingness to penetrate the autonomy of the community of practice and to ask, directly, how well it serves the public interest. But it is conservative in that it is unwilling to advise the reconstruction of a practice on principle alone, but only in relation to its own traditions and purposes.

The great uneasiness of orthodox liberals, of course, is that systematic consideration of the public interest in the various forms of rational enterprise will lead to centralized planning and comprehensive state control, an obliteration of the public-private distinction that is so essential to liberalism. To be sure, pragmatic liberals are somewhat more sanguine about the role of the state in economy and society than are other liberals. The important point, nevertheless, is that deliberation of the public character of the rational enterprises need not culminate in state action. It can also be addressed to the community of practice itself. The essential structure of liberal society is a matter for continuing reappraisal, as the distinctive patterns of organized endeavor that emerge are tested against the persisting foundations of liberal values. But this appraisal is not for the practitioners or the state alone. It is a matter for everyday political argument, part of the process of critical inquiry which is essential to rational performance itself.

Pragmatic liberalism is a political theory that is the unique product of our century and our civilization. This is a heritage of thought to which we might happily return once our current fascination with the more recondite aspects of liberal philosophy has ended. The very familiarity of this mode of thought, its closeness to the considerations of everyday life, is an advantage. And this is still, in many respects, a raw and unfinished tradition. It has not yet been fully articulated, and its implications are far from exhausted.

Notes

1. Philip Selznick, *Law, Society and Industrial Justice* (New York: Russell Sage Foundation, 1969), p. 12.

2. For a full discussion of the classical conception of reason in relation to liberalism, see Thomas A. Spragens, Jr., *The Irony of Liberal Reason* (Chicago: University of Chicago Press, 1981).

3. This case is often made in contemporary work on political theory and policy analysis. See, for example, Douglas T. Yates, Jr., "Hard Choices: Justifying Bureaucratic Decisions" in *Public Duties: The Moral Obligations of Government Officials*, ed. Joel L. Fleishman, Lance Liebman and Mark H. Moore (Cambridge: Harvard University Press, 1981), pp. 32-51; and David C. Paris and James F. Reynolds, *The Logic of Policy Inquiry* (New York: Longmans, 1983).

4. John Rawls, *A Theory of Justice* (Cambridge: Harvard University Press, 1971), pp. 48-51.

5. Relevant works include Roberto Unger, *Knowledge and Politics* (New York: Free Press, 1975); Alasdair MacIntyre, *After Virtue* (Notre Dame: University of Notre Dame Press, 1981); and Michael Walzer, *Spheres of Justice* (New York: Basic Books, 1983); Michael J. Sandel, *Liberalism and the Limits of Justice* (New York: Cambridge University Press, 1982), pp. 54-59.

6. MacIntyre, *After Virtue*, p. 175.

7. Stephen Toulmin, *Human Understanding* (Princeton: Princeton University Press, 1972), pp. 142-44. See also the "political" use of the concept in Spragens, *Irony of Liberal Reason*, pp. 357-95.

8. Wolfgang Friedman, *Law in a Changing Society*, 2d ed. (Hammondsworth: Penguin Books, 1972), p. 120.

9. John Ziman, *Public Knowledge* (New York: Cambridge University Press, 1968).

10. Friedrich A. Hayek, *The Constitution of Liberty* (Chicago: University of Chicago Press, 1960), pp. 56-59.

11. Paul Feyerabend, *Against Method* (New York: Schocken Books, 1975).

12. Albert O. Hirschman, *Exit, Voice and Loyalty* (Princeton: Princeton University Press, 1970).

13. Charles E. Lindblom, *Politics and Markets* (New York: Basic Books, 1977). See also Robert A. Dahl and Charles E. Lindblom, *Politics, Economics and Welfare* (New York: Harper & Row, 1953).

14. For the basic literature, see Sanford Lakoff and Daniel Rich, *Private Government* (Glenview, Ill.: Scott, Foresman and Co., 1973).

15. The best example is Theodore Lowi, *The End of Liberalism* (New York: W. W. Norton, 1969).

Index

Contributors

ALFONSO J. DAMICO is a political scientist at the University of Florida and the author of *Democracy and the Case for Amnesty* and a study of John Dewey, *Individuality and Community.* A frequent contributor to political science journals, he has written about such topics as pragmatism, marxism, and liberalism.

CHARLES W. ANDERSON, Hawkins Professor of Political Science at the University of Wisconsin—Madison, is the author or editor of many books. Among them are *The Political Economy of Mexico, The Political Economy of Modern Spain, Statecraft, Value Judgment and Income Distribution.* He is currently writing a book on the theory of "Pragmatic Liberalism."

DEBORAH BAUMGOLD teaches political theory at the University of Florida. A recent NEH fellow, she has just completed a book on *Hobbes's Political Theory.* Her articles on political interpretation and the history of ideas have appeared in both American and English journals.

STEVEN M. DE LUE is a member and currently chair of the Department of Political Science at Miami University. His many essays about modern liberalism, Kant, and Rawls have been published by such journals as the *American Political Science Review* and *Political Theory.* He is currently preparing a book on political obligation.

JAMES S. FISHKIN, a political scientist at the University of Texas—Austin, recently won the Eric Erickson Prize for his book *Beyond Subjective Morality.* His other books include *Tyranny and Legitimacy, Justice, Equal Opportunity and the Family,* and *Limits of Obligation.*

RICHARD E. FLATHMAN is a senior member of the political science faculty at The Johns Hopkins University. His books include *Political Obligation, The Practice of Rights,* and *The Practice of Political Authority.* His *The Philosophy and Politics of Freedom* is forthcoming.

WILLIAM A. GALSTON has taught political theory at the University of Texas—Austin and is currently the Director of Economic and Social Programs for the Roosevelt Center for American Policy Studies in Washington, D.C. He has written *Kant and the Problem of History* and *Justice and the Human Good.* His writings on liberalism, equality, and other topics have appeared in a variety of journals and books.

EMILY R. GILL is Professor of Political Science at Bradley University. Her studies of contemporary liberal thought and major figures in the liberal tradition have had a wide audience, having been published in political science, philosophy, and economic journals.

ELAINE SPITZ held a number of teaching posts, including appointments at the City University of New York, the New School for Social Research, Cornell, and Vassar. She wrote often about liberalism and democratic theory and was the author of the recently published *Majority Rule.*

THOMAS A. SPRAGENS, JR., a political scientist at Duke University, is the author of *The Irony of Liberal Reason, The Dilemma of Contemporary Political Theory, The Politics of Motion: The World of Thomas Hobbes,* and *Understanding Political Theory.*

RONALD J. TERCHEK teaches political theory in the Department of Government and Politics at the University of Maryland. He has written *The Making of the Test Ban Treaty* and coedited *Interactions: Foreign Policy as Public Polity.* His articles and contributing essays have been widely placed in journals and books in America, Europe, and India. He is currently completing a book on classical liberal thought.